AWS Certified Advanced Networking - Specialty Exam Guide

Build your knowledge and technical expertise as an AWS-certified networking specialist

Marko Sluga

BIRMINGHAM - MUMBAI

AWS Certified Advanced Networking - Specialty Exam Guide

Commissioning Editor: Vijin Boricha
Acquisition Editor: Heramb Bhavsar
Content Development Editor: Abhishek Jadhav
Technical Editor: Prachi Sawant
Copy Editor: Safis Editing
Project Coordinator: Jagdish Prabhu
Proofreader: Safis Editing
Indexer: Tejal Daruwale Soni
Graphics: Jisha Chirayil
Production Coordinator: Jayalaxmi Raja

First published: May 2019

Production reference: 1240519

Published by Packt Publishing Ltd.
Livery Place
35 Livery Street
Birmingham
B3 2PB, UK.

ISBN 978-1-78995-231-5

www.packtpub.com

`mapt.io`

Mapt is an online digital library that gives you full access to over 5,000 books and videos, as well as industry leading tools to help you plan your personal development and advance your career. For more information, please visit our website.

Why subscribe?

- Spend less time learning and more time coding with practical eBooks and Videos from over 4,000 industry professionals

- Improve your learning with Skill Plans built especially for you

- Get a free eBook or video every month

- Mapt is fully searchable

- Copy and paste, print, and bookmark content

Packt.com

Did you know that Packt offers eBook versions of every book published, with PDF and ePub files available? You can upgrade to the eBook version at `www.packt.com` and as a print book customer, you are entitled to a discount on the eBook copy. Get in touch with us at `customercare@packtpub.com` for more details.

At `www.packt.com`, you can also read a collection of free technical articles, sign up for a range of free newsletters, and receive exclusive discounts and offers on Packt books and eBooks.

Contributors

About the author

Marko Sluga has had the opportunity to work in computing at a very exciting time and has been privileged enough to witness the rise of cloud computing in the last 20 years. Beginning his career as a service technician, he excelled at solving difficult problems. He worked his way up the IT food chain to work on servers, operating systems, virtualization, and the cloud. In the past, Marko has architected numerous cloud computing solutions, and today works as a cloud technology consultant and an Authorized Amazon Instructor. He is AWS-certified, holding the Architect, SysOps, and Developer Associate AWS certifications, the DevOps and Architect Professional AWS certification, and the Security, Advanced Networking, and Big Data Specialty AWS certifications.

About the reviewer

Zubin Ghafari is an AWS cloud certified professional and a consultant in cloud engineering and architecture. He currently holds over 8 AWS certifications at the Associate, Professional, and Specialty levels. With a passion for consulting and the cloud, Zubin enjoys spending his time experimenting and developing customized solutions for the AWS Cloud Computing platform. He has immense gratitude for his peers at Slalom who have supported him in his career.

Packt is searching for authors like you

If you're interested in becoming an author for Packt, please visit authors.packtpub.com and apply today. We have worked with thousands of developers and tech professionals, just like you, to help them share their insight with the global tech community. You can make a general application, apply for a specific hot topic that we are recruiting an author for, or submit your own idea.

Table of Contents

Section 3: Managing and Securing Network-Attached Platform Services in AWS

Section 6: The Exam

Preface

Before we begin, let me thank you for choosing this book as your guide to the AWS Certified Advanced Networking - Specialty exam. The intention of this book is to provide you with a tool that will help you to gauge your AWS and general networking knowledge in order to determine your confidence level for passing the AWS Certified Advanced Networking - Specialty exam.

The goal of the book is to focus exclusively on the networking components of AWS. We will be discussing the networking services and their features in great detail and a lot of depth. This does, however, come with a caveat—I will be assuming the reader has previous experience of working as a networking engineer and is familiar with AWS services and concepts. This assumption will come at the expense of explaining basic networking concepts such as how the OSI model works, how the IP protocol operates, how we calculate IP addresses, and so on.

Furthermore, the assumption implies that the reader is familiar with AWS and the services AWS provides to run applications. The assumption will mean that some AWS services mentioned in this book will need to be read up on outside of the context of this book. If you cannot determine how comfortable you are with AWS services, I recommend picking up a copy of *AWS Certified SysOps Administrator - Associate Guide* or the *AWS Certified Solutions Architect - Associate Guide*, both available from *Packt Publishing*, because both of these books are great tools to get you started with AWS.

Who this book is for

If you are a system administrator or a network engineer interested in getting certified with an advanced cloud networking certification, then this book is for you. Prior experience of cloud administration and networking is necessary.

What this book covers

Chapter 1, *Overview of AWS Certified Advanced Networking – Specialty Certification*, outlines the AWS Certified Advanced Networking – Specialty exam and highlights the critical aspects, knowledge areas, and services covered in the official blueprint published by Amazon.

Chapter 2, *Networking with VPC*, describes how you can create a Virtual Private Cloud (VPC) and start building a secure network with a number of components of AWS networking services.

Chapter 3, *VPC Network Security*, describes how you can secure a VPC with a number of security features of the VPC and other AWS security services.

Chapter 4, *Connecting On-Premise and AWS*, provides an overview of the connectivity services available in AWS and the security features and controls provided for these AWS features.

Chapter 5, *Managing and Securing Servers with ELB*, describes the way to secure the ELB and elaborates on the critical aspects of the ELB service.

Chapter 6, *Managing and Securing Content Distribution with CloudFront*, provides an overview of some of the critical features of CloudFront to help you manage and secure it.

Chapter 7, *Managing and Securing the Route 53 Domain Name System*, introduces you to the Route 53 service and describes various components of the service.

Chapter 8, *Managing and Securing the API Gateway*, takes a look at how to maintain security and the highest possible uptime of the content being delivered through the API gateway.

Chapter 9, *Monitoring and Troubleshooting Networks in AWS*, describes how you can use CloudWatch, CloudTrail, and the VPC Flow Logs Services to collect and track network state and metrics, collect and monitor log files, set alarms, and automatically react to changes in your AWS resources.

Chapter 10, *Network Automation with CloudFormation*, provides an overview of the CloudFormation service as it relates to network services.

Chapter 11, *Exam Tips and Tricks*, provides elaborate guidance on how to prepare for the exam, and provides tips and tricks on the topics covered in the book.

Chapter 12, *Mock Tests*, consists of two mock tests for readers to test their knowledge. It tries to cover all the topics from the exam and challenges your understanding of the topics. Each mock test contains 60 questions. You should try to complete a mock test in 90 minutes.

To get the most out of this book

The knowledge that is required by readers in order to benefit from this book is as follows:

- A basic understanding of general cloud computing terminology and environments
- A basic understanding of networking, the OSI layers, and the IP stack
- A basic understanding of network function devices, such as routers, firewalls, load balancers, and content delivery networks
- A basic understanding of virtualization and server operating systems
- A basic understanding of user and security management
- A basic understanding of storage concepts (for example, object storage, block storage, and file storage)
- A basic understanding of database services
- A basic understanding of messaging in applications
- A basic understanding of serverless computing
- A basic understanding of automation and orchestration

In addition, a more in-depth understanding of the following topics will be beneficial:

- Designing applications for high availability and resilience
- Operating system scripting languages
- Database structures
- The JSON data format
- Programming languages and application design

Download the example code files

You can download the example code files for this book from your account at www.packt.com. If you purchased this book elsewhere, you can visit www.packt.com/support and register to have the files emailed directly to you.

You can download the code files by following these steps:

1. Log in or register at www.packt.com.
2. Select the **SUPPORT** tab.
3. Click on **Code Downloads & Errata**.
4. Enter the name of the book in the **Search** box and follow the onscreen instructions.

Once the file is downloaded, please make sure that you unzip or extract the folder using the latest version of:

- WinRAR/7-Zip for Windows
- Zipeg/iZip/UnRarX for Mac
- 7-Zip/PeaZip for Linux

The code bundle for the book is also hosted on GitHub at `https://github.com/PacktPublishing/AWS-Certified-Advanced-Networking-Specialty-Exam-Guide`. In case there's an update to the code, it will be updated on the existing GitHub repository.

We also have other code bundles from our rich catalog of books and videos available at `https://github.com/PacktPublishing/`. Check them out!

Download the color images

We also provide a PDF file that has color images of the screenshots/diagrams used in this book. You can download it here: `http://www.packtpub.com/sites/default/files/downloads/9781789952315_ColorImages.pdf`.

Conventions used

There are a number of text conventions used throughout this book.

`CodeInText`: Indicates code words in text, database table names, folder names, filenames, file extensions, pathnames, dummy URLs, user input, and Twitter handles. Here is an example: "To perform this, we can add `WaitCondition` to `CreationPolicy`."

A block of code is set as follows:

```
{
  "Transform" : {
  "Name" : "AWS::Include",
  "Parameters" : {
  "Location" : "s3://cftemplatebucket/simple-network-stack.json"
  }
  }
```

Bold: Indicates a new term, an important word, or words that you see onscreen. For example, words in menus or dialog boxes appear in the text like this. Here is an example: "Open the **CloudFormation** console and click on **Create stack**."

Warnings or important notes appear like this.

 Tips and tricks appear like this.

Get in touch

Feedback from our readers is always welcome.

General feedback: If you have questions about any aspect of this book, mention the book title in the subject of your message and email us at customercare@packtpub.com.

Errata: Although we have taken every care to ensure the accuracy of our content, mistakes do happen. If you have found a mistake in this book, we would be grateful if you would report this to us. Please visit www.packt.com/submit-errata, selecting your book, clicking on the Errata Submission Form link, and entering the details.

Piracy: If you come across any illegal copies of our works in any form on the Internet, we would be grateful if you would provide us with the location address or website name. Please contact us at copyright@packt.com with a link to the material.

If you are interested in becoming an author: If there is a topic that you have expertise in and you are interested in either writing or contributing to a book, please visit authors.packtpub.com.

Reviews

Please leave a review. Once you have read and used this book, why not leave a review on the site that you purchased it from? Potential readers can then see and use your unbiased opinion to make purchase decisions, we at Packt can understand what you think about our products, and our authors can see your feedback on their book. Thank you!

For more information about Packt, please visit packt.com.

Section 1: Introduction

Amazon publishes an official blueprint for each certification exam. The blueprint elaborates the scope of the exam, prerequisites to attend the exam, and the knowledge required to successfully complete the exam. This section outlines the AWS Certified Advanced Networking – Specialty exam and highlights the critical aspects, knowledge area, and services covered in the blueprint.

In this section, we will cover the following chapter:

- Chapter 1, *Overview of AWS Certified Advanced Networking - Specialty Certification*

Overview of AWS Certified Advanced Networking - Specialty Certification

In this chapter, we will be taking a look at the characteristics and structure of the AWS Certified Advanced Networking – Specialty certification exam. This chapter is intended to provide a baseline understanding of the approach to taking the exam and the type and depth of knowledge you will need to be able to successfully pass the exam.

The following topics will be covered in this chapter:

- The exam blueprint
- The exam requirements
- The exam structure
- Scoring
- Knowledge domains
- Taking the exam

Technical requirements

There are no special technical requirements to follow through and understand in regards to this chapter; however, familiarity with general networking concepts will help you get a better grasp of the concepts that will be discussed. The chapters that follow will require deeper knowledge of different aspects of networking, from IP to the OSI layer to security. Additionally, topics covering network connectivity with AWS will require that you have a broad understanding of WAN connectivity types and routing protocols, especially the **Border Gateway Protocol (BGP)** routing mechanism.

The exam blueprint

As with all the AWS certifications, the Certified Advanced Networking – Specialty certification will follow the AWS outlined blueprint. This blueprint will provide an overview of the objectives and requirements of the exam. According to the blueprint, for the AWS Certified Advanced Networking – Specialty exam, taking and passing the exam will prove the exam taker's experience and ability to design and implement network architectures of any scale within AWS and connect them to hybrid environments.

The exam blueprint outlines that the following skills will be tested:

- An understanding of the AWS network concepts
- An understanding of hybrid IT network architectures
- An understanding of network automation tools provided in AWS
- The ability to configure network services and integrate them with applications
- The ability to design and implement network security
- The ability to optimize and troubleshoot networking issues

The exam requirements

AWS outlines several different requirements as prerequisites so that you're able to pass the exam. These include both the understanding of the networking components and services within AWS, as well as general networking concepts. Alongside theoretical knowledge, practical experience on large-scale network deployments is a big bonus.

The ideal exam candidate should be able to identify that they have the following list of skills:

- A minimum of five years experience using AWS services with a focus on networking
- A detailed understanding of the OSI model
- The understanding and ability to implement AWS security best practices
- The understanding of the AWS storage options and their features
- The understanding of and the ability to integrate AWS networking components
- The understanding of global enterprise networking requirements

- The understanding of network high availability
- Deep understanding of the TCP/IP stack and IPv4 and IPv6 protocols
- Can demonstrate the ability to automate networks and deploy at scale
- Experience with advanced LAN networking architectures and WAN options
- Experience with routing architectures and IPv6 network transitions
- Experience with network security features such as WAF, IDS, IPS, and DDoS protection

The exam structure

The exam was designed in a multiple choice, multiple answer question format. There are approximately 65 questions in the exam, and you will have 170 minutes to complete them. The questions in the exam are content heavy, so this time should be used wisely. The exam is available in English, Japanese, and Simplified Chinese, and you can also sign up for an online practice exam before taking the exam with a registered exam proctor. The registration fee for the actual exam is $300 USD, and that of the practice exam is $40 USD. The exam questions come in three different formats:

- **Multiple choice**: You will need to select the option that provides the best answer to the question or select an answer that completes a statement. The question may come in the form of a graphic, where you will be able to point and click on the answer.
- **Multiple response**: You will need to select more than one option that best answers the question or completes a statement. Multiple response questions are limited to a maximum of four correct answers.
- **Sample directions**: You will read a statement or question and must select only the answer(s) that represent the most correct or logical response.

Scoring

When scoring the exam, the score for each of the questions is given only for fully correct answers. This means that the question will be deemed as correctly answered only when the correct answer or all of the correct answers are selected. A single incorrect answer in a multiple-response question invalidates the entire question.

The exam pass/fail grade is independent of the number of correct answers, and is calculated based on the score that's achieved out of 1,000. Each question carries a different number of points since each question is considered to be of a different level of difficulty. This means that even if you were to answer 70% of the questions correctly, you can get scored at 60% or lower if all the questions that were answered correctly carried a lower score. I encourage you to answer all the questions during the exam, as even a few unanswered questions can affect the scoring dramatically.

AWS does not disclose the passing score publicly, but you can discern the passing score by examining the pass/fail scores of the community of test takers that have posted their pass/fail scores on various forums. The official stance of AWS is that the certification passing score is heavily dependent on the statistical analysis of multiple metrics that AWS receives from several sources.

Historically, the community has determined that the passing scores of different AWS exams has been set to between 650 and 750 points out of a possible 1,000. The benefit of this variable passing score is that the more difficult the exam, the lower the passing score will usually be, although depending on being able to pass the exam due to a low threshold is not recommended. Once the exam is released, the metrics that are received from the exam takers are taken into account and the passing score of a particular AWS exam is adjusted periodically. This implies that the actual passing score at the time when you attempt the exam might not reflect the definition set out in this chapter. Because of this, I recommend that each exam taker has the confidence that they can answer at least 80% or more mock questions correctly before attempting the real thing.

Knowledge domains

The questions in the exam are broken down into knowledge domains. Each knowledge domain will have a defined percentage of questions in the exam. However, the exam blueprint specifies that the knowledge domains might not match the number of questions exactly, and the percentages are posted for orientation purposes only.

The following knowledge domains are defined for the AWS Certified Advanced Networking – Specialty exam:

- **Domain 1: Design and implement hybrid IT network architectures at scale – 23%**: The questions focus on assessing the exam taker's ability to demonstrate the understanding of external network connectivity options and their characteristics. Expect questions on Direct Connect, VPNs, IPSec, bandwith, BGP routing, and prioritizing traffic.

- **Domain 2: Design and implement AWS networks – 29%**: This domain represents the core of the exam and will assess the exam taker's ability to understand and design AWS network concepts. Expect questions on VPCs, subnets, gateways, routing, and NAT.
- **Domain 3: Automate AWS tasks – 8%**: Automation is a big part of AWS, and domain 3 will assess the exam taker's ability to use CloudFormation to automate the deployment and management of networks and their topologies at scale. Expect questions on CloudFormation, with a focus on networking.
- **Domain 4: Configure network integration with application services – 15%**: This domain assesses the exam taker's ability to implement and integrate networking components with applications running in AWS. Teams in the cloud will have to understand each other's components and responsibilities, meaning that network engineers will now be required to understand both the application and the services the application depends on to correctly and efficiently configure the network. Questions will require a general understanding of AWS services and their relationship to the network.
- **Domain 5: Design and implement for security and compliance – 12%**: This domain focuses on security. Questions will assess whether the exam taker is able to design and configure networks in a secure and compliant manner and apply AWS best practices to the network configuration. Expect questions on NACLs, security groups, DDoS prevention, WAF, CloudFront, and the API gateway.
- **Domain 6: Manage, optimize, and troubleshoot the network – 13%**: The last domain focuses on testing and assessing the exam taker's ability and understanding of management, optimization, and the troubleshooting tools that are available and practiced in AWS. Expect questions on network service configuration techniques and procedures, as well as tools for optimizing and troubleshooting networks, such as flow logs.

Taking the exam

The first step to being prepared for this exam is, of course, the level of practical experience you have on AWS. No book can replace your day-to-day hands-on experience, and your years spent working, troubleshooting, and learning about networking technologies. The goal of this book is to provide the next step and allow you to focus on passing the exam with a well-structured approach that will enable you to rapidly prepare yourself for a pass.

Once you have acquired the relevant knowledge that's covered in the knowledge domains, you will need to assess your confidence level at passing the exam. I personally recommend that my readers and students need to achieve a confidence level of 80% or higher before taking the exam, as this is a good indicator that they can pass the exam, no matter the passing score that AWS sets for that day. To determine your confidence level, you will need to run through some practice questions. The final two chapters of this book provide you with a total of 130 original questions that simulate the types of questions and content you might find in the real exam. The ability to answer 80% or more of the mock exam questions correctly should assure you that you will be able to pass the exam. In case you require additional assurance, I would also recommend that you take the practice exam, as the questions in the practice exam will be very close to the ones in the full exam.

Summary

In this chapter, we have taken a short look at the blueprint, requirement, structure, and knowledge domains of the AWS Certified Advanced Networking – Specialty exam. We have also discussed the scoring of the exam and determined that the best strategy for passing the exam is having high confidence in passing by being able to answer mock questions correctly at a very high rate.

In the next chapter, we will be taking a look at the core networking component of AWS, the **Virtual Private Cloud** (**VPC**). The VPC gives us the ability to build a private, layer 2, isolated networking layer for our applications in the cloud.

Section 2: Managing Networks in AWS

2

Virtual Private Cloud (VPC) forms the basic building blocks of networking on the AWS cloud. It enables the user to create a private network on AWS infrastructure. This section describes how you can create a VPC and start building a secure network with a number of components of AWS Networking Services. We will also see how you can secure a VPC with a number of security features of the VPC and other AWS Security Services. One of the requirements for a lot of modern businesses is the need to connect existing infrastructure with the AWS data centers and services. In this section, we will get an overview of the connectivity services available and the security features and controls provided for these AWS features.

We will cover the following chapters in this section:

- Chapter 2, *Networking with the Virtual Private Cloud*
- Chapter 3, *VPC Network Security*
- Chapter 4, *Connecting On-Premises and AWS*

Networking with the Virtual Private Cloud

2

In AWS, the core networking component is the **Virtual Private Cloud (VPC)**. It serves as a private, layer 2 isolated networking layer that allows us to build applications in the cloud. VPCs can be connected to each other, on-premise locations, and AWS services, and give us a lot of flexibility when it comes to choosing built-in and custom security solutions.

This chapter will walk you through all you need to know about VPCs. First, you'll install and configure a basic VPC. Then, you'll learn about its networking components and even set some of them up. Finally, you'll engage with some best practices to ensure that you not only know everything about VPCs, but also learn how to use them in the best possible manner.

The following topics will be covered in this chapter:

- Introduction to the VPC
- Working with VPCs
- VPC networking components
- Best practices

Technical requirements

You need a solid understanding of IT networking terminology, including the ability to identify and manage resources, including, but not limited to, **local area networks (LANs)**, routing, **network address translation (NAT)**, the OSI layers, **Internet Protocol Version 4 (IPv4)** and **Internet Protocol Version 6 (IPv6)**, and the differences between these two protocols. The exam will also require that you have the ability to calculate IP address ranges and their characteristics, which falls under a basic prerequisite knowledge of networking and will not be covered in this book. You should also have experience with AWS. Familiarity with the most frequently used AWS services, such as EC2, S3, RDS, and DynamoDB, is also required. At least one year of hands-on experience in configuring AWS services and their networks is recommended.

Introduction to the VPC

The VPC service provides us with the ability to provision logically isolated networks in AWS. With VPC, we are able to design, create, and manage all aspects of networking in the AWS Cloud. When creating a VPC, we start by creating a range of IPv4 and/or IPv6 addresses that we can then split into subnets. We also have the ability to configure all aspects of routing and control how and where we attach network gateways. The VPC is the main environment that provides logical network isolation and grouping of resources, such as **Elastic Compute Cloud (EC2)** or **Elastic Container Service (ECS)** instances, and other AWS services that we want to connect to via private IP ranges.

VPC networks

When creating a VPC, we always specify a network range for the VPC. This range is limited to sizes between /28 and /16 according to the **Classless Inter-Domain Routing (CIDR)** definition of network addressing. Each VPC network can then be further subdivided into subnets. Addressing in VPC defaults to IPv4, but IPv6 and dual stacks can be run in a VPC if required. When running IPv6 or dual stacks, we need to be aware of the implications of the protocol and its effects on how traffic will pass through to the internet and back.

When creating a network, we need to be aware of the approximate number of addresses we will be consuming in each VPC and each subnet. This is important as the provisioning process in VPC is irreversible – when we provision a network, we cannot change it. We should try and make sure that we have designed the VPC with ample space for our application to run and possibly grow with time.

We should also consider that there will be some services running in the VPC that are reserved by AWS; for example, an IP address will be consumed for the **internet gateway** (**IGW**), the DHCP service, the NAT gateway, and the reserved addresses that AWS keeps unused for future services.

Private and public subnets

AWS defines two types of subnets that can be created within a VPC network – public and private. By design, the only difference that makes a subnet public rather than private is that instances running in a public network will be able to access the internet by default and also be made public by attaching a public or Elastic IPs to them. The public subnet would also be identified easily as it will have an IGW attached to it and a route for all addresses pointing to the IGW.

We can think of a public subnet as a sort of DMZ in classical network terms. The subnet is hidden from public view via a router (the IGW) with 1:1 DNAT rules attached that map the public or Elastic IPs to the IPs of our instances running in the subnet.

Private networks are completely cut off from any access to the internet by default, but can communicate with any instances running in all subnets that exist in the VPC. We can also control the traffic between all subnets through the VPC's **network access control lists** (**NACLs**) and define rules that will prevent certain subnets from communicating from each other. Private subnets are also able to connect to other networks via a NAT gateway that will allow outbound traffic, as well as through a VPN Gateway or Direct Connect connection that will allow the private subnets to communicate without on-premise systems.

This holds true for IPv4, but when we're using IPv6, there is no such concept as NAT due to the fact that all IPv6 addresses are global unicast addresses. This means that the only way to allow an IPv6 subnet to communicate with the internet is to attach an IGW to the subnet. All IPv6 addresses in a subnet with an IGW attached are inherently able to access the internet and instantly become accessible from the internet. But what if we want to keep our instances private and still communicate with the internet? For this purpose, AWS has introduced a so-called egress-only gateway that can be used to allow instances with IPv6 addresses to communicate with the internet, but does not allow any traffic into the subnet since ingress traffic is automatically blocked. This is an easy way of making an IPv6 subnet private.

Public, elastic, and private IPs

When we use IPv4 networks and have created some resources in a VPC subnet, we will need to make them available on the internet. As we've already mentioned, we can attach an IGW to the subnet and make it public. Once we have spun up some instances in the subnet, we can either attach a public IP address or an Elastic IP address.

Public IPs are sourced from one or more AWS-controlled public IP address pools and are attached to the instance randomly whenever an instance is started. When an instance using a public IP address fails and is recreated or shut down and restarted, it will not maintain the same public IP address.

This is probably the biggest advantage of Elastic IPs. An Elastic IP address is associated with your account and is persistent. This means that you have the ability to assign the Elastic IP to your instance to retain the address when it is shut down and restarted, or you can attach the same Elastic IP the failed instance was using to an instance that was recreated.

A public or Elastic IP attachment means that a virtual 1:1 DNAT connection between the public or Elastic IP is established with the instance's private IP. When the user inspects the IP address within the instance with operating system tools, they will not be seeing the public or Elastic IP. However, we do have an option to see the public or Elastic IP address from the instance itself by looking at the instance metadata. The instance metadata is available on an APIPA address of `169.254.169.254`. We can see the contents of the metadata by browsing or issuing a command to inspect the address and retrieve information about our instance that would normally be invisible in the operating system. For example, when searching for the public IP, we can browse to the following URL: `http://169.254.169.254/latest/meta-data/public-ipv4`.

The following diagram represents a fully redundant VPC deployment with two private subnets and two public subnets. The following numbers correspond to what is labelled in the diagram:

1. The VPC is deployed within an AWS region.
2. The VPC network address range is designated as `10.0.0.0/20`.
3. Two public subnets are created with IP ranges `10.0.1.0/24` and `10.0.2.0/24`.
4. Two private subnets are created with IP ranges `10.0.3.0/24` and `10.0.4.0/24`.
5. All traffic between any subnets in the VPC is allowed by default as the local route points to the VPC address range of `10.0.0.0/20`. Any additional subnets that are created in this network will also be accessible to all subnets.

6. The public subnets have a connection to the internet gateway.
7. Any EC2 instances with public or Elastic IPs assigned are accessible on the public subnet.
8. Any private EC2 instances in the private subnet can reach the NAT gateway.
9. The NAT gateway needs to be deployed in a public subnet and will NAT all the traffic from the EC2 instances in the public subnet in the outbound direction to the internet.
10. The NAT gateway has an Elastic IP assigned, and any traffic being sent to the internet through the NAT gateway will always be seen as originating from this EIP:

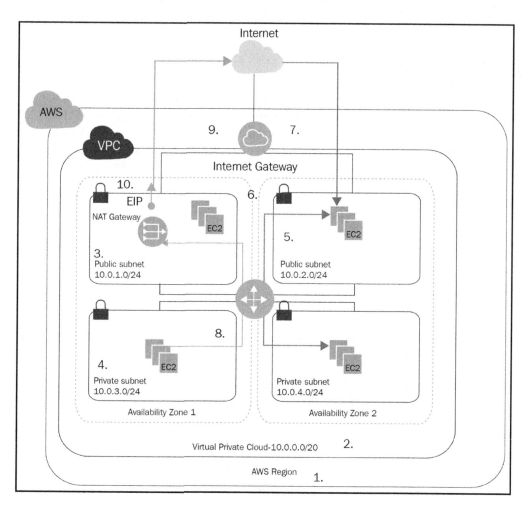

Working with VPCs

We need to consider that VPCs are regionally bound, so before creating a VPC, we need to make sure that we select the region where we would like the services or application to run. Once we have selected a region, we need to be aware of the AWS VPC limitations. By default, we are only able to create five VPCs in each region. However, this limit is a soft limit that's imposed by AWS for the sake of sanity, so if we have a certain use case that would require us to create more than five VPCs, then we should contact AWS. Each VPC network can be divided into 200 subnets at most, and we are able to assign up to five IPv4 CIDR blocks to each VPC. Both of these limits can also be increased if required. However, we are limited to only one IPv6 CIDR block per VPC. This is a hard limit and cannot be increased.

Creating a VPC

In this section, we will look at an overview of the VPCs, subnets, route tables, internet gateways, and other networking components that are created in all regions. Unlike most AWS services, the overview in the VPC dashboard is global, which allows us to get a really good understanding of our network and the number of VPCs and other network components in our entire AWS environment. Let's follow these steps to get started:

1. To create and configure a VPC, we need to navigate to the **VPC Dashboard**, as shown in the following screenshot:

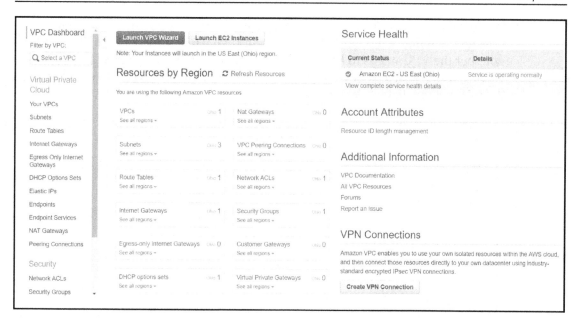

2. We will be creating a VPC and all its component by navigating to the appropriate sections of the **VPC Dashboard**. First, we will create a VPC from the **Your VPCs** section by clicking on **Create VPC**:

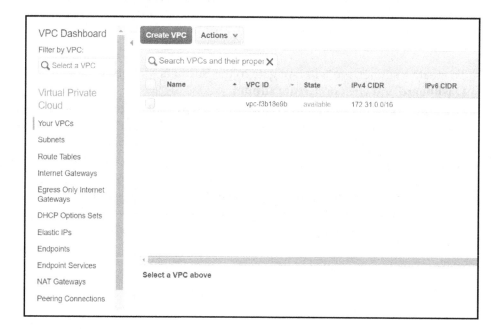

3. We will name our VPC and assign a network CIDR. We also have the option of selecting whether we would like to have an IPv6 CIDR added to the VPC, and whether the VPC needs to have dedicated tenancy. For our purposes, we will create a network CIDR of 10.0.0.0/16 and leave advanced options at their defaults before clicking **Yes, Create**:

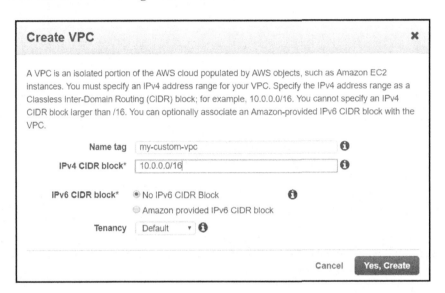

Now that we have created the new VPC, we will need to create the subnets for the VPC.

4. To create a subnet, we will navigate to the **Subnets** section of the **VPC Dashboard** and click on **Create subnet**.

5. Once in the **Create Subnet** dialogue, we have the option to give the subnet a name and select the VPC in which we will be creating it. Please choose your newly created VPC.

6. Next, we will select the availability zone and create a new CIDR block for the subnet. We should be creating multiple subnets if we would like to have the services in the subnets highly available and separated into public and private subnets. A minimum of four subnets is recommended: two public and two private, with each pair spread across two availability zones.

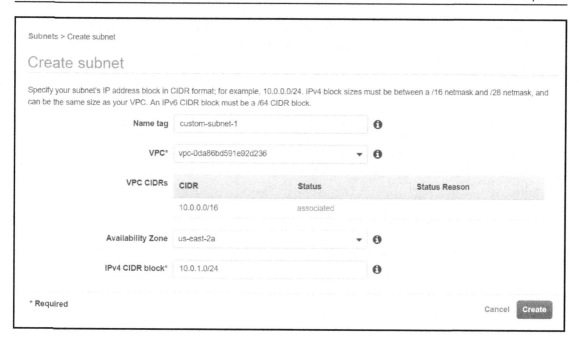

7. Next we will create an **Internet Gateway** to support internet connectivity and make the subnet public. We need to navigate to the **Internet Gateways** section of the **VPC Dashboard** and click the **Create internet gateway** button. Once in the **Create internet gateway** dialogue, we simply need to name our IGW and click **Create**:

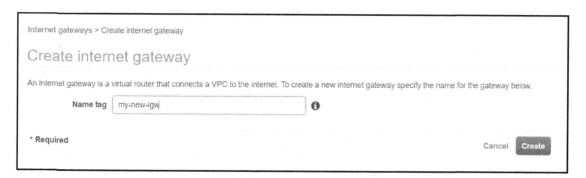

Once created, the IGW is detached.

8. Now, we need to select the newly created IGW and attach it to our newly created VPC by clicking on **Actions** and selecting **Attach to VPC**:

9. In the **Attach to VPC** dialogue, we select our VPC and click on **Attach**:

Now that we have attached the IGW to the VPC, we need to create a new route table so that our public subnets can have access to the internet.

10. Navigate to the **Route Tables** section of the **VPC Dashboard** and select the route table that was created for your VPC. This route table is also called the main route table. It is predefined to allow all subnets within the 10.0.0.0/16 network to communicate with each other. All of the subnets that are created are associated with this route table by default.

11. Now, let's create a new route table by clicking on the **Create Route Table** button:

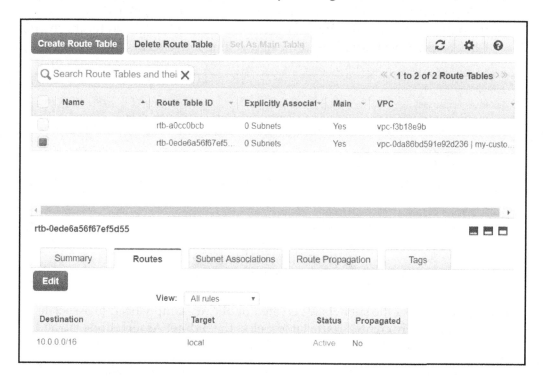

12. In the **Create Route Table** section, we need to give it a name and select our VPC, and then click **Yes, Create**:

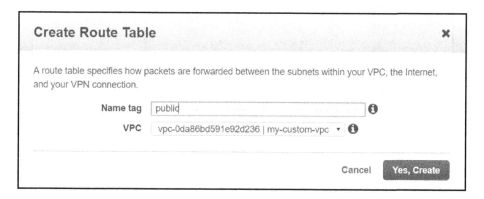

Now that the route has been created, we need to allow access to the internet via this route.

13. Select the newly created route, click on the **Routes** tab, click **Edit**, and then click **Add another route**. We need to select our IGW as the target and 0.0.0.0/0 for the destination – this denotes all routes and is the default CIDR for the internet. Click on the **Save** button to put the new setting into effect:

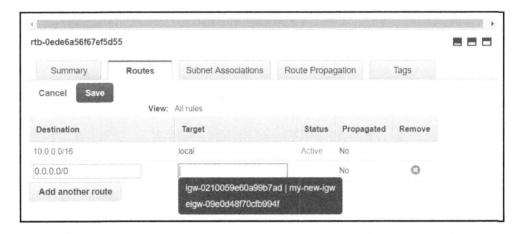

14. To make any of the subnets we created public, we simply need to associate them with this newly created route table. Select the **Subnet Associations** tab and click **Edit**. Select the subnets you want to make public and click **Save**:

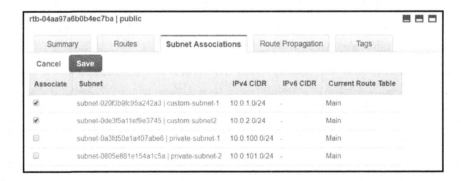

15. To allow the instances being deployed in the public subnets to be automatically available from the internet, we can configure the public IP assignment so that it's performed automatically. This is an optional step. To configure automatic IP assignment, navigate to the **Subnets** section of the **VPC Dashboard**, select any of your public subnets, click on **Actions**, and click on **Modify auto-assign IP settings**:

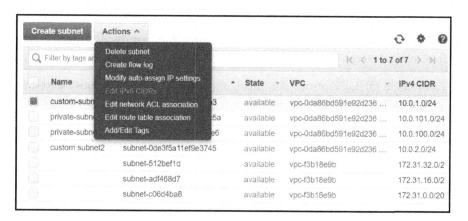

16. Select the check mark next to **Auto-assign IPv4** and click on **Save**. Make sure that you repeat this step for the second public subnet:

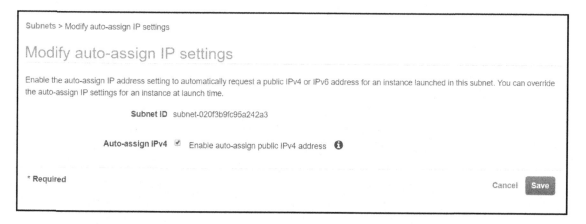

Configuring DHCP options

All the subnets we create have automatically configured DHCP options to provide default AWS settings. In case we ever need to control DNS, NTP, and NetBIOS address distribution in our VPC, we can create a DHCP options set and then set and attach that new set to the VPC. A VPC can only have one DHCP options set attached to it at a time, so consider that the default AWS options will not be effective if we attach a new DHCP options set to the VPC. This is useful when we would like to provide hybrid infrastructures that would require the use of our own or on-premise DNS servers that can resolve some private addresses that are not present in AWS. Let's follow these steps to get started:

1. To create a DHCP options set, navigate to the **DHCP Options Sets** section of the **VPC** management console and click **Create DHCP options set**:

2. In the **Create DHCP options set** dialogue, we will need to enter the following information:
    *   **Name**: Name of the DHCP options set
    *   **Domain name**: The name of the domain that we would like to be passed in during DHCP configuration
    *   **Domain name servers**: A comma-separated list of DNS server IP addresses
    *   **NTP servers**: A comma-separated list of NTP server IP addresses
    *   **NetBIOS name servers**: A comma-separated list of NetBIOS server IP addresses
    *   **NetBIOS node type**: The method to use to resolve a NetBIOS name into an IP address:

This dialogue has a neat feature that provides us with the command-line input for our configuration. This can be used as a template when we are configuring numerous VPCs with our own DHCP options. It will make much more sense to use the AWS CLI when working with very large environments since creation and configuration can be easily scripted:

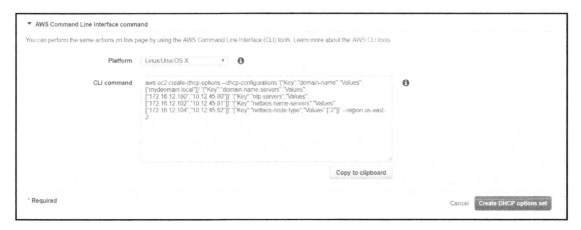

In this example, we have created a custom VPC that gives us the ability to spin up instances in two separate availability zones and thus provide high availability to our application. We have also configured the DHCP options that will allow us to control the way the DNS, NTP, and NetBIOS server addresses are provided to the instances we create in the VPC.

VPC networking components

The VPC itself is designed to contain services running inside AWS in a private network. The design is based around a standard IPv4 approach to networking with NAT. As we've already discussed in this chapter, the design also supports IPv6. Essentially, the goal of the VPC is to deliver a private network environment where we can connect virtual instances, containers, AWS services, and other VPCs through private IP addresses. To connect these, we will be using the following networking components:

- **Elastic Network Interface (ENI)**
- Routing NAT and internet access
- VPC endpoints and PrivateLink
- VPC peering

ENI

The ENI is a virtual network adapter that allows us to connect operating systems, containers, and other components to a VPC. When an EC2 instance is created, a special kind of ENI is created and permanently attached to it. This ENI is also called the primary network interface, and will be shown as **eth0** in Linux instances or **Local Area Connection** in Windows instances. The primary network interface has all the characteristics of an ENI, except it cannot be detached from the instance it was created with.

We also have the ability to create an ENI independently of an EC2 instance and arbitrarily assign its characteristics. When created separately, the ENI is created with a persistent MAC address. Once attached to an instance, this adapter will show up as a secondary network interface and the MAC address will be visible in the operating system. This ENI is completely independent of the EC2 instance it is connected to and its characteristics will persist through stops and starts, and will remain unchanged even when the instance is terminated.

We are also able to detach the ENI and attach it to another instance. This is of great benefit when we use licensing that is tied to a MAC address. Instead of tying the license to the primary network interface and hoping that the instance never fails, we can assign the license to a separately created secondary ENI. In case of a failure of the instance, we simply reattach the ENI to another instance with the same software or recover the instance from an AMI and attach the ENI to the newly created instance.

To create an ENI, we will need to execute the following steps:

1. Navigate to the **EC2** management console, scroll down to the **NETWORK & SECURITY** section, and select the **Network Interfaces** section. There, we click on the **Create Network Interface** button:

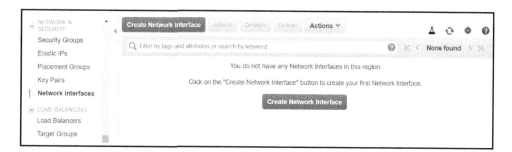

2. In the **Create Network Interface** dialogue, we need to specify the following:
   - **Description**: An optional description of the interface.
   - **Subnet**: The subnet to attach the ENI to.
   - **Private IP**: The IP address for the network interface. An IP will be automatically assigned if you leave this blank.
   - **Security groups**: The security groups to control access to the network interface:

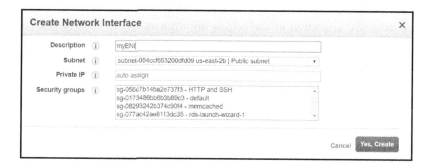

To control security on the ENI adapter, we use security groups. By default, we are able to assign up to five security groups to each ENI, but since this is a soft limit, we can contact AWS support for the soft limit to be raised if required. The absolute maximum is 16 security groups per ENI. However, increasing the number of security groups we can assign will not increase the number of security group rules that we can assign to an ENI since the absolute maximum number of rules per ENI is 300. This is distributed across the security groups so that when we're using five security groups, we can create 60 rules within each security group (for example).

Once created, we can manage the ENI. For example, we can manage the IP addressing of the ENI separately from the instance it is connected to. In the ENI features, we can specify a primary IP address from the VPC subnet primary IPv4 address pool and any number of available secondary private IPv4 addresses. Additionally, we can assign one or more IPv6 addresses:

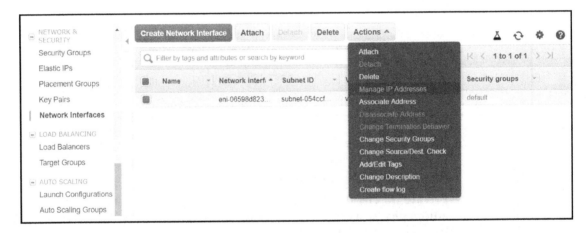

Each ENI can also have a public or Elastic IP assigned to it. Assigning an Elastic IP is very useful when we require an unchangeable IP address for any of our instances. To assign a new address navigate to Elastic IPs and select **Allocate new address.** The dialogue for requesting a new EIP is shown in the following image:

When troubleshooting and diagnosing network flow issues, we can enable VPC flow logs for each ENI separately. This allows us to diagnose the traffic flow to and from a particular ENI. This is especially valuable when using containers that have an ENI attached as we are able to granularly diagnose and determine the traffic flow pattern to each and every endpoint.

As you can see, the ENI is the virtual connectivity device that gives us the flexibility, performance, and control that we would expect from a modern virtual network device. Now, we will take a look at how any traffic from an ENI can pass outside the subnet and get routed to the internet and other networks.

Routing, NAT, and internet access

To allow access from private networks to the internet, we will need to configure a device that will allow us to connect to the internet. There are several scenarios within AWS that will determine the type of device we will be using to connect to the internet. As we discussed at the beginning of this chapter, we can create either public or private subnets in a VPC.

Connecting public subnets to the internet

When using IPv4, we will be connecting an IGW to the public subnet, which will allow us to assign public and Elastic IPs through 1:1 NAT to our instances. This means that any traffic coming into the public or Elastic IP will be directed by the IGW to the internal IP address of the instance (the IP address will be sourced from the subnet IP range). When using IPv6, the addresses are assigned directly to the instances in the public subnet, and by connecting an IGW, we allow the traffic to flow in and out of those instances.

The IGW is designed to be horizontally scaled, redundant, and highly available by default, so there is no need to configure any redundancy when attaching an IGW to our public subnet.

To allow the traffic from the instances to flow to and from the internet, we will also need to create a default route in the routing table of each public subnet that has an IGW attached to it. For IPv4, we will need to create a route for `0.0.0.0/0`, whereas a route for an IPv6 will have a destination of `::/0`. Both routes will need to define the target as the ID of the IGW that is connected to the subnet. When creating a route in the AWS management console, simply start typing `igw` in the target for the default route and the IGW ID will pop up as a recommended value, as shown in the following screenshot:

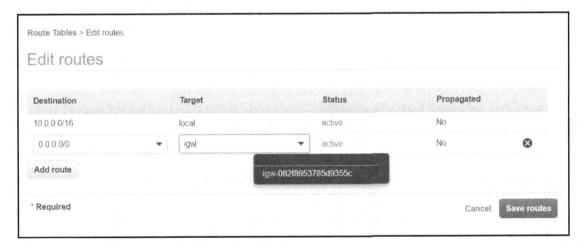

Connecting private subnets to the internet

To connect an IPv4 private subnet to the internet, we can use a NAT gateway. The NAT gateway will allow all outgoing traffic to pass to the internet and is used when we require the instances in the private subnet to access the internet.

This allows us to access external services even from the private network, such as the following:

- Retrieve operating system and application updates and patches
- Communicate with external services, such as payment gateways and processing tools
- Synchronize time with an external NTP service
- Access external DNS and other services

A NAT gateway has the following features:

- Supports 5 GBps of bandwidth and automatically scales up to 45 GBps
- Supports up to 55,000 simultaneous TCP, UDP, and ICMP connections to each unique destination
- Can associate exactly one Elastic IP address with a NAT gateway – once created, it cannot be dissociated
- Cannot associate a security group with a NAT gateway, but access can be controlled at the instance level with security groups
- A NAT gateway has an automatically assigned private IP in your subnet that can be viewed in the AWS management console

If the performance of a single NAT instance is not satisfactory, we can create multiple NAT gateways.

In case we are using an IPv6 environment, we will need to use an egress-only internet gateway. The egress-only gateway has all the characteristics of an internet gateway, the only difference being that it blocks all incoming traffic to the IPv6 address space that we assign to our private subnet. We are thus able to achieve the same kind of operation as we would with an IPv4 NAT gateway without all the limitations that come with the NAT gateway.

There are also scenarios where the NAT gateway or the egress-only gateway are not the right solution. This would happen in cases where we require a single instance to handle greater volumes of IPv4 traffic or to retain control over the IPv4 or IPv6 traffic being passed to the internet. In certain situations, allowing all traffic to the internet via a NAT instance or egress-only gateway is not allowed or would not be compliant with certain rules. In this kind of scenario, we can spin up our own NAT instance with our own custom software running on it. We are also able to do additional traffic shaping and security checks with our own NAT instances, especially when they have some kind of packet inspection and firewalling software installed on it. To control IPv6 traffic, our instance will be using routing instead of NAT and control the flow of the traffic on the firewall level.

VPC endpoints and PrivateLink

There are certain situations where we require services in private subnets with no access to the internet to be able to connect to an AWS service such as S3, SQS, KMS, and DynamoDB. We could also put instances in a public subnet, but with a requirement that no data within the application is passed over the public IP space. In both of these cases, we can implement a VPC endpoint to connect a service to the VPC and allow for communication to the service within a private IP space. VPC endpoint connections come in two different types:

- Gateway endpoints
- Interface endpoints

Gateway endpoint

A gateway endpoint is generated for a specific AWS-supported service and is designed as a route within the VPC routing table. Any instance running within the VPC will need to consult the routing table to access the AWS service. At the time of writing, Amazon S3 and DynamoDB support gateway endpoints and will probably remain the only services to be supported in this way.

The following diagram shows an S3 VPC gateway endpoint that's connected to the VPC. The private subnet will now see an identifier for the S3 service and a route to the VPC endpoint device. This allows our EC2 instances in the private subnet to connect to the S3 service without requiring a NAT instance:

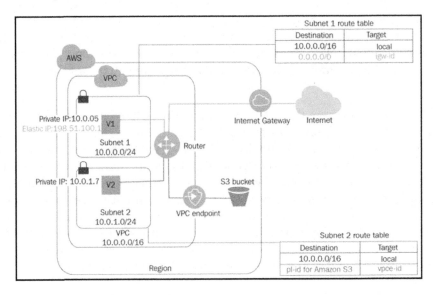

Interface endpoint – powered by AWS PrivateLink

An interface endpoint is essentially a service-level ENI. The service is attached straight to the VPC subnet through the ENI. This allows us to assign a private IP address from the subnet pool directly to the service. By using an interface endpoint, we have the ability to address the AWS service directly through the private IP of the ENI instead of going to its public endpoint. This allows us to communicate with the service on the private network and maintain any data to the service within our subnet. Basically, it is like having a complete copy of an AWS service sitting right in your VPC subnet.

The following diagram shows an SQS VPC interface endpoint connected to the VPC. Our EC2 instances in the private subnet will now be able to directly connect to the SQS service by connecting to the private IP of the SQS service. Any SQS queues we create will be assigned a DNS name, and any DNS name within the private subnet with a VPC interface endpoint link will automatically resolve to the private IP of the VPC endpoint network interface:

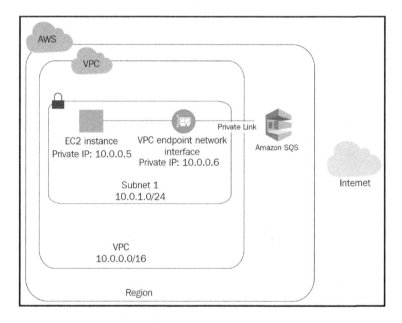

To get a full list of services where the service endpoint is supported. please consult the VPC endpoints link in the *Further reading* section of this chapter.

This service is supported by AWS PrivateLink. PrivateLink also allows any other service and software providers to provide a private interface link straight to your VPC subnet. This way, we can exchange information with the provider via a seamless private connection, keeping our traffic off the public networks.

Configuring an endpoint

You can navigate to the **Endpoints** section to see how a service or other VPC endpoint can be created. Note the ease of configuring these features within the VPC dashboard:

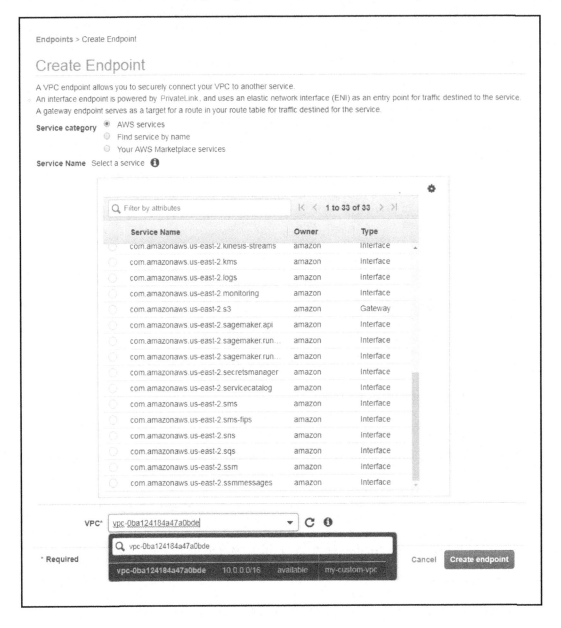

VPC peering

When operating a large application that spreads across VPCs or regions, we sometimes have a requirement to connect that application via a private connection. We always have the option to create VPN connections between VPCs, but that will require us to maintain the configuration of the VPN devices and ensure the security of those.

A simpler way to connect VPCs together is through VPC peering. A VPC peering connection is a networking connection between two VPCs that allows you to route traffic between them privately and have the ability to connect instances in private subnets within separate VPCs to communicate directly, as demonstrated in the following diagram:

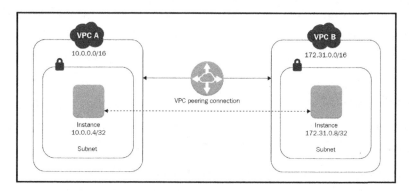

AWS provides the ability to create VPC peering connections between our own VPCs or with a VPC in another AWS account. The VPC peering connections can be established within one region or across different AWS regions. AWS uses existing, scalable network technologies with no single point of failure to enable VPC peering.

When enabling VPC peering between regions, AWS will take care of the VPN connection between the locations and maintain redundant pathways for the traffic. Since the traffic between regions will pass over the internet, standard inter-region charges apply when using VPC peering between regions. No charges to traffic within a region are applied.

Limitations of VPC peering

When setting up a VPC peering connection, we need to be aware of the following limitations:

- It is not possible to peer VPC with overlapping IPv4 or IPv6 CIDR blocks.
- Transitive peering is not supported; for example, peering A to B and B to C does not establish a link between A and C.

- Unicast reverse path forwarding in VPC peering connections is not supported.
- Tagging a VPC peering connection is only applied in the account or region in which you create them.

Additionally, inter-region VPC peering connections have the following limitations:

- The peer VPC's security groups cannot be referenced in security groups that are created in the other VPC.
- DNS resolution of hostnames that have both public and private IPs will only resolve public IPs when queried from the peered VPC.
- Communication over IPv6 is not supported.
- Communication over ClassicLink for EC2-Classic instances is not supported.
- Jumbo frames are not supported across the inter-region VPC peering connection.

Best practices

Now, let's take a look at the best practices that we should adhere to when designing a VPC. Generally, we should make sure that we follow these principles:

- Design our networks and subnets in the appropriate sizes
- Design our networks with high availability requirements in mind
- Understand special requirements for routing
- Understand the limitations of VPC peering when required
- Understand general VPC limits

Network and VPC sizing

When designing a VPC, we first need to look into network address configuration. Make sure that you design the network and subnet addressing with enough space to comfortably accommodate both the existing size and any future requirements for your application. The general rule when designing a VPC network and subnet ranges is that bigger is better. Don't lock yourself into small little subnets that will not allow your application to grow. Remember: once you create a VPC network, it cannot be changed. In case you require a larger network for your instances, you will need to create a new VPC and move the instances to the new VPC subnets.

High availability

When designing high availability, there are further considerations that you need to take into account. If public access is required, we would start by creating at least two public subnets in two different availability zones. This will allow us to spin up instances in two fault-isolated environments. The same approach would be used for private subnets – we would create at least two private subnets within two different availability zones. With private subnets, the high availability of your NAT gateway, NAT instance, or egress-only gateways should also be considered.

Routing

When parts of an application have unique routing requirements, add additional subnets and perform the routing at the subnet level. Put the parts of the application into separate subnets. The application will be able to inherently communicate since all subnets can communicate with each other by default. Each subnet will have the ability to provide specific routing to the part of the application that requires it.

VPC peering recommendations

When you require VPC peering, always consider the IP addressing of the existing VPCs so that you don't create an environment with overlapping IPs – VPC peering connections will not support overlapping IP ranges. Make sure that you always keep a design in mind that will allow you to grow. A good approach is to build sequential network ranges, for example, `10.0.0.0/16`, `10.1.0.0/16`, and `10.2.0.0/16` for the VPC networks, and then divide those networks into subnets, for example, `10.0.1.0/24`, `10.0.2.0/24`, `10.1.1.0/24`, and `10.1.2.0/24`. None of these ranges will ever overlap.

VPC limitations

Consider the limitations of VPCs. By default, you are allowed to create 5 VPCs per region. This number can be increased by contacting AWS support. However, you are limited to 200 subnets per VPC, so when you're designing subnets, there is no need to leave room for more than 200 subnets in your VPC network range. The 200 subnet limit is a hard limit. You can also create up to 5 IPv4 network ranges (one primary and four secondary) per VPC. This limit can be increased if needed. For IPv6 ranges, you are only allowed to create one IPv6 range per VPC. This is a hard limit and cannot be increased.

Summary

In this chapter, we have taken a look at VPCs and the features they provide. We have learned how the concept of private and public subnets are defined in AWS. We have also taken a look at how to enable traffic so that it can be passed to and from public subnets with an IGW and how to enable private subnets to communicate with the internet by attaching a NAT gateway or an egress-only gateway. We have discussed the ENI and the way we can attach services to the VPC via VPC endpoints, and also looked at an overview of VPC peering connections.

In the next chapter, we will take a look at network security. We will discuss security from the aspect of the OSI layers, talk about securing the VPC and its instances, and delivering advanced security with the AWS tools provided.

Questions

1. Name five components of the VPC.
2. How does accessing private subnets via the internet differ between IPv4 and IPv6?
3. What considerations should you keep in mind when deciding on CIDR sizes?
4. What is the difference between an IPv4 and an IPv6 public subnet?
5. What is the difference between a gateway and an interface VPC endpoint?
6. VPC A is peered to VPC B. VPC B is peered to VPC C. How can traffic flow be designed to allow for instances in VPC A to communicate with the instances in VPC C?
7. You are configuring the network for your highly available application. You are required to maintain a strict separation of layer 2 broadcast traffic between four different tiers of the application. The web frontend tier is the only tier that's allowed to communicate with the internet. All other tiers will exchange information via SQS queues. Describe the most appropriate approach for designing the network environment with one or more VPCs for this application.

Further reading

Refer to the following links for more information regarding what has been covered in this chapter:

- **AWS VPCs and Subnets**: https://docs.aws.amazon.com/vpc/latest/userguide/VPC_Subnets.html
- **AWS ENI**: https://docs.aws.amazon.com/AWSEC2/latest/UserGuide/using-eni.html
- **VPC IGW**: https://docs.aws.amazon.com/vpc/latest/userguide/VPC_Internet_Gateway.html
- **Egress-Only Internet Gateway**: https://docs.aws.amazon.com/vpc/latest/userguide/egress-only-internet-gateway.html
- **VPC Peering Basics**: https://docs.aws.amazon.com/vpc/latest/peering/vpc-peering-basics.html
- **VPC Endpoints**: https://docs.aws.amazon.com/vpc/latest/userguide/vpc-endpoints.html
- **VPCs and Subnets**: https://docs.aws.amazon.com/vpc/latest/userguide/VPC_Subnets.html
- **Practical VPC Designs**: https://medium.com/aws-activate-startup-blog/practical-vpc-design-8412e1a18dcc

3
VPC Network Security

One of the key aspects of operating any application, whether on-premises or in the cloud, is network security. This is well understood in AWS, and there is a whole range of security services and devices that can provide us with the required security mechanisms to keep our application protected on the network.

This chapter will walk you through all you need to know about securing VPCs. You will learn about the security components and how and when to use them in the best possible manner.

The following topics will be covered in this chapter:

- An overview of network security
- Securing the VPC
- Securing EC2 instance operating systems
- Delivering advanced network security in AWS

Technical requirements

You should be familiar with general network security concepts and terminology, including firewalls, firewall state, ports, WAF, DoS, and DDoS mitigation. Familiarity with widely used AWS services such as EC2, S3, and RDS is essential as well. Hands-on experience in configuring these services and their network security is a bonus.

An overview of network security

When dealing with network security, we should always strive to implement as many security mechanisms as our application design and budget will support. Think of network security as an onion – the more layers the onion has, the more work there will be to get to the middle of it. The same idea applies to providing network security.

The more security devices we implement, the harder it will be for malicious traffic to reach our application. We should be thinking about network security at all the layers of our application. We need to be careful, especially when it comes to identifying our entry points and protecting each of them with the appropriate security measures.

The following diagram breaks down the attack vectors according to **Verisign**. The diagram represents the security breaches that were successful in 2018 and network security only accounts for about one fifth of the attacks leading to a breach:

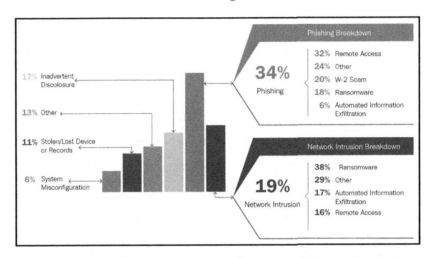

Contrary to popular belief, it is not the lone hacker intent on penetrating our network firewall that's the biggest concern when we talk about network security. Network security is, in fact, a small part of an overall strategy in securing our applications.

Understanding network security vulnerabilities

We should treat network security as our first line of defense when it comes to stopping attacks from external sources. However, attacks that can be prevented with good network security devices range in type and severity, and are roughly broken down into the following categories:

- Network layer attacks
- Service layer attacks
- Exploiting vulnerabilities
- Application layer attacks

Network layer attacks

There are several types of network layer attacks, including but not limited to the following:

- **Automated port scans**: Port scans attempt to discover open ports for attackers to try and compromise.
- **Spoofing**: An attacker sets up their own server with an IP address of the server being attacked and tries to intercept traffic intended for the legitimate IP.
- **DoS**: An attacker or a group of attackers (DDoS) attack an application entry point (such as website or email server) with traffic that is designed to overwhelm the system, either with volumes or with packets that will cause errors to accumulate.

AWS inherently prevents IP spoofing and port scanning within EC2 networks. Any attempt at spoofing an IP or scanning ports within an EC2 environment is treated as a violation of the AWS terms, and any system attempting to perform either of those will be automatically and immediately blocked from any further access.

AWS provides a set of guidelines on how to protect an application against DoS and DDoS attacks and allows for the ease of management of the security features that help to achieve this with AWS Shield and AWS WAF. We will discuss this in more detail in the *Delivering advanced network security in AWS* section of this chapter. We can also use WAF to prevent injection attacks and session hijacking, and we can use the AWS Shield service to help us mitigate DoS and DDoS attacks. We will discuss these two services in the *Delivering advanced network security in AWS* section of this chapter.

Service layer attacks

Service layer attacks are designed to attack a service that an application relies on to function correctly. One of the most frequently used attacks is DNS and domain hijacking. An attacker will try to intercept DNS traffic by taking over a domain and/or inject incorrect DNS information into a compromised application. The requests from the application will be sent to the attacker's DNS instead of the legitimate DNS service. We can prevent these attacks from happening by using the AWS Route 53 service.

Exploiting vulnerabilities

There are several types of vulnerability attacks that can be executed over the network:

- **Exploiting a vulnerability**: An attacker exploits a known vulnerability of an unpatched system for DoS or to gain access
- **Zero-day attacks**: An attacker exploits a newly released vulnerability of the system for DoS or to gain access before the vendor provides a patch
- **Unknown vulnerability**: An attacker exploits a known vulnerability of the system for DoS or to gain access

Protecting from vulnerabilities is a complicated matter as it requires tight coordination between the network, security, and the operations team to detect, identify, and prevent vulnerability attacks from being carried out. However, AWS WAF offers features that help prevent the exploitation of the most important security flaws, as named by the **Open Web Application Security Project (OWASP)**.

Application layer attacks

Application layer attacks come in the highest variety and severity, and include but are not limited to the following:

- **Brute-force attacks**: An attacker tries to gain access by trying to breach an application entry point (remote desktop, SSH, web login) with a dictionary attack or similar
- **Session hijacking**: The attacker intercepts credentials or tokens and pretends to be an active user to gain access
- **Injection attacks**: An attacker exploits poor application security to inject information into the application for DoS or to gain access
- **Account hijacking**: Accounts are hijacked through phishing or inadvertent disclosure of credentials for DoS or to gain access

We can easily detect brute-force attacks with a monitoring solution such as CloudWatch, which can provide an alert when a certain user has reached a certain threshold of invalid logins over a certain period of time.

To protect from session hijacking, we could use encryption. Since the traffic is encrypted, it will make it very difficult for an attacker to perform a session hijack. We can also implement mechanisms that allow you to check network packets on several layers. This helps our application determine whether the packet has been altered, thus indicating an interception and a possible attempt to hijack the session.

AWS WAF can be used to prevent injection attacks, but the wisest way to protect your application is to secure it at the application layer.

Possibly the most difficult attack to detect and protect from the network layer would be account hijacking. Phishing or inadvertent credential disclosures can lead to an attack that is hard to detect. An attacker can easily fool any automated system and pretend to be a legitimate user while trying to gain deeper access or transferring confidential data from our application. The recommended way to protect from account hijacking is to use **multi-factor authentication (MFA)**. AWS has built-in MFA for AWS accounts and IAM users. We should always make sure that any developers building any type of publicly accessible application understand the need for MFA. Building MFA capability into the application level will raise the security of any application accounts dramatically.

Security in the OSI model

Network security spans several layers in the OSI model. The following diagram gives us a breakdown of the different attack vectors and the representation of the percentage of attacks that succeeded in compromising an application in 2018:

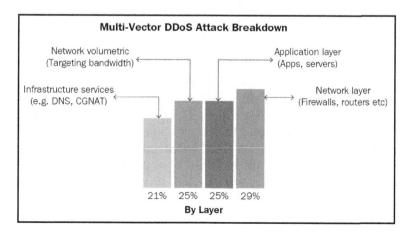

As we can see, more than half of all attacks are represented by network layer attacks. These are spread out over multiple layers of the OSI model. Network attacks are most commonly layer 3 and layer 4 attacks, and they usually do the following:

- Attack the network service's availability by overloading the network link
- Attack the services on the network that deliver packets to the application such as routers, firewalls, and load balancers

The other half is shared by the other two types of attacks, which are intended to attack the application itself or the services that support the application being available on the internet:

- Application attacks that send malformed or malicious packets on layer 7 directly to the application
- Infrastructure service attacks, which include network attacks against the infrastructure supporting the application

In this section, we will look at all the relevant layers of the OSI model where our services typically reside and look at the approaches to security on these layers.

Layer 2

Traditionally, layer 2 security is the first level of defense we have from rogue devices within our on-premise local area network. In the cloud, this would be replaced by AWS Config. AWS Config allows us to detect any changes (creation of instances and network interfaces) that could be connected to the VPC. An alert can be sent out that would act in the same fashion as an alert from a network switch that detected a device connection. AWS Config can also be integrated with Lambda, and in cases where strict compliance is required, Lambda can automatically detach and isolate these unauthorized resources so that an incident response team can investigate.

Layer 3

The next layer of security would be on layer 3, which should secure all IP communication. Layer 3 spans all our subnets and all of the internet. Essentially, when we talk about layer 3 protection, we are talking about stateless firewalls. These work in a way that allows everyone to connect from the get-go and then once bad actors on the network are detected, the IP addresses or ranges of these actors are blocked. Layer 3 firewalling can also help with specific network isolation requirements that need to be implemented due to compliance reasons. For example, we would only want a certain IP address range to communicate with another specific IP address range.

This can be simply implemented with layer 3 stateless rules. Stateless firewalls also seamlessly operate without any performance or latency impact on the packet flows. The **Network Access Control Lists (NACLs)** in the VPC take the form of stateless layer 3 firewalls. Layer 3 firewalls are great at stopping the volumetric attacks from the internet once the source has been identified by stopping the attacker at the perimeter of the network. Layer 3 firewalls can also stop some network layer attacks but not all, as the traffic source and destination sometimes isn't enough to identify whether the traffic is legitimate or not.

Layer 4

To prevent more sophisticated network attacks, we need to allow firewalling at the transport layer. Layer 4 firewalls can get some insight into the types of packets being sent and can prevent any kind of malformed packets being dropped at the perimeter where the firewall operates. Layer 4 firewalls also have the ability to maintain session state and, therefore, much easier to manage since once we open the incoming port, the return response will be allowed, no matter what port the return comes from. In AWS security groups, the operating system firewall, AWS Shield, and AWS WAF all play a role in stopping layer 4 attacks and provide a multi layered approach to network security.

Layer 7

With applications becoming more sophisticated every day, we also need to start thinking about more sophisticated ways to protect our applications. At the application layer, we need a device that understands the application and the type of traffic that will be flowing to and from the application. Application firewalling is perhaps the most difficult and wide-ranging subject, and there are numerous ways to approach it. AWS offers WAF, which can help with securing web applications, but there are also other third-party solutions for different application types and for centralized security that's been designed by mainstream firewall vendors and is available from the AWS Marketplace.

As you can see, network security has many different aspects to take into consideration. When designing network security for our application, we need to consider any and all connection points of our application and think about which types of communication protocols we will be using. We should then map these protocols to the OSI network layers to discover the vulnerabilities we might be introducing. Finally, once we have categorized our potential weaknesses, we need to implement appropriate security solutions for each and every layer. In the following sections, we will take a look at how to design our AWS services with security in mind and how to implement security for our application at all the relevant OSI layers.

WAN to LAN access patterns

When the primary source of legitimate connections to our application is the internet, the same will be true for any malicious packets. Any time an application is internet facing, it will need to be protected with as many mechanisms as possible.

Initially, we will need to determine what type of traffic is being sent between the internet and the local network to determine how to secure our application. We should also be aware of the underlying IP protocols in regard to both secure the IPv4 and IPv6 protocols with the same mechanisms.

After analyzing the traffic, we should focus on minimizing the footprint of the attack. This means that we should disable any unnecessary access and limit the incoming traffic only to the legitimate sources. For example, when using an ELB, we should always build a security group that only allows access to the ELB IP instead of both the ELB and the instances it load balances traffic to. The instances should only be accessible from the ELB itself. It is easy to implement this with security groups, as we will see later in this chapter.

Controlling port-based traffic

The primary approach to implementing security is to control ports on which the traffic is being received. There are two types of firewalls that allow port-based traffic control:

- **Stateless firewalls**: All rules are uni directional and no state is maintained. The stateless firewall requires us to specify the incoming ports and the outgoing ports the application will communicate on. This was simple in the early days of the internet with services such as DNS using port 53 and active FTP using port 21. But modern applications mostly use ephemeral ports for the return response, so stateless firewalls are hard to control.
- **Stateful firewalls**: All rules are bi directional. The stateful firewall will maintain a state of the incoming versus return traffic, and will automatically allow a return on any port that matches a request being allowed in the session information. So, essentially, if we allow port 443 for SSL, the firewall will automatically allow a response on any ephemeral port the operating system supports.

Controlling access to applications

To completely control access to the applications, we will use a multi layer, multi firewall, multi solution approach. The types and number of security barriers between the application and the internet will, of course, differ from application to application.

In AWS, we have most of the tools that will give us the ability to implement control at each and every point of access and build as many security barriers as it makes sense to make. Remember, security is like an onion – it should have many layers and it should make the person trying to peel the layers cry more and more!

Now, let's take a look at what security components AWS makes available and how we can implement them.

Securing the VPC

One of the more important aspects of computing is network security. The features of the VPC allow us to put all the basic checks in place to ensure that only the services that we want to expose are reachable. The VPC introduces two network security mechanisms:

- **The security groups**: These protect instances within the subnet.
- **The NACLs**: These protect our network subnets.

Security groups

The primary layer of defense for our instances is the security group. When creating new instances, we will always need to assign a security group to the EC2 instance's primary network adapter or any other ENI that we connect to the instance. The security group acts like a personal stateful firewall protecting each ENI with the security group rules that we assign to it. The security group has stateful port filtering capabilities and allows both the traffic coming into a certain port defined in a rule as well as any return traffic.

For example, a typical modern Linux-based web server would require access to the SSH console on port 22 and to HTTP/HTTPS on ports 80 and 443. To allow access to this server, we would simply create one or more security groups with the appropriate rules that would allow access on ports 22, 80, and 443. We would then assign the security group(s) to the instance, thus allowing access.

For the source, we can specify either IP ranges or other security groups. Specifying security groups is good practice as it allows much easier management as they will be dynamically applied to any instance that has the security group assigned, no matter what subnet the instance is started on.

If we needed to scale the application to multiple instances, we would simply assign the same security groups to them, and the services running on those instances would become accessible on the ports defined in the policy within the group.

Since all inbound ports are implicitly denied by default, all other ports would not be accessible. All outgoing traffic is allowed by the security group by default.

Another best practice is to specify security groups in the incoming rules of other security groups. The security groups are designed as follows:

- **A**: Allows access from the internet to the public IP of the ELB
- **B**: Allows access from only the load balancer security group to the web service security group
- **C**: Allows access from the web service security group to the database service security group:

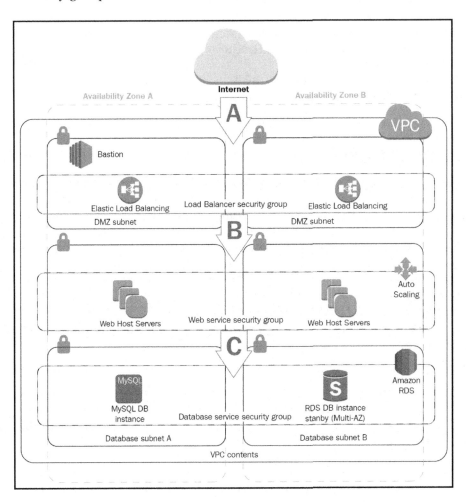

However, there are some limitations in regards to security groups. An ENI of an instance can be a member of only five security groups. We can have multiple ENIs attached to the instance (the maximum depends on the instance type). If we require more than five security groups to be assigned to an instance, we can open a request on AWS support to raise this limit to up to 16. This will not affect the maximum number of security group rules as that is always set at 300, no matter how many security groups we are attaching to an ENI.

NACLs

The second layer of defense is our NACLs. NACLs allow or deny traffic that's coming in or out of the subnet, and are defined as stateless rules that work in exactly one direction. An ACL can be used to define strict rules on network access and provide protection at the network level. The NACLs reside at the entry point to the subnet, and each subnet has a default NACL that is modifiable and can be used to control the traffic when it goes in and out. We can also create additional NACLs, but a subnet in a VPC can only be assigned to one NACL at a time.

NACLs protect subnets within our VPCs in a very similar way to how security groups protect instances. Unlike security groups, NACLs allow all traffic between subnets and gateways by default, so that the security approach that needs to be implemented with NACLs is closing the ports instead of opening them. Also, ACLs can be used when a certain set of IP addresses need to be prevented from accessing our networks; for example, if we need to block certain geographies or a certain set of IPs that have been determined to be malicious.

The following diagram shows how security groups and network ACLs apply within a VPC:

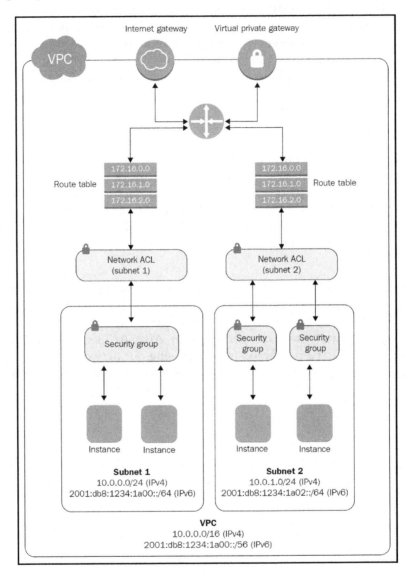

Controlling access

Combining NACLs and security groups gives us complete control of the application. We have the ability to both statelessly control traffic at the edge of the network as well as statefully control access at the perimeter of the elastic network adapter. This gives us a lot of flexibility in regards to what kind of traffic we allow into our instances.

For example, when we need to block malicious traffic from a certain IP address range, we can quickly and easily enter that address range into the NACL, which allows all traffic by default. On the other hand, when we want to only allow access from one very specific IP address, we can enter that IP into a rule on a security group, which is designed to deny all and only allow the sources we enter into the security group by default.

But establishing more layers means that we are generating more complexity, as we need to correctly configure both the stateless settings at the network perimeter and the stateful control at the ENI level. We might not get it right the first time when configuring security, and we might need to diagnose the traffic flow. Here is where VPC Flow Logs come into play.

VPC Flow Logs

When setting up network security with NACLs and security groups, we can sometimes get into a situation where the flow of traffic is not passing through the target as expected. In these cases, VPC Flow Logs provide us with the ability to gain a deeper understanding of the IP traffic going to and from any network interface within the VPC. The Flow Logs capture the status of each packet and the state of the packet in question. We can publish Flow Logs to CloudWatch Logs and view the VPC Flow Logs directly from the management console. We are also able to store the Flow Logs in S3 so that we can store and view the data for historical purposes.

VPC Flow Log examples

A flow log record always displays the values in the following order:

- `version`: The version of the VPC Flow Logs output
- `account ID`: The ID of the account capturing the data
- `ENI ID`: The ID of the ENI adapter on which the flow logs are enabled
- `source IP`: The source IP address sending the request
- `destination IP`: The destination IP address receiving the request

- `source port`: The source port of the sender
- `destination port`: The destination port of the receiver
- `protocol`: The IANA protocol number
- `packets`: The number of packets captured during the time the flow log was enabled
- `bytes`: The number of bytes captured during the time the flow log was enabled
- `start`: The start time in the UNIX timestamp
- `end`: The end time in the UNIX timestamp
- `action`: The action taken by the security groups or NACLs – either `ACCEPT` or `REJECT`
- `log status`: The status of the log – either `OK`, `NODATA`, or `SKIPDATA`

The following is an example of a Flow Log record in which HTTPS traffic was allowed:

```
2 887726112345 eni-f219da8c 10.1.1.12 10.1.2.33 32782 443 6 34 6872
1550695366 1550695395 ACCEPT OK
```

From this record, we can see the following information:

- `version`: In this example, the version is 2.
- `account ID`: The ID of the account is 887726112345.
- `ENI ID`: The ID of the ENI adapter is `eni-f219da8c`.
- `source IP`: The source IP address is 10.1.1.12.
- `destination IP`: The destination IP address is 10.1.2.33.
- `source port`: The source port is 32782.
- `destination port`: The destination port is 443, indicating HTTPS.
- `protocol`: The IANA protocol number is 6, indicating TCP.
- `packets`: The number of packets captured is 34.
- `bytes`: The number of bytes captured is 6872.
- `start`: The start time in the UNIX timestamp is 1550695366.
- `end`: The end time in the UNIX timestamp is 1550695395.
- `action`: The action taken is `ACCEPT`.
- `log status`: The status of the log is `OK`.

The following is an example of a Flow Log record in which HTTPS traffic was rejected. As you can see, the major difference is at the end of the line, where the action that was taken was recorded as REJECT. This means that the NACL or security group blocked the packet from being transmitted to the ENI:

```
2 887726112345 eni-e42989ad 10.1.2.33 10.1.1.12 55421 443 6 14 3218
1550695423 1550695483 REJECT OK
```

The following is an example of a Flow Log record in which no data was recorded while the Flow Logs were being captured. As you can see, we can see the version, account ID, ENI ID, the timestamps, and the status, which is NODATA:

```
2 887726112345 eni-f219da8c - - - - - - - 1550695566 1550695632 - NODATA
```

The following is an example of a Flow Log record in which records were skipped while the Flow Logs were being captured. This can happen due to an error or a performance bottleneck during the time of the capture. The status that's being displayed is SKIPDATA:

```
2 887726112345 eni-e42989ad - - - - - - - 1550695672 1550695782 - SKIPDATA
```

Securing EC2 instance operating systems

Once we have secured the instance with the AWS services, we shouldn't forget the operating system firewall. For example, instances in the same security group are unable to communicate with each other, which means a lot of times, administrators will not think to even start up an operating system firewall. However, not using an instance operating system firewall is bad practice.

For example, multiple teams or individuals might have the ability to manage the AWS environment. One of the teams or individuals could create a rule to allow communication between all the instances in a security group. The change might even be required as there are many cases where an application might require the ability to maintain contact with its peers over the network. If the operating system firewall is not enabled, all of the ports on the machine are exposed to all of the other instances in the same security group. If only one of the instances is compromised, all of the instances in the security group would be instantly vulnerable.

Implementing a firewall in the operating system as well as in AWS decreases the attack footprint of our application and is a security measure that does not come with any drawbacks. The implementation of appropriate security rules in all modern operating system firewalls is well-documented and should be easy for even the most inexperienced network security administrator. I highly recommend using the operating system firewall as I have personally seen issues in environments that could have easily been prevented by simply starting up and configuring the operating system firewall service (and in some cases, not even configuring it!).

EC2 network adapter characteristics

The EC2 network adapters are ENIs. There is a special type of ENI that is attached permanently to the instance called the primary network interface. This interface will show up as the first network interface in the operating system, and we can always define rules based on this principle. The EC2 network adapters will receive IP addresses from the DHCP service. The DHCP service running in the VPC will assign the address based on the VPC subnet that the network adapter is connected to. This means that we should make sure we do not hardcode any static IP addresses into the firewall rules of the EC2 instances, since their IP addresses are dynamic.

Controlling traffic to and from EC2 instances

We can control access to and from each EC2 instance with security groups. Security groups provide us with a basic definition of what kind of traffic will be allowed on which ports from the network. Beyond the network, we can further control the traffic through NACLs and other security features that we will discuss further in this chapter.

Controlling access with the OS firewall

To fully control access to instances, we need to make sure that we are also appropriately configuring the operating system firewall. The initial benefit of the operating system firewall is that it protects our instance from any possible misconfiguration of the security groups while also allowing us another level of traffic logging at the perimeter of the operating system. The operating system firewall might also be configured differently than the security group in certain cases.

An example of this is when an application requires awareness and needs to maintain contact with its peers. This could be because the cluster needs to maintain a certain state that's distributed across the instances or some data being replicated among them. Or, it could simply be a heartbeat that determines the master or lead node in the cluster. In this situation, we need to think about securing the operating systems with the appropriate firewall rules that might be beyond the scope of the security groups since we will need to maintain some open ports for this type of communication to be allowed. We would, however, not want to allow the firewall to be disabled on the instance, as theoretically, a single compromised instance might be able to attack another instance on ports that are left open for no reason.

Advanced EC2 operating system security

By going beyond port-based security, we can discover a whole range of scenarios where the firewall simply isn't enough. One case would be awareness of the traffic flowing through the open ports. When we open port 443, we would usually expect to find HTTPS traffic to our application to be the only thing that would flow there. But many other application protocols such as VPNs, chat, and file transfers can utilize port 443. Because of this, there are options for implementing advanced firewall tools, such as next-generation firewalls and deep packet inspection tools, that will allow us to determine the exact traffic that is passing through the open port. There are many different reasons for doing this, such as compliance and preventing data leakage, which would require us to implement such tools within the operating system or within a certain portion of the network where the packet inspection device operates.

One way to increase security above the capabilities of the operating system firewall would be to implement a software solution within our instances, but the sheer power that's required to analyze all the traffic would mean that the instances would be experiencing a lot of performance overhead to be able to make sense of the content of the packets. But as with all the other features AWS has provided, there are ways to deliver advanced security as a service with advanced security tools.

Delivering advanced network security in AWS

Security groups, NACLs, and the operating system firewall offer us the ability to control the traffic to the OS, ENI, and the subnet with great flexibility. The control mechanisms provided by these three features rely on proven industry-standard stateless layer 3 firewall rules with NACLs, whereas security groups and the OS firewall allow for a stateful layer 4 firewall mechanism in the setup.

However, modern applications require that we maintain security at all the levels of the OSI layer. There are numerous commercial devices that are able to inspect and control traffic, as well as AWS's own features, such as the AWS WAF and AWS Shield, which provide us with the right tools.

In this section, we will take a look at the types of attacks and the advanced network security tools in AWS that will allow us to protect our environment. Namely, we will look at the following:

- Threats to modern applications
- AWS WAF concepts
- DDoS mitigation
- Packet security
- Advanced network security patterns

Threats to modern applications

One of the primary goals in meeting the SLA is the ability to maintain the desired availability of the application. Network security is a crucial factor in maintaining availability as there are many forms of attack that can bring down even the most secure publicly available application. These attacks can be directed either at our application or are designed to disrupt the services our application is depending on.

As we have already mentioned, the ability to protect our application at each and every entry point is crucial. Additionally, we should be implementing security wherever possible. We have already discussed the layers of protection that come with the VPC and within the operating system of the EC2 instance, but today's attackers are very sophisticated and will try and disrupt our service in a way that will mimic real-life traffic and try to overwhelm our application, bringing it to its knees.

AWS outlines several aspects of how to be prepared and mitigate DDoS attacks:

- **Scaling**: The ability to scale our application is crucial. Within AWS, we have all the necessary tools to withstand anything the attacker might throw at us. Though it may be expensive to mitigate an attack through scaling, it is one of the features that will allow us to survive an attack and maintain the SLA.
- **Minimizing the attack surface**: We need to make sure that any unnecessary or unused entry points to the application are removed. We also need to identify all the possible mitigation strategies for any entry points that are crucial for the operation of our application and implement them.
- **Identify traffic patterns**: We need to make sure that we understand the typical traffic pattern of our application. We also need to maintain watch over the traffic pattern and identify any anomalies. This can be automated through CloudWatch alarms in AWS.
- **Resiliency**: Finally, building our application in a manner where it will be resilient to attacks is also a crucial approach to reducing the impact a DDoS attack will have on our application.

To mitigate DDoS attacks and to make sure that our application is secure, we can use two different services in AWS:

- AWS WAF
- AWS Shield

AWS WAF concepts

WAF is a service that's provided by AWS, which lets you monitor and filter traffic that's intended for the following destinations:

- HTTP/HTTPS web servers behind an Application Load Balancer in EC2
- The API Gateway
- CloudFront distributions

WAF allows us to specify conditions like IP addresses or strings in the HTTP request, upon which we can control access to our content. With WAF, we are able to control the intricate details of each request and are able to achieve the following:

- The ability to block malicious scripts, XSS, and SQL injection attempts
- The ability to block queries with a length and type of any regex that should not be supported by our application
- The ability to block sources based on IP ranges, regions, and countries

WAF can be implemented at the edge location when protecting the API Gateway or a CloudFront distribution. This gives us the ability to filter the traffic at the edge location, as shown in the following diagram:

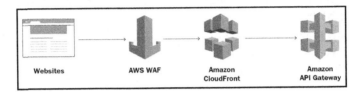

The WAF service can also be implemented as a scalable solution with the so-called **WAF sandwich** approach, where an ELB is put in front of a WAF or a group of WAF devices that can be scaled according to the incoming traffic. The WAF devices send the filtered traffic through to the second ELB that sits in front of our web instances. The naming comes from the WAF being *sandwiched* between two ELBs, as shown in the following diagram:

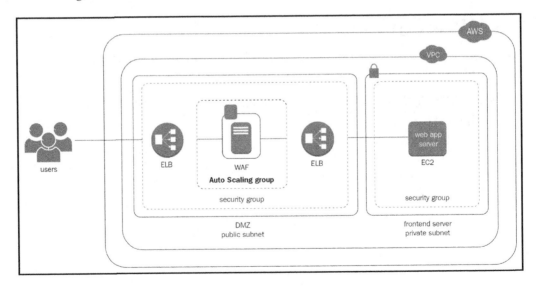

DDoS mitigation

AWS Shield is a DDoS protection service. It allows for automatic detection and mitigation of common DDoS scenarios. AWS Shield comes with the following two options:

- **AWS Shield Standard**: It provides protection at no additional cost when using CloudFront and Route 53. The service provides protection from layer 3 and 4 DDoS attacks.
- **AWS Shield Advanced**: In addition to the features of the standard version, it allows for the protection of EC2 instances and ELBs. On top of the layer 3 and 4 DDoS mitigation, it also provides higher level attack mitigation and near real-time visibility to the traffic. AWS Shield Advanced also allows for integration with AWS WAF to deliver a complete all-in-one mitigation strategy for protecting any kind of web application.

Packet security

The requirements of modern applications sometimes go beyond the security that's provided by both the WAF, AWS Shield, or any port-based firewalls we implement. To achieve complete packet security, we would need a device that would be able to implement a deep packet inspection or packet pattern analysis inside the traffic being sent through the network.

This would be perfectly viable if all the traffic flowing to our applications was unencrypted. However, encryption is becoming a standard approach to application security and this is the point at which AWS draws a line of separation of responsibility. To make sure your environment is always secure from intrusion, the shared security model delegates all security of content to the end user. It could be seen as a breach of security if AWS was able to implement a device that would decrypt, inspect, and encrypt any secure traffic over the internet. Essentially, it would be a man-in-the-middle attack for security purposes.

Advanced network security patterns

To achieve complete security at all OSI layers, we would need to implement a third-party device such as a next-generation firewall, IDS/IPS, or deep packet inspection device with a specially designed network architecture approach. We would either implement a subnet or a special VPC where the device (or cluster of devices) would be running, and then we would redirect all the traffic to the device(s) in the specially designed network.

The subnet approach is shown in the following diagram:

Essentially, the public subnet in the preceding diagram only hosts our network security device or devices. All the traffic from the private subnets to the internet and from the internet to the private subnets must pass through the network security device. Therefore, the device is able to screen the traffic, inspect the packet content, or simply understand the traffic patterns. This can help determine whether the traffic being passed through the device is legitimate or is a form of attack, attempt at an external intrusion, or represent an internal breach of security or disclosure of confidential data.

There are different types of network security devices that can be positioned in the public subnet to deliver the required security, including but not limited to the following:

- IPS/IDS devices
- Next-generation firewalls
- Network packet sniffers and deep packet inspection tools
- WAFs
- Data leak prevention devices

Summary

In this chapter, we learned about the security aspects of the AWS environment. We talked about the different components we can use to protect our networks and the way these components can be integrated together to provide comprehensive security measures for our application. We looked at the NACLs and security groups, the operating system firewall, and, going beyond packet security, we have also looked at the WAF and Shield services since their features can help us make our application available and secure on the network.

In the next chapter, we will look at the connectivity options for connecting our on-premises networks with AWS. We will learn all about how to create, manage, and secure hybrid cloud solutions.

Questions

1. Which component acts as a stateful firewall that can filter the incoming port-based traffic of our ENI?
2. You have opened port 80 in your NACL and all the security groups of your subnet. The web servers running in the subnet are still not responding. What is the reason for this?
3. Your web instances are running the Ubuntu Linux distribution. Your website is not accessible, even after you opened port 80 in the security group and verified that the NACL allows all traffic in both directions. You were instructed to run `ufw disable` inside the instance by a Linux administrator and now the website is accessible. Is this the right approach to providing access to the web service?
4. You are unable to establish a connection to your web server. You have enabled the VPC Flow Logs and are seeing the following output:

   ```
   2 887726112345 eni-fa9d12ad 10.0.0.10 103.0.1.172 55421 443 6 7
   1132 1550832406 1550832456 REJECT OK
   ```

   What could be the reason for the server being unavailable?

5. You need to secure your EC2 instances behind an ELB with a WAF. What architecture approach would you consider in this scenario?

6. You have a single stateless EC2 instance running your website on a t2.medium instance. The web gets hit by a lot of traffic once a week for about 45 minutes, during which it is unavailable. You have identified the traffic as coming from a single public subnet of IPv4 addresses. You have determined that the amount of traffic would require at least three instances of the same type to handle. How can you improve your scenario and make sure that your server is available during the spike in traffic?

7. You are running a S3 static website with a dynamic component running behind an API Gateway. You are looking to implement DDoS mitigation on the website. How could this be achieved?

Further reading

Refer to the following references to learn more about what was covered in this chapter:

- **Ephemeral ports**: https://en.wikipedia.org/wiki/Ephemeral_port
- **AWS WAF for vulnerability mitigation**: https://aws.amazon.com/about-aws/whats-new/2017/07/use-aws-waf-to-mitigate-owasps-top-10-web-application-vulnerabilities/
- **AWS network ACLs**: https://docs.aws.amazon.com/vpc/latest/userguide/vpc-network-acls.html
- **AWS security groups**: https://docs.aws.amazon.com/vpc/latest/userguide/VPC_SecurityGroups.html
- **Protocol numbers**: https://www.iana.org/assignments/protocol-numbers/protocol-numbers.xhtml
- **Security Group Rules Reference**: https://docs.aws.amazon.com/AWSEC2/latest/UserGuide/security-group-rules-reference.html
- **AWS WAF**: https://docs.aws.amazon.com/waf/latest/developerguide/waf-chapter.html
- **AWS DoS mitigation**: https://aws.amazon.com/answers/networking/aws-ddos-attack-mitigation/
- **AWS Shield**: https://docs.aws.amazon.com/waf/latest/developerguide/ddos-overview.html

4
Connecting On-Premises and AWS

We have now taken a look at how to create a private network with the **Amazon Virtual Private Cloud** (**Amazon VPC**) and how to secure the VPC and the applications and devices that will be connected within the VPC, but there are many companies out there that would like to migrate from their on-premises network to AWS. Also, there are many scenarios in which running solely in the cloud is not an option. In this chapter, we will take a look at connecting the AWS environment with other private and on-premises networks.

This chapter will walk you through all the things you need to know about connecting VPCs to on-premises networks. You will learn about connectivity options and services, and how and when to use them in the best possible manner.

The following topics will be covered in this chapter:

- An overview of on-premises connectivity
- Connecting VPCs and private networks
- VPNs with the virtual private gateway
- Connecting with Direct Connect
- Designing highly available and secure WAN links

Technical requirements

The reader is required to have a solid understanding of **local area network** (**LAN**) and **wide area network** (**WAN**) designs, WAN connectivity options, **virtual private networks** (**VPNs**), the **Open Systems Interconnection** (**OSI**) model, and WAN routing. Hands-on experience in configuring WAN/LAN/VPN-related devices, services, and their networks is a bonus.

An overview of on-premises connectivity

An on-premises environment can have quite a complicated setup from a network point of view. It might be represented as a data center with a well-organized structure, several layers of switching, every port labeled, and every connection accounted for. Security systems in all spots, from multi-factor access to video surveillance to all kinds of network security devices, are connected and scanning the network for threats. However, in a lot of cases, the term *on-premises* describes not just one network or one data center, but a complicated set of different networks, different devices, mismatched equipment, a mix of servers, office workers, road warriors and home office users, remote sites, collocation sites, and partner sites. An approximation of a typical network you might find when talking about *on-premises* is shown in the following diagram:

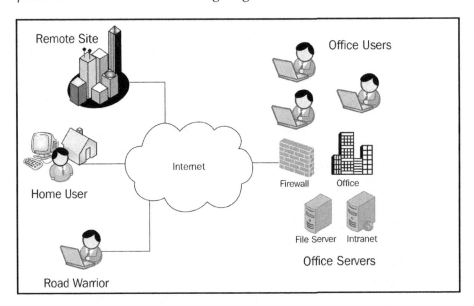

You'll quickly notice that the *ideal* on-premises environment that we all think of when talking about the hybrid cloud is rarely represented by modern, fairly complicated corporate networks and that the challenge of connecting all of the bits and pieces of a modern corporate network to a cloud environment might get quite complicated. A typical on-premises environment might need any of the following connectivity types:

- Connectivity to the internet
- Connectivity for the users to access the office and servers (with a client VPN)
- Connectivity from one location to another (with a site-to-site VPN)
- Leased lines or optical fibers to collocation and data center sites

The advantage that AWS has is that it can cover any of these requirements with managed services that provide several options for connecting to AWS, including the following:

- An AWS-managed VPN with a virtual private gateway
- AWS VPN CloudHub
- Using a VPN instance that we build ourselves
- Using a VPN instance from the AWS Marketplace
- An AWS client VPN for OpenVPN clients
- Direct Connect private optical links to AWS

Connecting VPCs and private networks

Essentially, when we talk about connecting a VPC, we need to talk about connecting the private subnets of a VPC to another network. The concepts behind connecting subnets with other private networks are very similar to the VPC peering discussed in `Chapter 2,` *Networking with Virtual Private Cloud (VPC)*. Essentially, a private connection is established across a public network and routing is configured to allow private networks to communicate with each other.

In this part of the chapter, we will be looking at the following topics to get a good understanding of the requirements of connecting a private network to the AWS environment:

- Connectivity across networks
- Public IPv4 and IPv6 traffic patterns
- Public routing and BGP

Connectivity across networks

When connecting private networks, a typical approach is to create a private link in the form of a VPN or a leased line. The private link establishes either a layer 2 or layer 3 connection between the networks. When a leased line is used, the devices connecting the networks can actually be designed to allow layer 2 traffic to pass between the two sites. Unfortunately, using layer 2 links to connect different private networks is, however, not very cost effective, as the cost of the leased line increases dramatically when increasing the distance between the sites.

The most common modern approach to connecting private networks is by using layer 3 connections. When using connections based on layer 3, we introduce the context of routing. This implies that the traffic can be passed between devices and routed over higher level connections, such as the internet. The biggest benefit of using layer 3 connections is lower cost. It is actually no different when we are connecting two computers in the same room or two devices on the opposite side of the planet (or perhaps multiple planets, in the future). The biggest drawback of using layer 3, however, is the increase in latency. Layering increases latency by itself and so does each device routing the traffic. In high-performance applications, in which latency is crucial, layer 2 connectivity is the preferred approach.

Essentially, AWS provides both options for connecting the on-premises environment with a VPC:

- **Direct Connect**: This is a fast, low-latency, layer 2 connection established on dedicated private links between the on-premises location and the VPC.
- **VPN with a virtual gateway**: This is a layer 3, IPSec-encrypted connection between the VPC and an on-premises network over the public internet.

Public IPv4 and IPv6 traffic patterns

Since we are connecting on layer 3, we will be using the IP protocol to connect as it is the de facto protocol of the internet. As we all know, IP comes in v4 and v6 variants. With IPv4, there is a clear distinction between private and public networks – private ranges sit in predefined private IP ranges, whereas with IPv6, there really is no such concept as all of the addressing being assigned in IPv6 belong to a global unicast scope (with the exception of `fc00::/7`, reserved for ULA, and `fe80::/10`, reserved for auto-configuration, which are special-purpose addresses but still belong to the global scope). This means that there will be quite a lot of distinction between the way two private networks are connected on IPv4 versus how two IPv6 networks can be defined as private and connected.

IPv4

With IPv4, a private network is inherently private, even when a gateway with a NAT device is attached to the network to connect the members of the network to the internet. The NAT device allows for the connection of a public IP address with which all devices connected to the private network will be able to access the internet. The NAT device will be the gateway to the private network and will keep a mapping of internal IPs to external targets that each of the IPs is connecting to, and forward the traffic accordingly, as demonstrated in the following diagram:

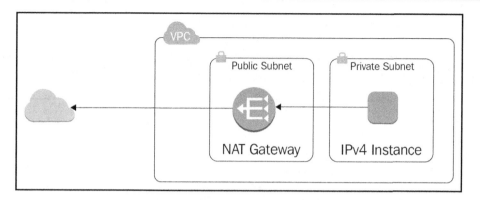

We can selectively make certain addresses within the private network public by adding a 1:1 destination NAT to our NAT device, where we connect a private IP with a fixed public IP. This is exactly how public VPC subnets work:

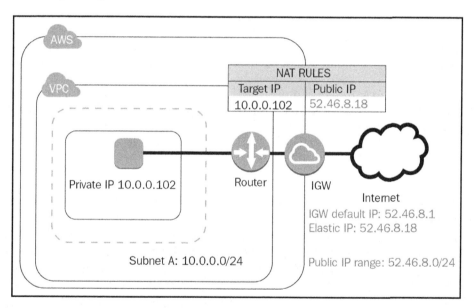

As demonstrated in the preceding diagram, the EC2 instance with a private IP has been connected to a router and an **internet gateway (IGW)**. The IP address of this instance is in the private range of subnet A, but an elastic IP is also assigned to the instance. The elastic IP, in fact, resides on the IGW device as a secondary IP address on the IGW adapter, as only the IGW is connected to the public IP range. The IGW will consult its NAT rules to send traffic to the internal private address of the instance. The instance will always be visible to the outside world with its elastic IP address.

To connect two private networks, the networks need to establish a connection. For example, the NAT device can also work as a VPN gateway and the two private networks can be connected. However, the limitation of the IPv4 VPNs is that the network ranges must never overlap, as there would be a routing failure if such overlapping occurred:

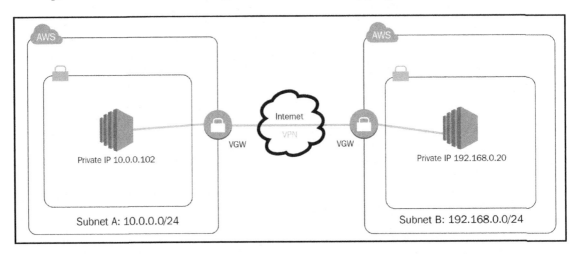

The VPN connection example is demonstrated in the preceding diagram, where two IPv4 subnets are connected via the internet with a VPN connection. The VPN allows both private networks to directly access each other.

IPv6

As IPv6 is a protocol based on global unicast addressing, the network is only private when it is not connected to the internet. This means that as soon as we connect a gateway to the IPv6 subnet, all the addresses in the network will gain access to the internet and become accessible from the internet. No concept of NAT exists in IPv6 networks, so instead of the networks being inherently private, they are inherently public. To retain privacy on an IPv6 network, but still have the ability to connect to the internet, we would need to configure the gateway in a way that blocks the incoming traffic to the subnet it serves. This is exactly how the egress-only gateway in a VPC operates to maintain private IPv6 networks.

Public routing and BGP

Once we have connected the subnets to the internet, the context of routing comes into play. Each packet in the IP space is routed either through IPv4 or IPv6 routing mechanisms to reach its final destination. Since the IP protocols live in the network layer, the devices that transmit the packets across the internet need to use some kind of mechanism to determine where to send the packet so it will reach its intended destination. Each device that is connected to the internet will need to determine its own gateway to exit the network, and the gateway will need to understand which other devices host which sets of IP addresses.

On today's internet, the **Border Gateway Protocol (BGP)** is used to route traffic between so-called **autonomous systems (AS)**. Each AS has an AS number assigned and each AS is allowed to maintain routing for certain network ranges as defined by the **Internet Assigned Numbers Authority (IANA)** and maintained by the **Regional Internet Registries (RIRs)**. An autonomous system can be any kind of provider that has registered a public network with an RIR. This means an autonomous system will be assigned to each ISP, a cloud provider such as AWS, a large organization, or commercial entity with a certain requirement for handling and delivering their own IP ranges independently on the internet. BGP is designed to allow the exchange of routing and reachability information for sets of IP addresses for each of the AS routes in its network:

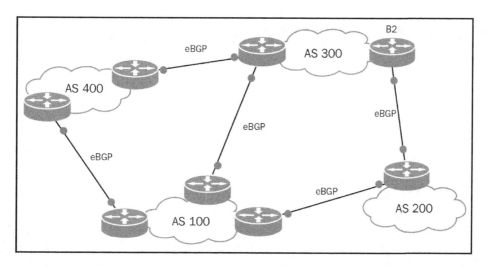

The preceding diagram is a very simplified schematic of how the BGP protocol allows different autonomous systems to communicate with each other and share routes. For example, in the diagram, AS 100 and AS 300 both have three routes with direct connections to all the other AS environments.

AS 200 and AS 400 only have two routes each, connecting them only to AS 100 and AS 300. BGP allows all the autonomous systems to advertise all the known routes to each other and enables the delivery of packets across links that otherwise would not be possible. For instance, when a system connected to AS 400 needs to communicate with another system in AS 200, it can simply send the traffic toward AS 100 or AS 300. In turn, routers in AS 100, which have an existing route to AS 200, will simply forward the packets over to the router of AS 200.

Being able to understand the IPv4 and IPv6 patterns is crucial to understanding the way private networks are defined and connected. AWS is proficient in routing, and in some cases, BGP routing is a must before we can consider connecting our private on-premises environment with a VPC.

The solution we choose will always be dictated by the requirements of our application. If our application requires very high network performance with low latency, then we can think about using a Direct Connect private layer 2 link. If the requirement is to establish a connection as cheaply as possible, then a VPN with a VGW is the right option. In the next two sections of this chapter, we will be taking a look at these two connectivity options provided by AWS.

VPN with the virtual private gateway

AWS makes it fairly easy to connect your on-premises network with the cloud environment. The simplest way to achieve this is to use the connectivity that is already available – the internet. We can simply establish a VPN connection with the AWS environment and allow for the delivery of a secure and reliable solution that can be used in most scenarios in which VPN-type connectivity to AWS is required.

Working with VPN

The Amazon VPN gateway is a managed service solution available from AWS that can be a very cost-effective way to connect our on-premises environment with an AWS VPC. The virtual private gateway is a logical network device that allows us to establish an IPSec VPN tunnel from our VPC to our on-premises environment. We have the ability to connect each and every subnet from our VPC to the VPN connection.

For each VPN connection, two public tunnel endpoints are created to enable automatic failover from your gateway device, as demonstrated in the following diagram:

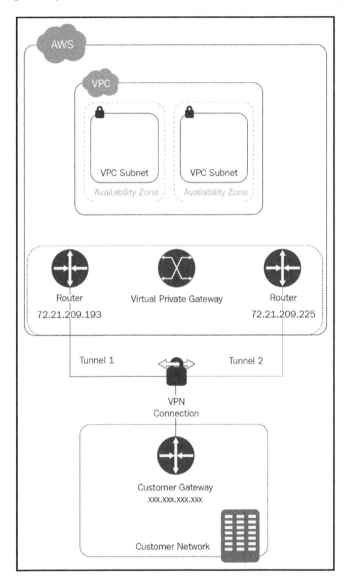

We have the ability to connect to multiple remote sites from one AWS VPN gateway; however, no transient traffic can pass through a VPN gateway. If we require a certain subnet to communicate with a certain on-premises network, a separate VPN connection needs to be established to that network, as demonstrated in the following diagram:

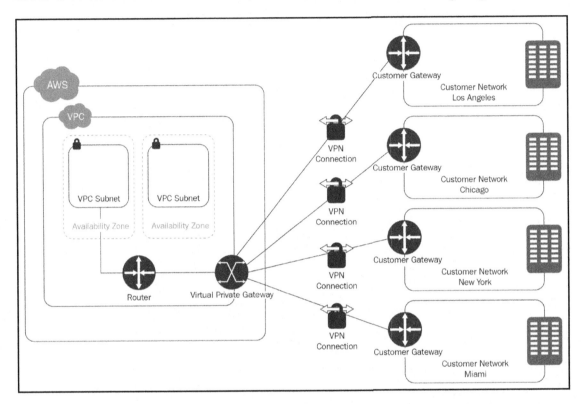

The VGW service limits

By default, each AWS account is allowed to create up to 50 site-to-site connections per region and up to 10 site-to-site connections per VGW. If those limits need to be increased, we are always able to open a support request and get them raised. The VGW supports NAT traversal out of the box and can be configured to connect to networks with a 2-byte or 4-byte ASN. We should also consider that each VGW only supports IPSec VPN throughput up to 1.25 GBps.

Securing VPNs

The AWS VPN connections support IPSec tunnels with IKEv2 and AES-256 encryption, SHA-2 hashing, and Diffie-Hellman groups, meaning all the steps of the authentication, key exchange, and traffic transmission phases are secured by default. When building a solution that requires encryption in transit, using a VPN will ensure the encryption is established from the local VPN device to the VGW over the internet. If our application requires end-to-end security, however, we still need to think about the encryption of the traffic between the server and client when not on the VPN (for example, during transit in the VPC or during transit in the on-premises network). This would usually be achieved by securing the traffic above the network level (for example, HTTPS, SSL encryption, or TDE for a database).

Connecting with Direct Connect

There are definite limitations when connecting over the internet with virtual devices. If we find that the throughput of a VGW does not meet our demand, or when running a huge VPN instance just wouldn't be economical, we have a better option that creates a fast, reliable, private link – AWS Direct Connect.

The following diagram shows how Direct Connect can be utilized to connect with AWS resources:

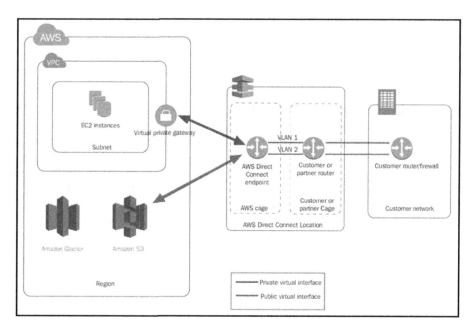

The connection between AWS and the customer is split into two different sections:

- The connection between the AWS region and the Direct Connect location
- The connection between the Direct Connect location and the customer location

When connecting to AWS with Direct Connect, we will need to deliver a device that will terminate the optical link between AWS and our equipment and install it into a designated Direct Connect location rack. From there onward, we will need to ensure a way to connect our on-premises network to the Direct Connect location and establish the second part of the link. The Direct Connect partners will provide the options required to establish the connection.

To connect to different VPCs and public AWS endpoints, we will need to create a VLAN that will connect us to each private or public interface created. A private interface will allow for connecting to the VPC, and, optionally, establishing a VPN connection over the Direct Connect link to encrypt our traffic.

When the Direct Connect provider uses an MPLS connection, they might require us to use their own provider VLAN to separate our traffic. In this case, we will need to use Q-in-Q VLAN encapsulation to provide the ability to connect to different AWS resources.

For example, a Direct Connect provider assigns VLAN 1234 to the MPLS link between the Direct Connect location and our on-premises data center. In AWS, we have designated VLAN 1 and 2, each connecting us to a separate VPC. This setup would require us to enable Q-in-Q between our on-premises network device and our customer router in the Direct Connect location that connects directly to AWS. The Q-in-Q connection would encapsulate VLANs 1 and 2 into VLAN 1234, while in transit on the MPLS link.

Working with Direct Connect

AWS Direct Connect allows you to establish a dedicated layer 2 network connection between your network and one of the AWS Direct Connect locations around the globe. The providers use private optical links with 802.1q VLAN support so that we have complete control over the traffic going to AWS. The traffic can, thus, be directed over multiple virtual interfaces to access multiple private subnets or public AWS services, such as S3, each over its own VLAN. AWS Direct Connect is the right solution whenever there is a requirement for the following:

- Lower latency
- Predictable performance
- Higher throughput

- Large amounts of data are being transferred daily between your on-premises environment and AWS
- Security and compliance requirements prevent the use of internet links

AWS Direct Connect can also save you money on transfer costs from AWS to your data center, as it is much cheaper to transfer data through the Direct Connect link than it is to transfer it over the internet. You can configure a lot of services to be directly accessible via the Direct Connect link, by creating a public virtual interface for those services or by adding those services as VPC endpoints to the subnet you are connecting to.

Direct Connect requirements

To be able to use Direct Connect, you have to, of course, be located in an area or building being serviced by an AWS Direct Connect partner. This usually means a data center with collocation services being provided by the partner, but in some cases, even metro area networks are serviced by these partners. To find a partner, visit the link provided in the *Further reading* section of this chapter.

You will also be required to have a device that can connect to a single-mode fiber connection with a 1000BASE-LX or 10GBASE-LR transceiver. The device must allow for the port speed and full-duplex mode to be configured manually. The device needs to support BGP and BGP MD5 authentication. Furthermore, 802.1Q VLAN encapsulation must be supported across the entire connection.

Securing Direct Connect

The Direct Connect links are private by design, but that private network might be passing through several provider devices before it reaches your VPC. The layer 2 connection between your VPC and your on-premises environment can be subject to sniffing on compromised equipment or even on compromised links between devices. In case we require an even higher level of security, AWS allows us to establish an IPSec VPN connection through the Direct Connect connection and, thus, automatically encrypts traffic passing between our on-premises location and AWS. This is a really good solution when compliance requirements dictate that any link can be encrypted, even if the layer 2 network is considered private. The drawback of securing links in this manner is that the same VGW is used for establishing the IPSec tunnels, so the limitations of the VGW device apply to any IPSec connections established over Direct Connect.

Designing highly available and secure WAN links

What about when even one Direct Connect link is not enough? When a requirement for high availability or more performance is expressed, then we should be looking at multiple connections to provide connectivity from on-premises to AWS.

When designing a highly available solution, we should always consider the following aspects:

- Reliability
- Routing
- Encryption

Reliability

So, how do we achieve reliability when connecting our hybrid network? With the basic VPN, high availability is already included. Each VPN connection will have two tunnels that can be configured to route the same network through BGP priorities. This built-in redundancy is demonstrated in the following diagram:

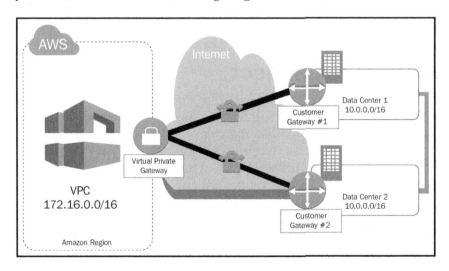

For Direct Connect, the design for reliability becomes a bit more complicated. The simplest thing to do is to connect a separate VPN connection with the same routes, so, if the Direct Connect link is down, the VPN connection can take over.

AWS has designed Direct Connect to always have priority over VPN when routing the same networks over BGP. A setup with a Direct Connect link with a VPN backup for redundancy is demonstrated in the following diagram:

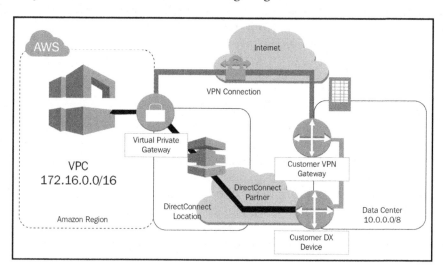

To achieve full redundancy of Direct Connect links, we can establish two Direct Connect connections to two different partner locations. If feasible, this can also be done from across two separate regions to increase the redundancy. The following diagram demonstrates the redundancy of two Direct Connect links:

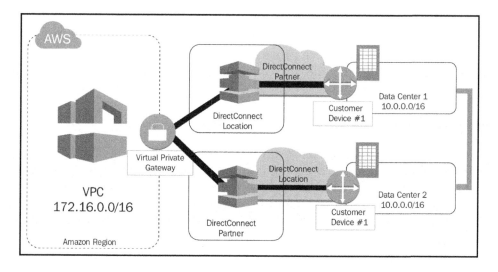

Each of these solutions is designed to deliver redundancy at a different level and at a different price point. The built-in VGW redundancy is the cheapest way to deliver a basic level of redundancy that will protect us from most common outages. Establishing two Direct Connect links, on the other hand, is going to be the most expensive, but will deliver the most redundancy and can protect from outages of whole regions if the Direct Connect links are terminated in different regions.

Routing

We also have the ability to connect two (or more) separate Direct Connect connections to our on-premises location. Now here, we need to make sure that we also configure the routing appropriately. In this case, both Direct Connect links have the same priority, so the only way to control the flow of traffic is to define the routes on the devices. The easiest way to configure high availability is to allow for dynamic routing across two or more Direct Connect links. When dynamic routing is enabled, the failover from one to another Direct Connect link can be done automatically. We can ensure this by enabling **Bidirectional Forwarding Detection (BFD)** on the devices connecting to the Direct Connect links.

However, dynamic routing does not make sense in all situations. When required, we do have the option to control the priority of traffic across a given Direct Connect link. To achieve priority, we can either specify a more specific BGP route or BGP AS-path, prepending with a higher priority for each network that we would like to route through a specific link. If the link fails, the more broadly defined route on the secondary link can take over.

When using two Direct Connect links, always make sure to determine the sites that the links will be established to, and which providers you are using, to avoid issues with the site or a provider, and make sure that the connections will truly be following different paths.

Encryption

As we have already discussed, we can secure a Direct Connect link by allowing an IPSec tunnel to be established over the Direct Connect link. To enable this functionality, we would need to configure a public virtual network interface on the Direct Connect connection between AWS and our on-premises environment. To deliver high availability in this scenario, we would use BGP to advertise the public IP address of both our VGW and our customer gateway on each Direct Connect connection where the VPNs would be running.

The implications of this setup mean that our Direct Connect connections simply become layer 2 carriers for the layer 3 IPSec tunnels established on our VGWs. What this means is that each direct connection encrypted with this approach will now essentially become equal to any other VGW-established connection.

For example, we would have a primary link designated to send traffic across a Direct Connect link. All this traffic needs to be encrypted. A secondary link can be established as a VPN over the internet. When the Direct Connect link is encrypted through a VGW-enabled IPSec VPN on top, it becomes equal to the secondary VGW-enabled VPN IPSec connection over the internet. We have previously said the Direct Connect link is designed with priority over any VGW traffic. But in this case, the BGP endpoint is the VGW in both cases, so, essentially, we now have two AWS site-to-site VPNs, so the traffic being advertised over the VGW will need to be routed appropriately if we want to maintain the correct primary-secondary relationship.

Summary

In this chapter, we took a look at the requirements and details when connecting on-premises and cloud environments. Starting with an overview of general requirements, we worked our way to VPNs and Direct Connect connections, and described the approaches to making the connections secure and encrypted, as well as offering a glimpse into how to make these connections highly available.

In the next chapter, we will discuss the **Elastic Load Balancer** (**ELB**) and the ability to use the ELB to securely distribute traffic across our EC2 instances and ECS containers.

Questions

1. How do IPv4 private networks differ from IPv6?
2. What is the benefit of using layer 3 connections over layer 2 across long distances?
3. In BGP, what does AS stand for?
4. What kind of tunnel is established between a VGW and an on-premises gateway?
5. What is the throughput of a VGW?

6. Name three features that need to be supported on the customer device when using Direct Connect.

7. You are looking to establish a securely encrypted, reliable, and predictable low-latency 1 GB network link from on-premises to AWS. What solution would you recommend?

8. You are required to establish a highly available connection from your AWS VPC to the on-premises environment. The connection needs to be highly available and as cheap as possible. What would you recommend?

Further reading

- **AWS VPN Connections**: https://docs.aws.amazon.com/vpc/latest/userguide/vpn-connections.html
- **AWS Direct Connect**: https://docs.aws.amazon.com/aws-technical-content/latest/aws-vpc-connectivity-options/aws-direct-connect-network-to-amazon.html
- **Direct Connect Partners**: https://aws.amazon.com/directconnect/partners
- **HA from on-premises to AWS**: https://aws.amazon.com/answers/networking/aws-multiple-data-center-ha-network-connectivity

3
Section 3: Managing and Securing Network-Attached Platform Services in AWS

Elastic Load Balancer (**ELB**) is a load balancing service which distributes incoming traffic across multiple EC2 instances, containers, or IP addresses and increases the fault tolerance of the environment. This section describes the way to secure the ELB and elaborates on the critical aspects of ELB service. Network administrators are expected to maintain low latency, security and the highest possible uptime of the content being delivered from their servers. For this purpose, AWS introduces the CloudFront **Content Delivery Network** (**CDN**), which can securely handle content distribution at any scale.

This section provides an overview of some of the critical features of CloudFront to help manage and secure it. Amazon Route 53 is a highly available and scalable cloud **Domain Name System** (**DNS**) web service. This section introduces you to the service and describes various components of the service. One of the ways to expose our services on the network is through the API gateway. We are going to take a look at how to maintain security and the highest possible uptime of the content being delivered through the API gateway.

We will cover the following chapters in this section:

- Chapter 5, *Managing and Securing Server with ELB*
- Chapter 6, *Managing and Securing Content Distribution with CloudFront*
- Chapter 7, *Managing and Securing the Route 53 Domain Name System*
- Chapter 8, *Managing and Securing API Gateway*

5
Managing and Securing Servers with ELB

In the previous chapters, we discussed the high availability of networks. This chapter will continue with the high availability theme and discuss how to make our applications that are running in the cloud highly available. We will also take a look at how to distribute traffic among a set of instances serving the same content through load balancing by taking a look at the AWS **Elastic Load Balancing** (**ELB**) service.

This chapter will walk you through all you need to know about the ELB service. You will learn about the functionality of the different ELBs and how and when to use them in the best possible manner.

The following topics will be covered in this chapter:

- Introduction to ELB
- Types of ELB
- Working with the ELB
- Securing traffic on the ELB

Technical requirements

To follow along with this topic, a familiarity with load balancing technologies and the delivery of network load distribution to groups of servers is required. A clear understanding of the **Elastic Compute Cloud** (**EC2**) service is also needed as common EC2 concepts will be discussed in this chapter. Any hands-on experience with load balancers and supporting technologies is a bonus.

Introduction to ELB

The AWS ELB service delivers a high performance, highly available, highly scalable cloud-based load balancing managed solution. The ELB service provides us with all the features that are required for the distribution of load across multiple instances or containers within our AWS environment. The service has the ability to automatically distribute and detect failures, therefore allowing high availability targets to also be met. The ELB service also integrates with CloudWatch and the EC2 Auto Scaling service to enable the Auto Scaling of our instance clusters according to the load being experienced or the connection increases and decreases.

Types of ELB

The ELB service was initially started as a single solution that provided some layer 4 and layer 7 support. However, as the applications in the cloud evolved, so did the requirements of the users. Modern applications require us to implement load balancing solutions that can either fully understand the structure of the traffic on layer 7, or support extremely high performance on the network layer and let the application handle what the application knows best. At the time of writing, there are three types of load balancing that can meet various application requirements:

- **Classic Load Balancer**: With both layer 4 and some layer 7 load balancing features
- **Application Load Balancer**: A pure layer 7 load balancer
- **Network Load Balancer**: A pure layer 4 load balancer

Classic Load Balancer (CLB)

Everyone used to refer to the CLB as the ELB. This was due to the fact that, for some years, what we now call the CLB was the only load balancing solution. The CLB is essentially a quite powerful but fairly simple load balancer. The service provides us with a highly available and secure load balancer that supports both IPv4 and IPv6. The CLB is able to load balance requests on the connection level as well as perform some basic request-level traffic control, mainly with support for X-Forwarded HTTP headers and sticky sessions. The CLB can also simplify the application configuration and reduce performance overheads by offloading HTTPS traffic at the entry point of connection from our clients. As with any other service on AWS, it is fully integrated with CloudWatch metrics, from which we can extract real-time metrics and set it up with alarms that can integrate with Auto Scaling and other services.

Application Load Balancer (ALB)

The ALB is the first part of the next generation of the ELB service. It provides many of the advanced features that are required by modern applications to deliver more flexibility when routing traffic based on layer 7 requests. The ALB features full layer 7 traffic shaping capabilities, as well as the layer 7 features found in the CLB. Its main power lies in the ability to target multiple backends that can respond to different types of requests, with different types of content. The ALB can distinguish and determine the destination based on the following:

- **The browser or initiator type**: It can send desktop browsers to the default page, mobile clients to mobile pages, and API calls to the API
- **The path being accessed**: It can determine which service is responsible for a certain path, for example, `website.address/images` to the image frontend, `website.address/forum` to the forum backend, and `website.address/uploads` to the uploads frontend

The following diagram demonstrates an example of an ALB load balancing to multiple target groups based on the requested path:

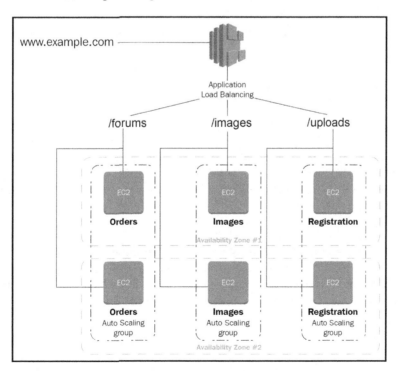

The ALB is also able to send traffic to the following targets:

- Any reachable IP in the same VPC
- Any reachable IP within a peered VPC in the same region
- An EC2 instance connected to a VPC via ClassicLink
- An on-premises resource connected via VPN or an AWS Direct Connect connection

Network Load Balancing (NLB)

The second next-generation load balancer from AWS ELB service is NLB. This highly available, fully managed service was introduced to deliver a very high network throughput (in the millions of connections) and very low latency to client services at the network level. NLB can deliver consistent performance, even for very spiky application operating patterns. Since it works on the network layer, it cannot deliver any higher-layer features, like those provided by the ALB or the CLB. Being network bound also means it will only be able to serve a specific static or Elastic IP address, or a specific target availability zone or zones—that is the trade-off for performance. The benefit of NLB is that it can forward the packets transparently with the source address fully intact, giving us the ability to control session behavior within our application backend.

Working with the ELB

The ELB service works by receiving traffic from different sources over the internet on a so-called listener. The listener is configured when you're creating an ELB, and it will define what type of traffic on which port the ELB will listen on. Any listener that we configure will also be associated with a single target group. If we are working with the ALB, we can also map multiple target groups to one listener, but we will need to define the listener rules so that the load balancer can determine how to send the traffic to the backend.

Once the correct target group is determined, the traffic is sent to one of the targets (instances, containers, on-premises, or external IP addresses) in the target group. All of the instances in a target group should be serving the same content so that when a client requests a certain page, file, and image, that content is delivered in the same way, no matter which target served the response. This operation of the ELB is demonstrated in the following diagram:

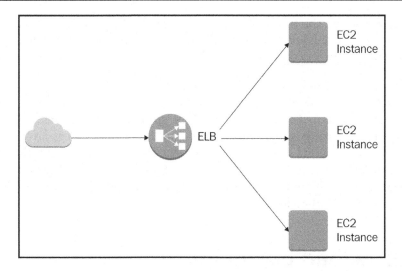

In order to maintain application availability, the load balancer will determine the health of the application. If one of the targets that the load balancer sends traffic to fails the health check, the load balancer can mark the target as unhealthy and send the traffic to another target in the same group. The health check can fail for any reason, such as instance failure, service failure, or another problem within the instance, for example, high CPU usage. The following diagram demonstrates the server load being high, therefore triggering a health check failure:

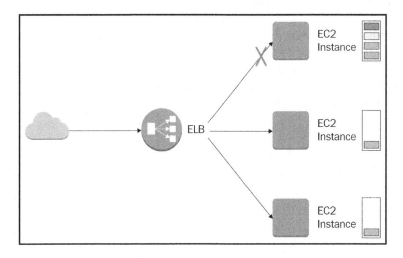

The ELB will stop sending the traffic to the instance due to the failure, but if the instance were to recover, the health check will pass again and the instance will again be included in the load balancing scenario.

In order to deliver high availability, the load balancer can load balance traffic across multiple availability zones. This way, the traffic can be directed to an environment that can withstand not just a single instance failure but the complete failure of an availability zone. When building a target group, we should ensure that the EC2 instances are deployed into subnets that reside in different availability zones. We should also consider the numbers of instances and how the traffic will be load balanced across the availability zones. If the number of instances in each availability zone might be uneven, then we should consider enabling cross-zone load balancing.

Cross-zone load balancing

Load balancing across multiple availability zones can be done in two different ways. When we're creating or configuring a load balancer, we have the ability to either enable or disable the cross-zone load balancing feature.

When cross-zone load balancing is disabled, each availability zone will receive an equal amount of load, regardless of the number of instances in the availability zones. For example, if we are load balancing across two availability zones, then each availability zone will be receiving half the traffic, whereas when we load balance across three availability zones, then each will receive one-third of the traffic. This is demonstrated in the following diagram, where the traffic is distributed across two availability zones, with one hosting two instances and the other hosting four instances. In this case, each availability zone is receiving half of the traffic, meaning availability zone A with two instances will need to serve a quarter of the traffic on each instance, whereas in availability zone B, only an eighth of the traffic will be served by each instance:

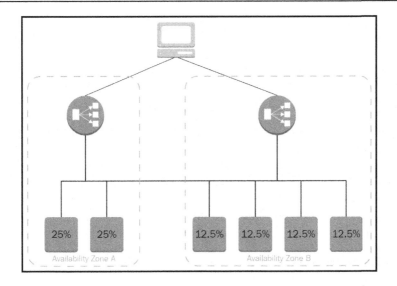

When cross-zone load balancing is enabled, each instance will receive an equal amount of load, regardless of the availability zone it resides in. This is demonstrated in the following diagram, where the traffic is distributed across six instances in two availability zones. In this case, each instance is receiving one-sixth of the traffic, regardless of the availability zone it resides in. In our example, availability zone A with two instances will be serving one-third of the traffic, while availability zone B will be serving two-thirds as it has double the instances of availability zone A, as demonstrated in the following diagram:

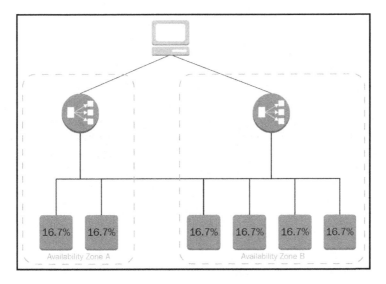

Now that we have understood the working of the ELB, we will have a look at how we can secure traffic on the ELB.

Securing traffic on the ELB

Security is one of the most important aspects of any modern application, especially if that application has a public-facing entry point, such as a public ELB interface. The ELB service itself is very scalable and able to serve quite a substantial amount of traffic. But even the ELB has its own limitations. As we have already discussed in Chapter 3, *VPC Network Security*, AWS provides guidelines on how to minimize the scope and mitigate a **Denial of Service (DoS)** attack. The ELB can play a crucial role in this mitigation, and we need to look at the following aspects of security governing the way traffic can be secured on the ELB:

- Security controls on the ELB
- Security of the traffic contents with encryption
- Protection against DoS attacks

Security controls on the ELB

Since the load balancer is used as a unified entry point into our application, AWS has made certain that the security on the load balancer can be implemented to control the incoming traffic and its behavior. To control port-based security, we will be using the VPC security groups. When defining access to the load balancer, we are required to use a security group when creating a load balancer. This makes sure that we only open the ports that we require. We should also make sure that we implement the security groups according to the best practices outlined in Chapter 3, *VPC Network Security*.

On top of port-based security, the ELB itself has the ability to control the encryption protocols and cipher mechanisms being used to connect to the ELB, and, of course, to connect to the backend server serving the content. For even higher protection, the ELB can be directly integrated with AWS **Web Application Firewall (WAF)**, and in the case of an ALB, also with AWS Shield.

Security of the traffic contents with encryption

When our application requires us to have the ability to control the encryption settings on the ELB, we will be using a load balancer security policy. The load balancer security policy controls the encryption and authentication mechanisms that can be used with the load balancer. This will determine how the clients connect to the ELB and how the secure HTTPS session is established. We have the ability to use built-in security policies, as well as create custom ones. AWS has also prepared security policies that are compliant with security standards such as PCI DSS, which mandate the use of only certain secure cipher suites and encryption protocols.

According to the SSL pulse from SSL labs, which conducts a monthly survey of the world's 150,000 most popular sites, there are still a lot of sites supporting old and insecure SSL and early TLS protocols. Their data shows that while over 90% of sites support TLS 1.2, there are still 80% supporting TLS 1.1 and over 70% supporting TLS 1.0. While TLS 1.1 is still considered somewhat secure, TLS 1.0 is considered insecure as it is very susceptible to attacks such as BEAST, POODLE, and DROWN. The most worrying fact is that almost 10% of the world's most popular sites still support SSL v3 and almost 3% still support SSL v2. As we all know, these two protocols are considered completely inadequate for protection in modern applications. On the bright side, we can see that TLS 1.3 is being adopted and comes in at about 10% of supported sites.

We can also control the target connection configuration. This gives us the ability to either allow for the load balancer to terminate the SSL connection and offload the encryption task from our targets, or we can choose to connect to the targets on a secure channel. We will need to configure the targets as secure servers whenever end-to-end encryption is required. End-to-end encryption is increasingly being used as a requirement of multiple different security standards and compliance policies being used in enterprises and modern applications.

For example, when a payment gateway service is operating in a cloud environment, the service needs to be PIC DSS compliant. At the time of writing, the standard in effect is PCI DSS 3.2. The standard governs SSL connections and allows the use of only TLS 1.2 with only the strong cipher suites. The ELB service has a built-in policy that allows for the use of only TLS 1.2. You would think that the ELBSecurityPolicy-TLS-1-2-Ext-2018-06 policy can be used to achieve this goal, as it limits the use of only the TLS 1.2 protocol, but the policy supports the same set of ciphers as the default ELBSecurityPolicy-2016-08 policy. This means that we would need to create a custom policy for our PCI DSS 3.2 compliance and remove the non-compliant ciphers in addition to the non-compliant protocols.

On top of this, PCI DSS 3.2 dictates that end-to-end encryption is required when processing credit card transactions. This would require us to ensure that the target of the ELB uses an encrypted SSL or HTTPS connection as well. This can get complicated when the application has multiple tiers, as the following diagram demonstrates:

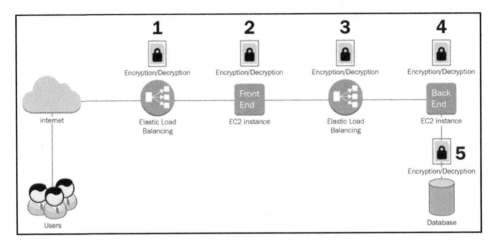

In the preceding diagram, the encryption/decryption scenarios are as follows:

1. The client establishes a connection with the external ELB and the connection is encrypted with the external ELB certificate.
2. The external ELB establishes a connection with the frontend service and the connection is encrypted with the frontend certificate.
3. The frontend establishes a connection with the internal ELB and the connection is encrypted with the ELB certificate.
4. The internal ELB establishes a connection with the backend service and the connection is encrypted with the backend certificate.
5. The backend establishes a connection with the database service and secures it with a database-specific encryption mechanism.

Once returned, the traffic is encrypted and decrypted several times for each response. Keep in mind that this is a fairly simple scenario and that there are applications that have multiple components distributed across many more tiers. The best practice for a multitiered application is to introduce automation to the certificate request and creation procedure, as with modern applications, each tier might consist of multiple instances in an Auto Scaling group that might get created and terminated multiple times a day. Special care also needs to be taken when designing containerized environments where the creation and distribution of the server certificates will be even more frequent.

Protection against DoS attacks

To protect the ELB service even further, we can introduce a WAF sandwich between two ELBs. When using the application load balancer, we also have the ability to augment the security of the ALB directly with a WAF integration option that has been supported since December 2016. The WAF will allow the service to catch any malicious traffic and throttle it at the perimeter, thus allowing our application to be protected from attackers and basic DoS attacks.

To increase security even further, we can use the AWS Shield or AWS Shield Advanced services to deliver full DDoS protection and mitigation to our application. When using Shield, all we are required to do is select the ELB service as the target for the Shield service to protect—the rest is taken care of by AWS. Shield is possibly one of the most valuable protection services in the industry, as it not only introduces standard DoS practices but also draws on the experience AWS has gained in well over a decade of experience running, operating, and protecting the services on AWS. Their response teams have seen it all and with advanced services, we are able to get directly in contact with a DDoS response team 24/7 if our website comes under attack. The response team will also ensure the highest possible level of protection from any additional costs incurred during a DDoS attack.

When implementing the AWS Shield service, we would typically take a two-pronged approach. The Shield can integrate with the Route 53 service and the ELB. The integration with Route 53 can help determine and cut off the bad actors at the DNS level by providing an invalid response to the requester once the requester is determined to be a bad actor. The second prong of protection is at the ELB where the bad actors are identified by analyzing the traffic and packet patterns being received by the ELB. The following diagram demonstrates this approach:

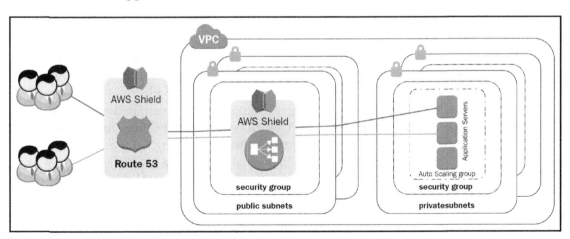

All of these security controls should be considered when determining the requirements for protecting our application. Each control mechanism provides another layer of the security onion, as defined in Chapter 3, *VPC Network Security*.

Summary

In this chapter, we have taken a look at the ELB service and the way it operates. We have received an overview of the three types of load balancers that are supported and looked at each one in detail. One of the key aspects of the ELB is security; this is why we provided an overview of the security principles and how to protect the ELB service and encrypt the traffic on the ELB. We have also indicated that the ELB can be straightened with the WAF and AWS Shield services.

In the next chapter, we will be looking at how to securely distribute content with the CloudFront service and make sure we can deliver the content to the user securely, in the fastest possible manner, and with the lowest latency.

Questions

1. What does the load balancer help us achieve?
2. Name the two next-generation load balancers.
3. An application running on a set of EC2 instances needs to collect metrics from thousands of temperature sensors in an industrial process that's sending out hundreds of data points each per second. You need a solution that will allow you to meet these performance requirements; which ELB would you choose?
4. You are looking for a solution to easily determine the browser and its compatibility with your application. If a browser is incompatible, a simple process for redirecting the user to a path with a backward-compatible mode is required. Would you be able to implement this with an ELB?
5. You need to provide a microservice application that's distributed across three peered VPCs with a load balancer. Your developers are pushing for an NLB to be used. Would this be the right solution for this setup?
6. Which AWS service would allow you to easily manage AWS X.509 certificates for your ELB?
7. Which service from AWS can help you protect your load balancer from DDoS attacks?

Further reading

Please refer to the following references for more information regarding what was covered in this chapter:

- **ELB features**: https://aws.amazon.com/elasticloadbalancing/features
- **ELB documentation**: https://docs.aws.amazon.com/elasticloadbalancing/latest/userguide/what-is-load-balancing.html
- **ALB**: https://docs.aws.amazon.com/elasticloadbalancing/latest/application/introduction.html
- **NLB**: https://docs.aws.amazon.com/elasticloadbalancing/latest/network/introduction.html
- **CLB**: https://docs.aws.amazon.com/elasticloadbalancing/latest/classic/introduction.html
- **SSL Pulse**: https://www.ssllabs.com/ssl-pulse/

6
Managing and Securing Content Distribution with CloudFront

When delivering content from AWS, we will always strive to serve that content as close to our users as possible. The global architecture of AWS allows us to make use of Edge locations, which are located in data centers across the world that are located close to urban population centers. At Edge locations, we can use the CloudFront content delivery network to deliver services to our users with the lowest latency possible. When content needs to be delivered in a secure and safe manner, there are some things to consider when on using CloudFront. In this chapter, we will examine all the ways to make sure that all our content is delivered securely and with the highest performance possible.

This chapter will walk you through all you need to know about the CloudFront service. You will learn about the functionality of CloudFront and how and when to use CloudFront in the best possible manner.

The following topics will be covered in this chapter:

- Introducing CloudFront
- Working with CloudFront
- Securing content delivery
- Encryption
- **Distributed denial of service (DDoS)** mitigation

Technical requirements

A basic understanding of content distribution, HTTP/HTTPS web protocols, and caching is required to follow along with this chapter. An understanding of DDoS attacks and CDN security is a bonus.

Introducing CloudFront

CloudFront is a fully managed content delivery network service. CloudFront is deployed at all Edge locations and allows very efficient low-latency delivery of different types of static content, such as website data, videos, and images. CloudFront improves the user experience when delivering static content, but it must be done in a secure manner. CloudFront itself has some built-in security features and we will take a look at how to use CloudFront to increase the overall security of our application.

Working with CloudFront

CloudFront is a content delivery network environment that can deliver web content with much lower latencies than if it is delivered from its original source. CloudFront services sit in Edge locations and enable the distribution of content to users all around the world with a user experience matching a local deployment. With CloudFront, we are able to deliver much higher-performance read and write operations over a standard HTTP/HTTPS interface.

CloudFront supports any origin that has a DNS-resolvable address on the internet or within AWS. Examples of CloudFront origins range from S3 buckets, EC2 servers, ELB load balancers, containerized applications with service discovery enabled, and any arbitrary IP addresses on the internet or within our cloud-connected on-premise environment.

CloudFront exposes a programmable API that allows us to control the behavior of the caching environment and deliver the services we would like to accelerate with great precision. Through the API, we can dynamically configure our CloudFront distribution and tune the features and performance characteristics of the application. When creating a distribution, we can choose which types of requests the CloudFront distribution will respond to and which ones it will forward to the backend origin servers.

The following HTTP methods are supported when creating a distribution:

- **HTTP GET and HEAD methods**: These are standard approaches to allow the caching of read operations in CloudFront. The service will respond to the GET and HEAD operations and perform a cache lookup. If the cache does not contain the object, then the service will forward the request to the backend. The service will also automatically pass any other calls to the backend.
- **HTTP GET, HEAD, and OPTIONS methods**: Additionally, GET and HEAD allows our caching service to respond to requests for HTTP communication options. Each OPTIONS response will be cached so that, when the backend service options change, we will need to force an update of the cache or expire the OPTIONS response.
- **The full set of HTTP methods**: We can also configure CloudFront to respond to GET, HEAD, OPTIONS, PUT, PATCH, POST, and DELETE methods. In addition to caching read operations, the service will respond to any write and delete HTTP requests. This allows the termination of the sessions at the CloudFront Edge location and can provide the end user with a faster response both to the read and write requests to the origin.

The full set of HTTP methods and the operations they support are displayed in the following screenshot:

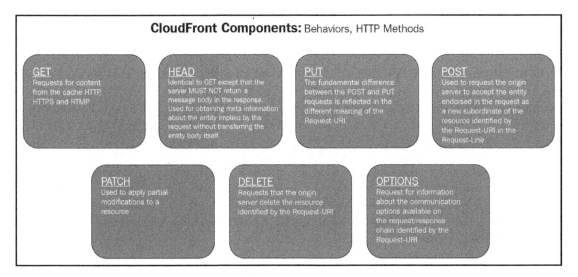

Any data in a CloudFront distribution will, of course, have a limited lifetime. When we change content on our origin servers, we will find that the CloudFront distribution will still be serving the cached content. This is why we also have the ability to control the **time-to-live (TTL)** of our cache in the CloudFront environment. We can control how long we want the content to be served for and when to set it to expire and be removed from the cache. We can also force the CloudFront distribution to frequently refresh the content on the origin and update its cache if necessary. The TTL configuration will be very much dependent on the life cycle of the content within your distribution. CloudFront provides us with the following options for controlling TTL:

- **The minimum TTL**: Determines the minimum time our content will exist in the CloudFront cache. This setting is only required when we configure all HTTP methods for our distribution. Once the minimum TTL expires, CloudFront will automatically refresh the content from the origin.
- **The default TTL**: When the origin does not enforce any caching configuration on the content, we can optionally set the default TTL. This determines the default caching time for our content. When a minimum TTL is set at the origin, the default TTL needs to be longer.
- **The maximum TTL**: Optionally, we can set the longest possible time for caching. This option can be set when the origin does have a caching configuration and is designed to override any defaults from the origin so that we can maintain our cache in CloudFront for longer and reduce the number of times the cache is refreshed from the origin.

Besides these methods and the cache, TTL's CloudFront allows us to control and shape traffic to our requirements. We can control compression and encryption with the `Compress` and `FieldLevelEncryptionId` options. These options increase performance by compressing and reducing the size of the data being transferred, and also increase security by adding encryption at the edge. Also, at the edge, we can control the execution of dynamic content with the `LambdaFunctionAssociations` option.

This option gives us the ability to associate a Lambda function and call the lambda function when the condition for dynamic execution is met. Through this association, we can also use Lambda@Edge, which allows developers to build execution patterns at the edge of the delivery and gives your application the ability to process dynamic data and requests from users within the Edge location.

The following diagram demonstrates how Lambda@Edge can be used to detect the browser or device type. The response from the website can be completely customized according to the device or browser type. We can perform other actions, such as putting up paywalls for our website or generating customized content based on other factors that can be detected by Lambda:

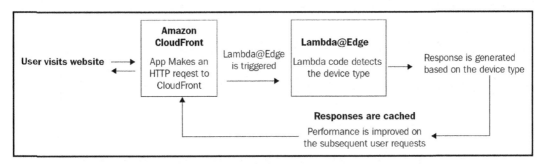

Moreover, the CloudFront distribution gives us the ability to control the cache at a very granular level by allowing us control over how CloudFront will handle strings, cookies, and patterns. We control these through the `ForwardedValues`, `PathPattern`, and `TargetOriginId` options. CloudFront is also very well suited for caching streaming content and allows us the ability to control both access to streaming content with the `TrustedSigners` option as well as improvements in the streaming performance with the `SmoothStreaming` option.

CloudFront can also help us save on costs, as any data being transferred between AWS services and CloudFront does not fall under data transfer costs. For example, when delivering content from S3, the price per request is about eight times higher than the price per request from CloudFront. CloudFront can both deliver content faster and with lower latency, as well as delivering at a better rate. So, the cost of delivering content from S3 increases more with the number of requests compared to CloudFront. We can think of a video sharing service that regularly posts viral videos. The videos will have millions of views. If a video is served from S3, the cost of request pricing is going to have the most impact on the cost of delivering that video. Since request pricing is much lower with CloudFront, the request cost will make much less of an impact.

As we can see in the following graph, delivering the same content through CloudFront will be more and more cost effective when the number of requests grows compared to S3:

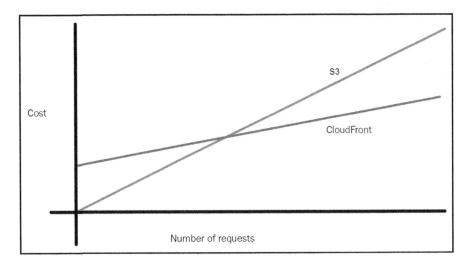

The CloudFront service is designed to deliver static content at a reduced price and with better performance. We can also terminate sessions for dynamic content at CloudFront and enable a better overall experience for our users. Each distribution is completely customizable so that we have complete control over what we cache and how content is delivered.

Securing content delivery

Delivering content to the right user in the right location can be a very daunting task. Some applications require us to deliver content from our environment in a secure manner and reach only the target audience that the content is intended for. This can be quite challenging to design and build in a typical web application, as the service will need to be able to clearly identify the user and their location. Luckily, CloudFront has been designed with a secure content approach in mind and has several features that give us complete control over content delivery.

When required, we can choose CloudFront to help us control access to our application content with signed URLs or cookies. A signed URL will help us define the access to the content in our application by specifying conditions on which the application will allow access to the content. For example, these conditions can be location- or time-based. We firstly need to identify the users that are allowed to access the content and provide them with signed URLs.

We then configure CloudFront with a key pair that will allow CloudFront to check the signature and determine whether it is valid. Once the user requests the content with the signed URL, the CloudFront distribution will verify the signature and then consult the signed URL policy to determine whether the conditions for using this signed URL are met. If the conditions are met, the content can be served by CloudFront. We can use application cookies in a similar manner to control access to content.

In the following diagram, we can see how the signed URL can be used with CloudFront:

1. The user signs in to the application.
2. Upon authentication, the application sends a signed URL to the user.
3. The signed URL points to CloudFront.
4. The CloudFront distribution verifies the signature against the policy and returns the content:

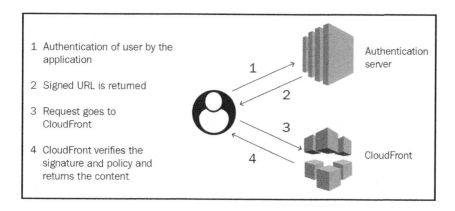

With CloudFront, we can also seamlessly control access to S3 buckets by using the **Origin Access Identity (OAI)** feature of CloudFront. When using signed URLs or cookies to control access to our application, we also want to control access to any S3 content. If the application that provides the content discloses the S3 URLs, users could bypass the signed URL and access the content directly from the S3 bucket. By creating an origin access identity in our distribution, we can control access to the S3 content in the same way that we control access with the signed URLs or cookies. Essentially, the user will be required to always connect through CloudFront to access the content and all requests for files directly on S3 URLs will be denied. The OAI can have a policy setup that can check the conditions of access to match the signed URL or cookie conditions, or it can be implemented independently and provide limited access to users without the need to use a signed URL or cookie.

This behavior is demonstrated in the following diagram. The end user is able to access the content via the CloudFront distribution, but is not able to access the same content when browsing directly to the origin server:

1. The user connects to CloudFront.
2. The CloudFront distribution OAI is allowed to access the content and responds with the content.
3. The user tries to go directly to the S3 URL and the connection is denied, since only the OAI is allowed:

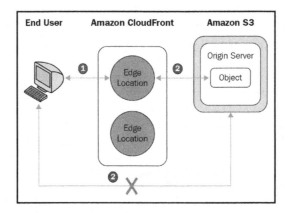

When content is public, but needs to be restricted to a certain region, we can use the geo-location feature in the CloudFront distribution. This is very helpful when we need to serve our content only within a certain region or country and do not have the necessary capacity to perform geo-location checks within our application. The service can be invaluable for video streaming and content providers looking to comply with their licensing agreements for their content.

Encryption

CloudFront can also help us to simplify the process of encrypting data in transit to and from our CloudFront distribution with SSL/TLS.

We can control the encryption between our client and the distribution by selecting any of the supported encryption protocols and ciphers. AWS will always ensure that only the secure protocols and ciphers are supported, but if we have special requirements laid out by certain compliance standards, then we have complete control over which protocols and ciphers we allow.

We can also use **AWS Certificate Manager (ACM)** with CloudFront, which allows us to create a completely free SSL certificate for our domain and attach it to our distribution. ACM also allows us to automatically update and renew the certificate for our domain so that we never need to worry about the SSL certificates expiring and we can dramatically reduce the cost of running highly trusted commercial certificates in our application.

The following diagram demonstrates this ability:

1. ACM automatically deploys the certificate to CloudFront.
2. Users connecting to CloudFront establish a secure session.
3. The CloudFront distribution can either offload the SSL encryption or connect via an encrypted protocol to the backend:

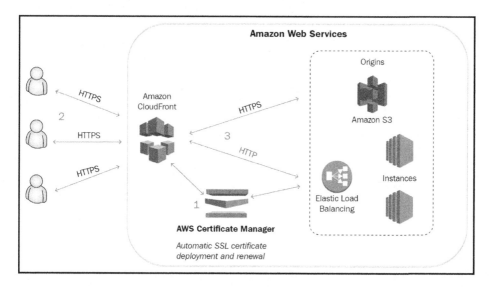

AWS recently introduced field-level encryption on CloudFront. Field-level encryption can greatly enhance the security of sensitive data within the traffic flow of our application by being able to determine which parts of the content need to be protected. This can be very handy for commercial websites that use credit card payments, as well as any other type of content where personally identifiable information (for example, social security numbers, social insurance numbers, or driver's license numbers) is shared with the application.

When configuring field-level encryption, we can specify up to 10 fields in a POST request that need to be encrypted. The encryption is done through a public key for encryption that has a corresponding private key on the origin server. This way, we can offload all of the HTTPS traffic on the CloudFront distribution while still leveraging field-level encryption to encrypt the sensitive data in the traffic between the CloudFront distribution and the origin server. We get the best of both worlds – better performance by offloading the SSL traffic at the Edge location and complete adherence to compliance requirements with end-to-end encryption of all sensitive data.

In the following diagram, the SSL connection from the client is terminated at the CloudFront location. This would usually mean that all the data being sent from the CloudFront distribution to our application is decrypted. But, since we can use field-level encryption within the CloudFront distribution, we are able to re-encrypt the fields containing sensitive data at the CloudFront location. The encryption is established using a public-private key pair so that only the custom origin can decrypt the contents:

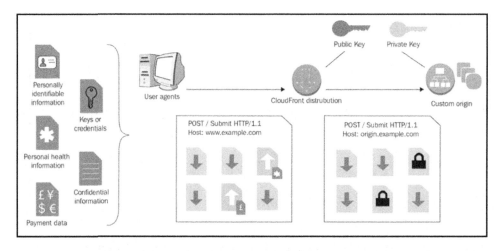

DDoS mitigation

CloudFront is, by itself, already inherently resilient to DDoS attacks, since it is integrated with AWS Shield Standard. There is no cost for this protection, and, due to the fact that DDoS mitigation is already in place out of the box, using CloudFront can be a big benefit for our applications. CloudFront itself can protect our applications and act as an extra layer of defense from attacks on the infrastructure and the availability of our web content. AWS Shield Standard automatically protects CloudFront from any layer 3 and layer 4 network DDoS attacks and can provide filtering of most DDoS traffic from the internet.

However, modern attack vectors know how to use even higher-layer DDoS attacks. When we need even higher security, we can use AWS Shield Advanced, which can provide our application with higher-level attack mitigation and near real-time visibility of the traffic events coming in to the CloudFront distribution. AWS Shield Advanced allows more control over the rate limiting for different types of network traffic and on a per-client basis with rate-based rules. We can also integrate AWS Shield Advanced with CloudWatch alarms. The feature gives us the ability to control notifications from AWS Shield and help us inform our security response team of any issues that need to be investigated. To enhance security on layer 7, AWS Shield Advanced can be integrated with the AWS **Web Application Firewall** (**WAF**) service with WAF rules that can be ran directly on the CloudFront distribution.

In the following diagram, we can see both the AWS Shield and WAF services protecting our application at the Edge location, well in front of any regional AWS resources:

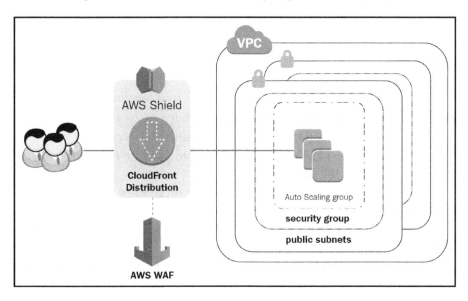

With AWS Shield Advanced, we are able to provide a comprehensive network attack protection mechanism at the initial entry point to our application and offload all of our application components sitting at the origin from having to perform threat mitigation. This can increase both the reliability and uptime of our application, as well as decreasing the cost of operating the application, since less unnecessary traffic will be reaching our target and less requests will be issued against the backend.

Summary

CloudFront is a fully managed CDN service that provides the ability to deliver content much faster to end users through caching. CloudFront gives us the ability to control and shape content in the cache and to terminate both read and write requests to our application at the Edge location. This can dramatically reduce the latency of the response from our application, as well as increasing the performance and the user satisfaction.

Not only that: with high volumes, CloudFront can help us save costs and stay compliant with full control over the encryption and security features. CloudFront can integrate with AWS Shield Advanced and WAF to provide full mitigation of any network attacks at the Edge location.

In the next chapter, we will look at the Route 53 service, which that gives us the ability to programmatically control our DNS setup.

Questions

1. What types of HTTP connections can CloudFront terminate at an Edge location?
2. In CloudFront, what does the maximum TTL for cache represent?
3. In CloudFront, what is the name given to a source server?
4. What service can be enabled on CloudFront to provide full mitigation of any network attacks at the Edge location?
5. Which feature can be used to control limited time access to our application through CloudFront?
6. What service integrates with CloudFront to provide SSL management for our domain?
7. What service can be integrated with CloudFront to provide dynamic content processing at the Edge location?

Further reading

- **Key features of CloudFront**: https://aws.amazon.com/cloudfront/
- **CloudFront Pricing**: https://aws.amazon.com/cloudfront/pricing/
- **HTTP Method Definitions**: https://www.w3.org/Protocols/rfc2616/rfc2616-sec9.html
- **Lambda@Edge**: https://aws.amazon.com/lambda/edge/
- **Signed URLs**: https://docs.aws.amazon.com/AmazonCloudFront/latest/DeveloperGuide/private-content-signedurls.html
- **Field-Level Encyrption**: https://docs.aws.amazon.com/AmazonCloudFront/latest/DeveloperGuide/field-level-encryption.html
- **Restricting Access to Amazon S3 Content by Using an Origin Access Identity**: https://docs.aws.amazon.com/AmazonCloudFront/latest/DeveloperGuide/private-content-restricting-access-to-s3.html
- **Supported Encryption and Ciphers**: https://docs.aws.amazon.com/AmazonCloudFront/latest/DeveloperGuide/secure-connections-supported-viewer-protocols-ciphers.html
- **CloudFront Cache Behavior**: https://docs.aws.amazon.com/cloudfront/latest/APIReference/API_CacheBehavior.html

7
Managing and Securing the Route 53 Domain Name System

Delivering modern applications depends on a catchy name. That catchy name can be the definition of success for some applications. In some places, the word internet and the names of big social networks are used completely interchangeably. To make our application successful, users need to be able to type in the name of the application and access it in a simple manner. This is where the **Domain Name System (DNS)** comes into play. A service conceived in the bygone era of ARPANET is one of the core components contributing to the success of today's internet applications. But the DNS service has essentially not changed much since its inception. Or has it? With Route 53, it has.

This chapter will walk you through all you need to know about the Route 53 service. You will learn about the functionality of Route 53 and how and when to use Route 53 in the best possible manner.

The following topics will be covered in this chapter:

- Introduction to Route 53
- DNS resource record types
- Routing policies
- Health checking
- Registering a domain name
- Best practices

Technical requirements

A basic understanding of domain internet addressing, DNS, FQDN, and bind name resolution is required to get a comprehensive grasp of the subject at hand.

Introduction to Route 53

At the core of modern web-scale applications is ease of access on the internet. Choose any name of a business, social network, or publication, wrap it up with a .com at the end and type that into a browser. The most likely thing to happen is a website belonging to that company, newspaper, TV channel, or social network will pop up. DNS is probably a technology everyone using the internet uses multiple times per day without even knowing it. And it is becoming crucial for both making the application respond on the internet, as well as giving the application the ability to be highly available, resilient, and scalable.

Traditional DNS servers map IP addresses to FQDNs in zone files. These are stored in text or binary format (binary can help with performance). Lots of times, these files are stored on one master server and one or more slaves. The master is where we can edit the zone and the slaves allow for redundancy in case the master goes down and vice-versa. The traditional DNS system is not well suited to changes, as the propagation times for changes in DNS can be long and will take up to 24 hours to propagate. Does that sound like a system that will help our application to be highly available and highly resilient? Not really.

This is why AWS decided to rewrite the book on DNS. Firstly, they deployed a traditional DNS system across all of their regions and decided to try and bring it down. They essentially discovered that the traditional DNS service is very vulnerable to multiple types of disruptions and that building a reliable DNS service on traditional out-of-the-box DNS servers is next to impossible. This is why the engineers and architects at AWS eventually decided to develop the Amazon Route 53 service.

The Route 53 service is what I like to call a *next generation* DNS service. Route 53 has none of the drawbacks of traditional DNS services. The management entry point is an API that stores the DNS information onto an extremely fast database layer instead of into files and then binaries. The service allows us to address it programmatically and manage the DNS entries in a completely automated manner. Route 53 also service-integrates with ECS for service discovery; it can allow us to create both public and private zones and—best of all—provides a 100% SLA for availability. That means that, short of a global disaster, the service will survive anything anyone can throw at it.

On top of all of that, Route 53 also supports the ability to route the traffic to different origins by checking the health of the origin and allowing the automatic exclusion of origins that do not respond correctly or fast enough, and always routing the users to the website that will provide the content in the fastest and/or most compliant manner.

DNS resource record types

When the service was conceived, the Route 53 creators had web applications in mind. Because of this, the service has been designed to host the most common DNS record types only. However, with advances in the way DNS is used to secure communication and perform authentication and encryption, the service has been extended with features that the most common record types used with modern internet-based applications. The following list, in alphabetical order, includes all of the resource types that are supported on Route 53 at the time of writing:

- **A and AAAA records**: These allow for resolving FQDN server names to IP addresses.
- **CAA**: This determines the **Certificate Authority (CA)** servers allowed to issue certificates for the domain.
- **CNAME**: This allows resolving of complex DNS names to simpler or more general DNS names. The name `www.packt.com`, for example, can have a CNAME record pointing to a CloudFront distribution DNS name.
- **MX**: This is used to determine the mail servers for a particular domain.
- **NAPTR**: This is used to dynamically determine application or service endpoints. NAPTR can be used, for example, to convert telephone numbers into SIP endpoints.
- **NS**: This is used to determine which DNS server is serving the domain.
- **PTR**: This allows for looking up DNS records in reverse by specifying an IP address.
- **SOA**: These are mandatory records that maintain versioning, timeouts, and authoritative DNS servers.
- **SPF**: This allows email systems to determine whether the email sender is authorized to send messages on behalf of the domain.
- **SRV**: This helps us to deliver information about the ports the host serves its services on.
- **TXT**: For the sharing of arbitrary strings of text within the DNS service, this allows us to extend the functionality or security of our domain.

Routing policies

To deliver the content to the user in a custom manner, the Route 53 service supports different routing policies. These routing policies enable us to shape the traffic according to different aspects of the user's request. For example, we can choose to send users from a certain geographical area to a certain region or regions, we can decide to respond with one origin or multiple, or we can send the response for only the fastest responding device. The following routing policies can be configured in Route 53:

- Simple routing
- Multi-value response
- Latency-based routing
- Weighted routing
- Failover routing
- Geo-location routing
- Geo-proximity routing

Simple routing

By default any A, CNAME, MX, or TXT record will be set to simple routing. Simple routing will respond with exactly one value for each single request. For example, the call for `packtpub.com` will return the following:

- Exactly one IP address of the host hosting website if the record is A
- Exactly one host name if the record is CNAME

The following diagram demonstrates a simple response from the Route 53 service:

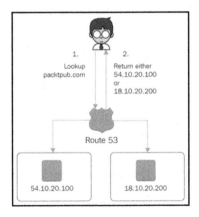

Considering the preceding diagram, we see the following:

1. The user requests the address, `packtpub.com`
2. The Route 53 service returns exactly one record at random from the records in that domain name

Multi-value response

Traditional DNS servers usually respond with any number of values for each request. Similarly, when this kind of service is required, multi-value response routing can be used. Each request will return up to eight possible responses. To extend the functionality of traditional DNS and deliver only healthy records, the Route 53 service can also perform a health check on the origin. This way, only the addresses that actually respond will be returned in the multi-value response. Applications requiring a list of possible servers to perform tasks in a distributed manner will benefit greatly from the multi-value response routing. Examples would be peer-to-peer applications, video streaming, and HPC.

The following diagram demonstrates a multi-value response from the Route 53 service:

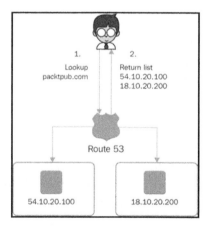

Considering the preceding diagram, we see the following:

1. The user requests the address, `packtpub.com`
2. The Route 53 service returns up to eight addresses from the records in that domain name

Latency-based routing

To determine the fastest server to serve the response, Route 53 latency-based routing can be used. The service will quickly measure the latency between the DNS service at the closest edge location to the user and the origin. The response to the user will include the address of the origin that has the lowest latency to the user. This is very beneficial if there are services in multiple regions that serve a geographical area where the request is coming from. The service can help to increase the performance of the application by serving the content from the fastest endpoint.

The following diagram demonstrates a latency check that is performed before returning the fastest host IP to the user:

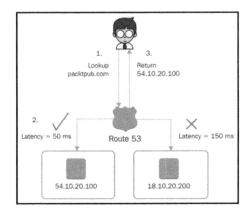

Considering the preceding diagram, we see the following:

1. The user requests the address, `packtpub.com`
2. The Route 53 service checks the latency to all origin addresses
3. The address of the host with the lowest latency is returned to the user

Failover routing

Similarly to the latency-based routing, the failover routing approach allows us to find a target that can serve the client. In the case of failover routing, an active endpoint is required. This active endpoint can represent our main data center or the region where our application usually serves all of the traffic. We then set a failover endpoint. This one represents a passive site that will be used in case the primary endpoint fails the health check. This routing policy is used when a primary site is replicating data only in one direction to a backup or a disaster recovery site.

If the failover policy detects that the primary site is unavailable, then all of the users are redirected to the failover site. Make sure you set your DNS TTL appropriately when using failover routing, as any cached DNS queries will not be looked up until the TTL expires. Luckily, the Route 53 service allows us to set TTLs as low as one second.

The following diagram shows how we can use Route 53 to fail over to a static version of our website hosted in S3, in case our primary EC2 instance fails:

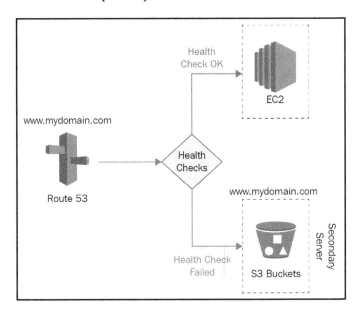

This is a really neat approach that can be used as a simple feature that maintains your website uptime even during major outages at very little cost.

Weighted routing

When the replication between multiple sites is multi-directional but the capacities of the sites differ, then weighted routing can be used. Weighted routing allows us to scale the amount of traffic depending on the capabilities of the endpoint, by specifying the weight of each endpoint. The weight is an integer between 1 and 255 that can determine what percentage of traffic will be sent to the endpoint. When two endpoints have a weight of 10, then 50% of the traffic will be sent to each endpoint.

If we add another endpoint with the weight of 20, then 50% of the traffic will go to this new endpoint while the other two endpoints will be receiving 25% of the traffic each. The traffic volume is based on the DNS queries, so we also need to consider the user behavior on the endpoints. Only if the behavior of our users is predictable can we scale very well with this approach. This can also be used for A/B testing, canary instances, or a blue/green deployment approach when upgrading applications.

The following diagram demonstrates how the traffic is distributed across two sites with different compute capacities deployed:

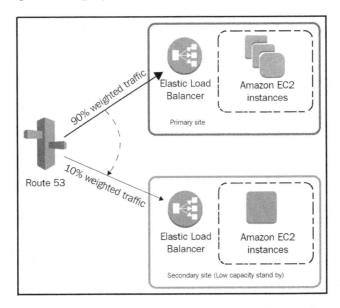

Both load balancer DNS names are entered into an alias record for the website. By implementing weighted routing on the record, the majority of the traffic (90%) is sent out to the primary site and a subset of the traffic (10%) is sent to the secondary site. The traffic is controlled by the routing weight of each value in the DNS entry. For example, for the DNS name of the **Elastic Load Balancer (ELB)** at the primary site, we enter a weight of 90, whereas the secondary record would have a weight of 10.

When a blue-green deployment is under way, the traffic weights can be increased for the green site (new version) while being decreased for the blue (previous version) until all traffic is on the green site and the blue site can be decommissioned.

Geo-location routing

Geo-location can determine the location of the user by their source IP addresses. This capability gives us the ability to shape the content based on the country or region the user is browsing from. Applications can be modified to match the user's language or comply with local laws and regulations. When running a global application, data sovereignty can be an issue since the storage of data is mandated differently by each country the users are browsing from. With geo-location routing, we can make sure we comply with the laws and regulations governing data sovereignty by routing the user to a region within their country or within the borders where the law applies.

In the following diagram, the user is directed only to the EU region because their location is determined to originate from the EU:

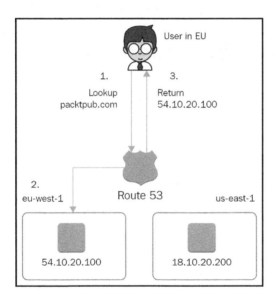

Considering the preceding diagram, we see the following:

1. The user requests the address, `packtpub.com`
2. The Route 53 service checks the geo-location database and that determines the user location is within the EU
3. The address of the EU host is returned to the user

Geo-proximity routing

Geo-proximity, on the other hand, will only determine the longitude and latitude of the user. The response will send the address of the origin that is closest in geographical terms. We can also shape the response by giving different origins different biases in the geo-proximity group. The bigger the bias is, the further the reach of each origin. This approach can be very useful when geo-location would always point the users to a random origin within the country. For example, in the US, there are four regions where we can have four origins. When one of the origins in one of the regions has a larger footprint, we can increase the geo-proximity bias so that it can serve a proportionally bigger group from a wider geographical area.

The following screenshot demonstrates the geo-proximity bias of **Endpoint A** in one of the `us-west` regions is serving a larger part of the continent than **Endpoint B** with a bias of 0:

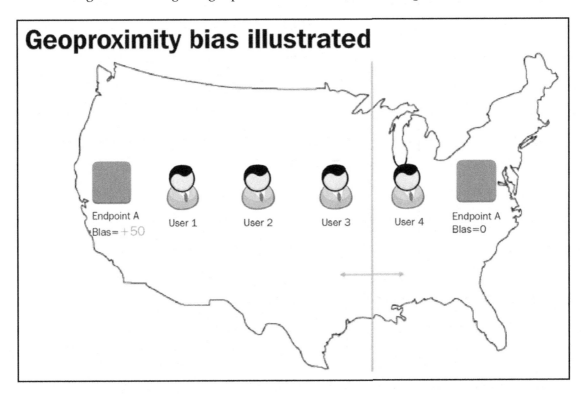

The routing policies allow us to shape the traffic in many ways, so that we can always cover all of the needs of our application. Next, we will take a look at how health checking works and how it can be integrated in the routing policies.

Health checking

Certain routing policies in Route 53 also support health checks. A health check will allow the DNS service to check the target and determine whether the response it receives is healthy or not. A Route 53 health check can either be TCP or HTTP/HTTPS based. The TCP check will simply check the response on the port, while a HTTP/HTTPS health check can also check for a specific string in the origin. Health checks can also include a maximum response time, which can also determine whether the site is responding too slowly to be of any use to clients.

The health-check operation is demonstrated in the following diagram:

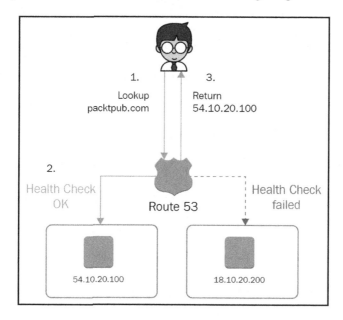

Considering the preceding diagram, we see the following:

1. The user requests the address, `packtpub.com`
2. The Route 53 service checks the origins and determines a healthy host
3. The address of the healthy host is returned to the user

Registering a domain name

The Route 53 service also serves as a self-service domain registrar and makes it very easy to register your domain name. Let's take a look at how we can register a domain and start using it in Route 53. This process should take less than five minutes:

1. First, navigate to the **Route 53** console and click on **Get started now** under **Domain registration**:

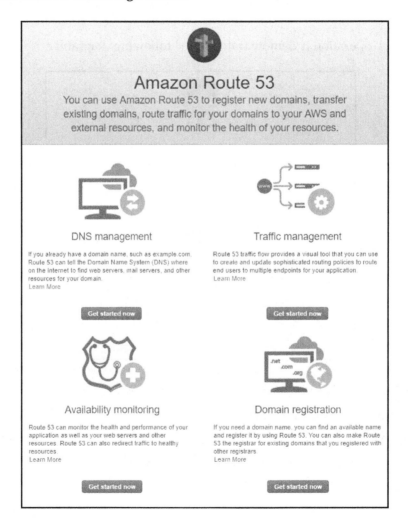

2. We can either register a new domain or transfer an existing one. We will take a look at registering a domain by clicking on the **Register Domain** button:

3. In the **Choose a domain name** dialog, choose a domain name you want to register and click **Check**. If the system finds the domain name to be already registered, it will offer suggestions on other domain names similar to ours.

4. Once you are ready to select your domain, just click on **Add to cart** and then click on **Continue**:

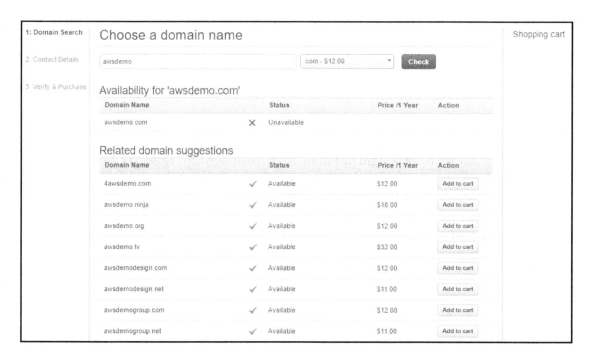

5. Next, fill out the contact information and click **Verify & Purchase** to verify the details and complete the purchase:

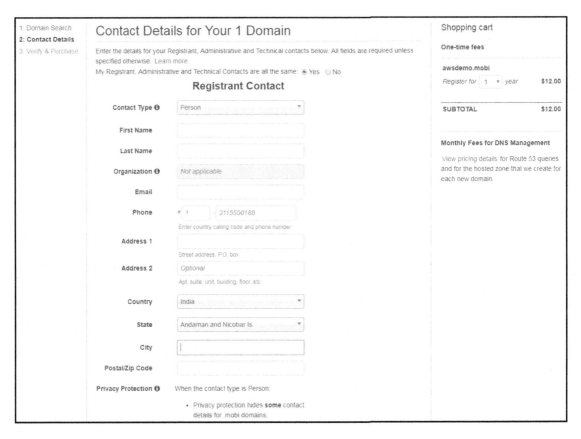

6. Now that we have bought our domain, we will need to create a hosted zone so that we can move the DNS records to AWS. Select **Hosted zones** from the menu and then click on **Create Hosted Zone**:

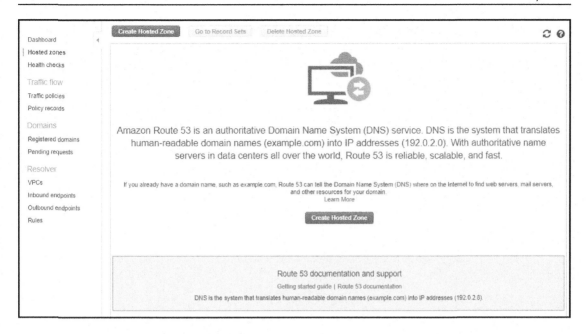

7. We will first need to name the domain and then select what kind of zone we are creating. A **Public Hosted Zone** will be available from the internet whereas a **Private Hosted Zone** can be used for internal domains reachable from our AWS account. Once you have entered the details, click on **Create**:

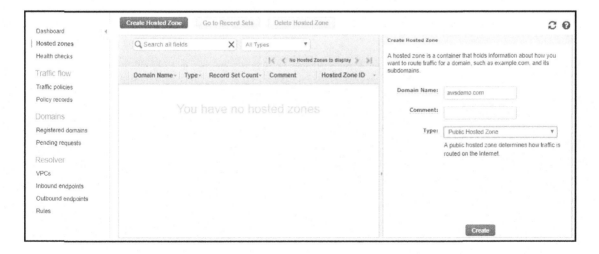

8. Once the zone is created, the SOA and NS names will be generated by AWS for us. Since the domain is registered with AWS, the NS names automatically propagate to the registered domain. Now, we can create records by clicking on **Create Record Set**:

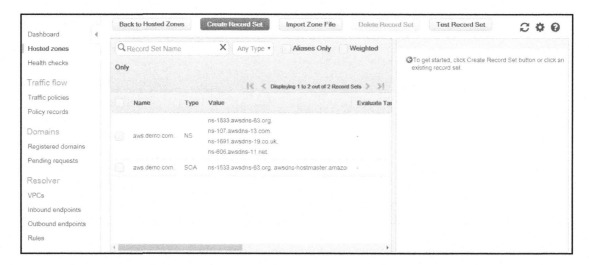

9. In the record set dialog, you can select the record name and type, set a TTL for the record and a value, and choose a routing policy. Once you have selected these, click on **Create**, and the record will appear in the list of records:

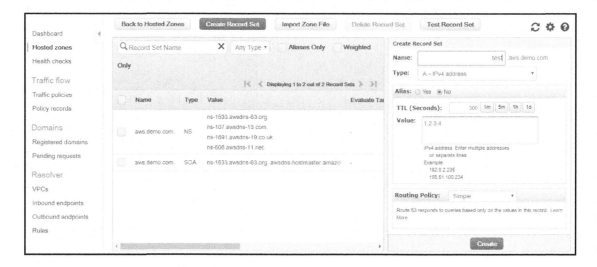

As you can see, registering a new domain and creating a DNS zone for the domain takes less than five minutes. Any records added will propagate within seconds across the Route 53 service and will be served through the NS names listed in the NS records.

Best practices

As with all of the other services in AWS, shared responsibility comes into effect. Even though the service is made highly available and ultra resilient, we should still ensure our DNS records are correct and reflect the best practices for security. When designing services on Route 53, we should be adhering to the following best practices:

- Domain auto renew can automatically renew your domain and protect it from hijacking on expiry
- Domain transfer lock can also help to prevent your domain from being hijacked at any time
- Privacy protection can be used to hide contact information
- Private records should not be entered into public zones
- You can protect your Route 53 configuration with AWS Config or CloudTrail so you can detect any rouge actions

Summary

The Route 53 service really takes a next generation approach to delivering DNS services. The service is fully managed and delivers a 100% SLA. The ability to manage the NS records in a simple browser interface or through the API is a great selling point, but not as important as the ability to perform routing and traffic shaping based on location, latency, and application capabilities. Reading this chapter should have at least enticed you to try and experiment a bit with Route 53, if not to move all of your domains there.

In the next chapter, we will be taking a look at managing security with API Gateway. The API Gateway service will give us the ability to deliver APIs in a uniform manner with great scalability and security features included.

Questions

1. How does Route 53 differ from traditional DNS?

2. You are developing an application that will store the data in a Global DynamoDB table in us-east-2, eu-west-1, and ap-northeast-1. Your locations will be serving users from their region in local languages. How can you direct the users to the right region?

3. Your application is budget-constrained. What services and features can you use to maintain uptime during major outages?

4. Your application allows for exchanging SIP packets over SSL on port 443 with the provider. To make the application highly available, you deploy three instances in three regions. How can you make sure the provider will not be trying to reach an instance that is down?

5. Your client is complaining that their domain got hijacked twice over the past year and they lost valuable customers because of this. How can Route 53 help?

6. You are working on an HPC cluster that will provide a backend to a genetics application. The application nodes need to be aware of at least three peers in the cluster at all times. How can you use Route 53 to deliver this insight?

7. You have registered a domain at an external provider before you knew about Route 53. You have created a public zone but the records do not seem to be propagating to the internet. What could be the issue?

Further reading

Refer to the following references:

- **Route 53 features**: https://aws.amazon.com/route53/features/
- **Route 53 record types**: https://docs.aws.amazon.com/Route53/latest/ DeveloperGuide/ResourceRecordTypes.html
- **List of DNS record types**: https://en.wikipedia.org/wiki/List_of_DNS_ record_types
- **Choosing a routing policy**: https://docs.aws.amazon.com/Route53/latest/ DeveloperGuide/routing-policy.html
- **Route 53 health checks**: https://docs.aws.amazon.com/Route53/latest/ DeveloperGuide/dns-failover.html

Managing and Securing API Gateway 8

Applications nowadays are designed with automation, resilience, and scalability in mind. In modern applications, multiple components need to be able to communicate with each other in a unified manner and with a standardized approach. To address communication between components, an **Application Programming Interface (API)** can be used. Because of this, AWS has built API Gateway, a solution that can help API developers to get off the ground quickly and efficiently.

This chapter will walk you through all you need to know about the API Gateway service. You will learn about the functionality of API Gateway and how and when to use it to unify, deploy, and secure your application APIs.

The following topics will be covered in this chapter:

- Introduction to API Gateway
- How API Gateway works
- Securing API Gateway
- Encryption
- **Denial of Service (DoS)** mitigation and enhanced security

Technical requirements

In this chapter, you will be required to have previous understanding of the HTTP protocol and the methods used to communicate in HTTP. An understanding of API design and the functionality that can be delivered through an API is a benefit.

The examples used in this chapter can be found at `https://github.com/PacktPublishing/ AWS-Certified-Advanced-Networking-Specialty-Exam-Guide/tree/master/Chapter08`.

Introduction to API Gateway

The API Gateway service is a fully managed solution from AWS that gives developers the ability to create highly scalable and highly secure API endpoints. The service is designed with the developer in mind and makes it very easy to write and deploy API endpoints straight out of the Management Console.

With API Gateway, we can expose different types of applications running in AWS EC2 or ECS to the internet and allow for direct communication with any HTTP/HTTPS-enabled managed services such as S3 or DynamoDB. The service also gives us the ability to create an API that will send queries to a Lambda function. Lambda functions are not exposed to the internet so API Gateway provides an entry point to the Lambda environment as well. Additionally, we can expose services completely external to AWS in our on-premises data center or anywhere on the internet.

The following diagram demonstrates different types of clients connecting to API Gateway. API Gateway can forward requests from the clients to different kinds of backends as described in the preceding paragraph:

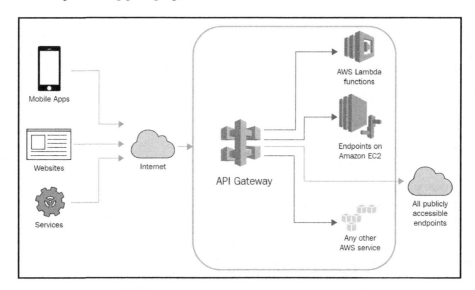

The main purpose of API Gateway is to build a unified approach to address our services. We can integrate all kinds of backends that might not be REST or WebSocket compatible and introduce an approach for communicating with these applications in a standard way. Additionally, API Gateway gives us the ability to secure our API against any denial of service attacks and allows us to throttle our users according to the expected performance of the application or according to their usage subscription.

How API Gateway works

API Gateway supports designing APIs in two different protocols—**Representational State Transfer (REST)** and WebSocket. The REST endpoints exposed by the API Gateway service adhere to standard HTTP protocol and methods and allow for the creation of completely stateless client-server communication to exchange information between application components, microservices, and different types of integrated devices. The WebSocket endpoints, on the other hand, allow for the creation of stateful, full-duplex APIs that also allow the routing of any incoming messages based on the message content.

For example, any application that performs transactions in an asynchronous manner can make great use of the RESTful API. REST is fast and stateless and all connection state is maintained outside the API itself. For example, in a website that tracks shipping across the world, the data for the location of vessels at sea does not change dramatically over short periods of time such as seconds or minutes. The site would allow the user to create a request to the RESTful API. The RESTful API then sends the request to the backend for processing. The backend looks up the information about the location of the ships and returns it to the RESTful API. The RESTful API responds to the user with the information. REST is great because a lot of users can make a lot of requests to the API at the same time and the API will only respond after the backend has responded to it.

On the other hand, any applications that perform transactions in a synchronous manner where the information flow in each direction requires an immediate response can be delivered off of a WebSocket API. Imagine a website that tracks traffic information in an urban area. The data about the traffic can change in seconds due to an accident or typical rush hour traffic. If the application was built on a RESTful API, all of the users would constantly need to send requests to the API for the same information. With WebSockets, we can create a stateful API that can maintain a session for such a request and deliver the changes in the application data in real time. Our users, for example, can now open their mobile application and continuously receive up-to-date information about traffic on their route. This approach is great for any type of application where the data updates need to be immediate, but has a drawback as WebSocket connections have a much higher level of resource usage than RESTful APIs.

The following diagram demonstrates the difference in operation when using a RESTful API versus using a WebSockets API:

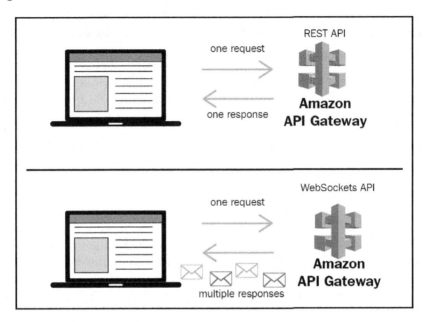

When we create an API Gateway endpoint, we essentially establish a service that will always be ready to take calls from clients. Those calls can be relayed back to the backend service that we are exposing. We then need to define the HTTP or WebSocket method to use and any transformation of data coming in when our backend is not compatible with the client request. The API Gateway endpoint can be deployed in three different ways:

- **Regional endpoint**: This serves the API on the internet from the selected region. This is very useful for compliance and governance.
- **Private endpoint**: This serves the API in a private VPC and is only accessible in the VPC. This type of endpoint is very useful when we host a heterogeneous private application where we would like to unify or standardize the communication
- **Edge-optimized endpoint**: This works in combination with CloudFront and delegates the session termination to CloudFront. In this case, users across the world get an experience that is similar to working with an application in their local region or even faster.

API Gateway can also perform caching of responses, making it very efficient in the way it responds.

The following diagram represents the full stack features of an edge-optimized API Gateway with caching enabled:

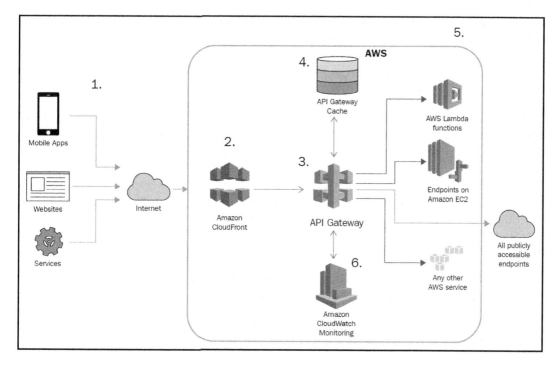

The preceding diagram can be interpreted in the following steps:

1. Different types of clients connect to the API gateway over the internet.
2. The CloudFront distribution terminates the session. If the request is looking for static content or read request, the CloudFront distribution can serve the static content directly, otherwise, it sends the request to API Gateway.
3. API Gateway receives the request and evaluates it.
4. If the same request has already been received and the response was cached, the service responds from the cache.
5. If the request has not yet been cached, the request is forwarded to the backend. API Gateway can perform transformation of data at this point and send the request in a format that will be readable by the backend. Once the backend responds, API Gateway can again perform transformation of data if required and then cache the response if configured to do so and, in parallel, respond back to the client.
6. Metrics about each response are sent to CloudWatch Monitoring.

Pricing

There is no cost for establishing the API Gateway service as the cost model for API Gateway is pay-per-request. For RESTful APIs, the request pricing is extremely low, starting at $3.5 USD per million requests. The pricing decreases with volume; after 333 million requests, the pricing gets a 15% discount, at 667 million another 15% kicks in, and at over 20 billion requests an additional 20% is sheared off the price per million requests. This makes API Gateway increasingly efficient with scale.

For WebSockets, pricing is done on a per-message basis. Any 32-kilobyte increment of data being transferred through the API, and any end of session increment regardless of its size, is considered a message. For example, a message with the size of 1 KB that terminates the session will be considered as one message. Another message of 33 KB will be considered as two messages: 32 KB for the first message increment and the 1 KB for the end of the session. But as you can see with applications that stream small updates in real time, it can be much more effective to maintain a session and rack up the 32 KB increment charges rather than resending the REST request over and over again. Pricing for WebSockets starts at $1 per million messages and includes a 20% discount when we reach over a billion messages.

The pricing mentioned in the preceding paragraphs is based on the pricing at the time of writing and the North Virginia (`us-east-1`) region.

When caching is in use, there is additional pricing that needs to be considered. The pricing is based on the amount of memory used for caching. Once deployed, you can enable and disable caching, re-configure it with different memory sizes, and determine which size provides the expected performance gain for your application. To determine the pricing for API Gateway, please refer to the *API Gateway pricing* link in the *Further reading* section of this chapter.

Securing API Gateway

The API Gateway service is a managed solution and is designed to be scalable to extreme capacity and receive any amount of traffic that is sent to it. But how does that work when the traffic coming into API Gateway is not legitimate? For example, how can we secure our API Gateway from a malicious attacker sending bogus requests and racking up our connection attempts and our AWS bill? We will try and answer all of the questions about the security of the API Gateway service in this section.

Authentication and authorization

To secure API Gateway, we can control the authentication, authorization, and control of access for any users accessing API Gateway. We have several mechanisms that will allow for controlling who can have access and when those mechanisms are in place, we can finely shape who to let in and which request is valid.

To secure our API Gateway, we can use the following:

- Authentication integration with Cognito and IAM
- Resource policies
- Lambda authorizers
- Usage plans

Cognito and IAM

We can use either AWS IAM or Amazon Cognito to authenticate users using API Gateway. When the users are authenticated by the AWS services, the AWS billing rule applies cost only to requests from valid, authenticated clients. Any other requests from any malicious actors that are not authenticated will be dealt with by AWS and will not fall under our billing obligations.

In the following diagram, this approach is demonstrated:

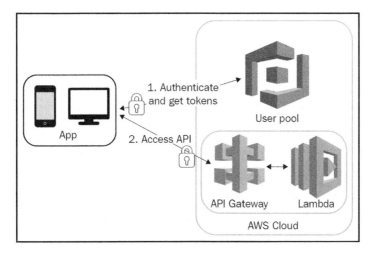

The preceding diagram can be explained as follows:

1. The user authenticates to Cognito and receives an authentication token.
2. The request is then signed with the authentication token and sent to the API Gateway endpoint. API Gateway can use the authentication token to verify the identity of the user with Cognito. If the token is valid, then user access is allowed and the request is forwarded to a Lambda function to process it.

Resource policies

When the service is designed as public, API Gateway also supports the creation of a resource policy where we can define the source IP addresses to allow or deny access from. In this scenario, any ranges in the policy that are denied will also not count against our usage.

Let's take a look at an example of a resource policy that can control the IP address ranges that are allowed or denied access. Remember, any explicit deny in AWS policies always takes precedence over any explicit allow, no matter the order of the rules.

Like any other policy in IAM, it always contains a statement that can have one or multiple effects. The effect can have a principal defined such as IAM users or groups and needs to state what kind of action over what kind of resource that effect will have.

Consider the following code block:

```
{
  "Statement": [
  {
  "Effect": "Allow",
  "Principal": "*",
  "Action": "execute-api:Invoke",
  "Resource": "arn:aws:execute-api:us-west-1:111122223333:myapi/*"
  },
```

The first part of this policy is as follows:

- Allows: "Effect": **"Allow"**
- Everyone: "Principal": **"*"**
- Invocation of API: "Action": **"execute-api:Invoke"**
- On an API called myapi in account 111122223333 in the us-west-1 region: "Resource": "arn:aws:execute-api:us-west-1:111122223333:myapi/*"

Here's another block of code:

```
{
  "Effect": "Deny",
  "Principal": "*",
  "Action": "execute-api:Invoke",
  "Resource": "arn:aws:execute-api:us-west-1:111122223333:myapi/*",
  "Condition" : { "IpAddress": { "aws:SourceIp": ["54.12.0.0/16",
"91.128.100.17/32" ] } } }
}
```

The second part of this policy is as follows:

- Denies: "Effect": **"Deny"**
- Everyone: "Principal": **"*"**
- Invocation of API: "Action": **"execute-api:Invoke"**
- On an API called myapi in account 111122223333 in the us-west-1 region: "Resource": "arn:aws:execute-api:**us-west-1:111122223333:myapi/***"
- Under condition that the *requests are coming from* the 54.12.0.0/16 network or 91.128.100.17 single IP: **"Condition"** : { **"IpAddress"**: { **"aws:SourceIp"**: [**"54.12.0.0/16"**, **"91.128.100.17/32"**] } } }

If we combine the two parts of the policy together, we can use this policy by simply modifying the source IP address condition. If you would like to learn more about how to write a policy for API Gateway, please visit the *Resource policy examples* link in the *Further reading* section of this chapter.

Lambda authorizers

If we would like to control access through our application, we can use Lambda authorizers. Lambda authorizers give us the capability to authorize or deny access according to any kind of custom authentication mechanism, text strings, values, and other content in the request itself. This way, we can define our own authorization mechanism that can be completely customized.

The following diagram represents a typical workflow of a Lambda authorizer-based authentication:

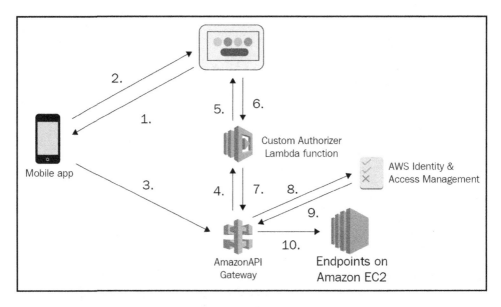

The preceding diagram can be interpreted as follows:

1. The user authenticates to a third-party authentication service using third-party credentials.
2. The third party provides the user with an authentication token.
3. The request is sent to API Gateway with the authentication token attached.
4. API Gateway detects the authentication token and forwards it to the Lambda authorizer.
5. The Lambda authorizer initiates a check of the token at the third-party provider.
6. If the token is valid, the third-party authentication system responds with the user group membership. If the token is not valid, then the third party responds with a denied request.
7. Lambda forwards the response of the third party to API Gateway. If the response is invalid, the user access is denied.
8. If the response is valid, API Gateway checks the group membership to role mapping with IAM.
9. IAM responds with the role that will allow access.
10. The request is sent to the backend using the IAM role.

Usage plans

API Gateway also supports usage plans. Usage plans give us the ability to create API keys that we can distribute to our users or subscribers. The API keys give API Gateway the ability to determine the level of access and track the usage of each user using a particular key. The end user will either be limited to a specific rate of requests, for example, 50 requests per second, and will not be allowed to exceed the number of requests by API Gateway. This can enable the building of several subscription levels where different API keys allow different users to use the application with different performance. We can also configure a volume-based request limit. For example, we can define that a user can make 100000 requests during a certain billing period. This approach lets the user use the service when required at any capacity of requests per second as long as they have not reached their quota.

The following diagram demonstrates how usage plans can be used to allow users who have purchased premium plans to communicate with API Gateway at a higher rate or higher volume than standard users:

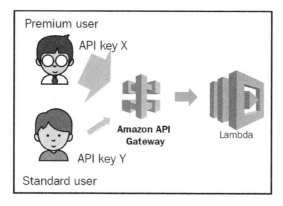

The plan is determined by the API key the user uses to access the API Gateway endpoint.

Encryption

To encrypt the traffic between the clients and API Gateway, we can use the HTTPS protocol for any connection made to the service. We will need to install a **Server Name Indication (SNI)** capable certificate on the API Gateway endpoint but that does give us the capability of offloading the SSL connection at API Gateway. When end-to-end encryption is required, we will need to configure each and every device in the path to have a separate certificate installed and managed.

The following diagram demonstrates an example of an end-to-end encryption using API Gateway that forwards the request to a group of EC2 instances behind an ELB:

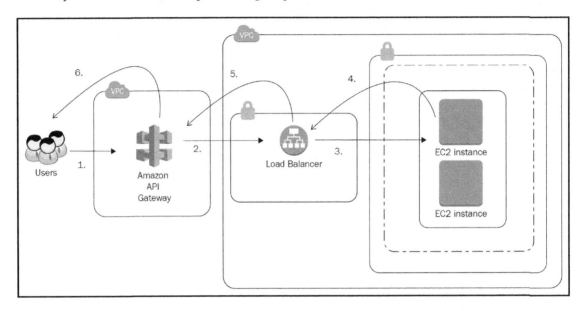

The preceding diagram can be explained as follows:

1. The user connects to API Gateway through the HTTPS protocol. The API Gateway SSL certificate is used to encrypt the request. The request is decrypted and evaluated by API Gateway.
2. API Gateway forwards the request to the ELB. The ELB SSL certificate is used to encrypt the request. The request is decrypted and evaluated by the ELB
3. The ELB forwards the request to the EC2 instance. The EC2 instance SSL certificate is used to encrypt the request.
4. The request is decrypted on the EC2 instance and processed. The EC2 instance responds with the EC2 instance SSL encryption. The response is decrypted by the ELB.
5. The response is re-encrypted with the ELB SSL. The response is received by API Gateway and decrypted.
6. The response is again encrypted by the API Gateway SSL and returned to the user.

We can also use the **AWS Certificate Manager (ACM)** with CloudFront, which allows us to create a completely free SSL certificate for our domain and attach it to our API Gateway and ELB.

The ACM also allows us to automatically update and renew the certificate so that we never need to worry about the SSL certificates expiring. Unfortunately, the ACM does not allow us to directly install any certificates to the EC2 instances so the last leg of the SSL still requires us to manage the creation and distribution of the certificates.

DoS mitigation and enhanced security

To implement **Denial of Service (DoS)** mitigation and enhance the security of our application, we can filter traffic with customized security rules, since API Gateway can be integrated with the AWS **Web Application Firewall (WAF)**. The WAF allows us to specify network-based rules and HTTP string-based filters so that we can remove any requests that would otherwise hit API Gateway at the WAF entry point. When the API Gateway endpoint is deployed in an edge-optimized manner, the service will be operating at the CloudFront layer and secure all our traffic at the entry point to our environment. With the WAF, we are able to control the intricate details of each API request, which allows us to protect our backends against malicious scripts, XSS, SQL injection attempts, and malformed queries with a length of query, type of query and any regex pattern of query that should not be supported by our application.

We can also combine the use of API keys and the WAF. We can expose our API Gateway directly and allow users with API keys to get direct access while any anonymous users without API keys will only be allowed to access our application via the WAF. The WAF will then evaluate the rules and either allow or block anonymous access to our application. This behavior is demonstrated in the following diagram:

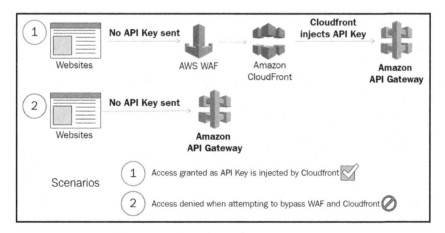

To conclude, the security features of API Gateway can be combined both with authentication and the WAF service to provide end-to-end security for our application.

Summary

We have taken a look at the features of the API Gateway service, the deployment modes, the pricing, and the security aspects of the service. API Gateway is a powerful tool for unifying the development of application communication. But since the tool is exposed on the network, any network engineer will need to understand how to control access and build advanced security mechanisms into the API Gateway service.

In the next chapter, we will delve even deeper into the monitoring and troubleshooting tools in AWS that will provide us with the ability to monitor and analyze the traffic flows as well as find issues with configurations and enhance the overall reliability and security of our network.

Questions

1. Which protocols are supported by API Gateway?
2. What kind of backends are supported by API Gateway?
3. You are building a public website. As part of your monitoring, you implement an alert that warns you when the API Gateway connection budget is at 50%. You get a warning the next day while the application is still in staging and no external users should be connecting to the application. How can you disable any external access during development?
4. You are using a third-party authentication mechanism and are planning to use API Gateway. You look in the documentation and see that only Cognito and IAM are supported as the authentication sources. What can you do in this case?
5. Your application requires you to implement end-to-end encryption. What tool can you use to simplify the issuance and renewal of the certificates on your API Gateway, ELB, and EC2 instances?
6. You are building a mobile application that will send live weather updates to any device with a browser open to your website. Can this be done with API Gateway?
7. You are building a mobile application that will exchange information with a backend DynamoDB database. How can you use API Gateway to secure access to the DynamoDB environment?

Further reading

Refer to the following references:

- **API Gateway documentation**: https://docs.aws.amazon.com/apigateway/latest/developerguide/welcome.html
- **API Gateway pricing**: https://aws.amazon.com/api-gateway/pricing/
- **REST**: https://en.wikipedia.org/wiki/Representational_state_transfer
- **WebSocket**: https://en.wikipedia.org/wiki/WebSocket
- **Controlling access to API Gateway**: https://docs.aws.amazon.com/apigateway/latest/developerguide/apigateway-control-access-to-api.html
- **Resource policy examples**: https://docs.aws.amazon.com/apigateway/latest/developerguide/apigateway-resource-policies-examples.html
- **Server Name Indication Certificates**: https://en.wikipedia.org/wiki/Server_Name_Indication

Section 4: Monitoring and Operating the AWS Networks

A network administrator is responsible for monitoring and managing IT resources of an organization. The job involves monitoring the availability and performance of the network. AWS eases up this job with CloudWatch, CloudTrail, and the VPC Flow Logs Services. This section describes how you can use these features to collect and track network state and metrics, collect and monitor log files, set alarms, and automatically react to changes in your AWS resources.

We will cover the following chapter in this section:

- Chapter 9, *Monitoring and Troubleshooting Networks in AWS*

Monitoring and Troubleshooting Networks in AWS

9

When we deploy services to AWS, we also need to make sure that we get an overview of what those services are doing, how many resources they consume, and whether they are operating efficiently. Monitoring is a very important aspect of operating any environment, as it helps to identify the metrics of resource usage, and gives us the ability to get insight into any issues and troubleshoot the environment in a much easier manner. AWS provides the CloudWatch service, an integrated monitoring environment that can help us understand the specifics of our environment.

The following topics will be covered in this chapter:

- Introducing CloudWatch
- How CloudWatch works
- Metrics, logs, and alarms
- Monitoring types – normal and detailed
- Creating a CloudWatch alarm
- AWS CloudTrail
- Working with VPC Flow Logs
- Monitoring network components
- Monitoring **Elastic Load Balancing** (ELB)
- Monitoring CloudFront
- Monitoring the **Application Programming Interface** (API) gateway
- Monitoring Route 53
- Troubleshooting

Technical requirements

You should be able to understand the basics of performance monitoring, metrics analysis, and network-flow troubleshooting in a typical enterprise environment in order to follow along with this chapter.

Introducing CloudWatch

Monitoring is a key component of running any production-grade application. Having insight into performance metrics and being able to understand resource usage is a crucial part of keeping any application running smoothly. In modern environments, monitoring takes on a whole set of functions that give us the ability to get both insight into the state of our application and deliver additional functionality by the way of alarming and triggering other systems. The typical tasks a motioning system will perform are as follows:

- **Metering**: The collection of metrics that give us insight into resource utilization and application performance.
- **Log collection**: The ability to collect system and application logs.
- **Graphing**: The creation of graphs based on resource utilization and performance metrics.
- **Alarming**: Sending notifications and triggering external systems based on predefined metrics or log triggers.

When operating an application, the ability to collect metrics and logs will help us form a usage pattern. The usage pattern will help us determine the state of the application and whether it is operating within the normal parameters. Having a definition of typical performance and resource usage can help us predict issues before they happen and take preemptive corrective actions. Using monitoring correctly can be very beneficial to our application up-time and can help us better adhere to the SLA.

In AWS, we have a choice to use the built-in monitoring system provided by CloudWatch and connect it to other AWS services, which can give us the ability to execute actions external to CloudWatch, based on the metrics and alarms coming out of CloudWatch. There are also many other monitoring platforms out there that have all of the preceding characteristics or are very specialized in their tasks. We have the ability to integrate many monitoring, log collection, graphing, and systems management tools with CloudWatch, which gives us the ability to utilize services that are familiar to us or where their use is mandated by an enterprise policy.

How CloudWatch works

The Amazon CloudWatch service is a serverless, fully managed, highly scalable metering, log collection, graphing, and alarming service that can collect metrics and the logs from our AWS components and services, as well as from any on-premise systems that have a CloudWatch agent installed. By default, all AWS services will send the relevant metrics and logs to CloudWatch, but we can augment and enhance the capability of CloudWatch by adding our custom metrics and logs into the collection service.

The following diagram gives a comprehensive overview of what CloudWatch can offer us:

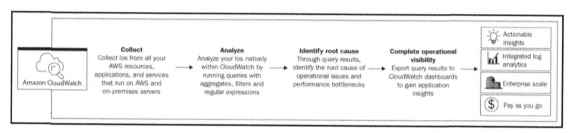

As seen in the preceding diagram, the benefits that CloudWatch can offer us are as follows:

- The service can collect metrics from all AWS services and any other sources.
- The built-in tools for analytics allow us to quickly and efficiently analyze data.
- With CloudWatch, we are able to perform alerting and can push data out to other systems, giving us a lot of flexibility at any scale.

The metrics and logs collected by CloudWatch are stored in the CloudWatch repository. The repository is regionally bound and will only display metrics from services in its own region and any on-premise services that are configured to send logs in that region. This implies that each region should be treated as a distinguished, unique entity, and the metrics that trigger additional actions should also be bound to that same region. Since regions are isolated environments, we should also be looking at regional logs and metrics when we are troubleshooting, so the fact that CloudWatch is regionally bound can be considered a benefit.

All CloudWatch metrics are available to view from the management console, the AWS **Command Line Interface (CLI)**, the **Software Development Kits (SDKs)**, and directly through the CloudWatch API. This means that any other systems can simply connect to the API and retrieve the relevant metrics from CloudWatch. For example, a benefit of using external tools on CloudWatch would be when we need to analyze an application that runs across multiple regions and we need to aggregate the data and visualize it as a single set.

While viewing metrics is beneficial in itself, the real power of CloudWatch comes through the alarm functionality that is available in CloudWatch. We can define certain triggers based on metrics and log content. If CloudWatch detects that the metric has breached the trigger, or that the logs contain a certain pattern, it can issue a request to other AWS services, which can then perform automated actions or notify the appropriate person or team to perform any kind of manual intervention. An architectural overview of CloudWatch is shown in the following diagram:

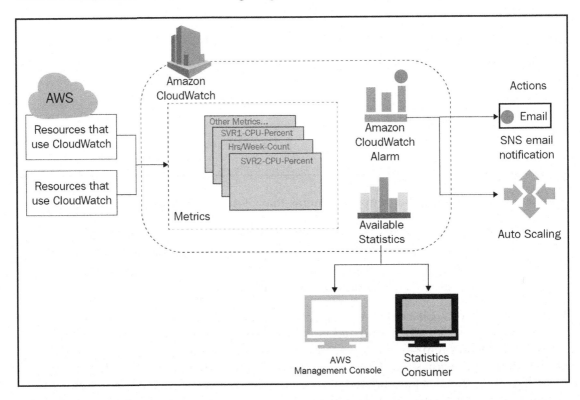

CloudWatch also has a dashboard where we can get a quick overview of the metrics that have been collected for our services. The following screenshot demonstrates how to select different dashboards according to each service:

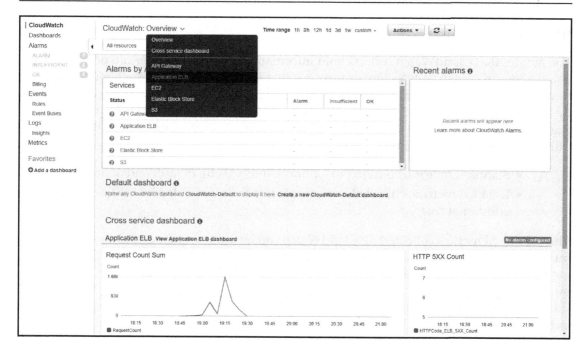

In the preceding screenshot, you can see the **Overview** dashboard, which gives us a general overview of aggregated metrics for our region, but to get a service-specific overview we can choose metrics that are presented in the drop-down menu when clicking on the arrow next to **Overview**.

Metrics, logs, and alarms

So, as you can see, the CloudWatch environment is a powerful tool that we can use to determine the state of our application. The basic functionality comes at no cost and enables us to perform powerful and automated actions on our environment by using the following core elements of CloudWatch:

- **Metrics**
- **Logs**
- **Alarms**

Metrics

The metrics that CloudWatch collects hold information, collected at a certain point in time, about a certain system, subsystem, or resource that is being consumed. Each metric will have a certain value that will represent the state of the system or the level of resource usage by that system. For example, the metrics collected by the CloudWatch service include the state of a health check of an instance, the CPU resource utilization, the disk write utilization, and so on. These metrics come in two types:

- Standard metrics, collected in 5-minute intervals by default and at no cost
- Detailed metrics, collected in 1-minute intervals if enabled by the user, at an additional cost

The volume of metrics collected by CloudWatch can be quite immense, and, as you can imagine, the data storage system to collect those metrics in the backend stores billions of metric points every day. The scale of the backend system determines the capabilities of the motioning platform, and the CloudWatch team has done a great job at making this whole thing work. But, the amount of metrics also means that all metrics cannot be kept for an indefinite amount of time. CloudWatch sets out a retention period for the metrics that are being collected:

- Custom metrics with below 1-minute interval – 3 hours
- 1-minute metrics – 15 days
- 5-minute metrics – 63 days
- 1-hour metrics – 15 months

Once the retention period for a certain metric level expires, the service will aggregate the detailed metrics to the next tier. For example, any 1-minute metrics will be aggregated to 5-minute metrics after 15 days. In turn, 5-minute metrics will be aggregated to 1-hour metrics after 63 days. The detail provided by CloudWatch is designed to provide more than enough time for the existence of detailed metrics, as the systems relying on detailed metrics will be consuming those metrics and performing actions in near real time.

To overview metrics, you can head to the CloudWatch management console and select the **Metrics** menu option, as shown in the following screenshot:

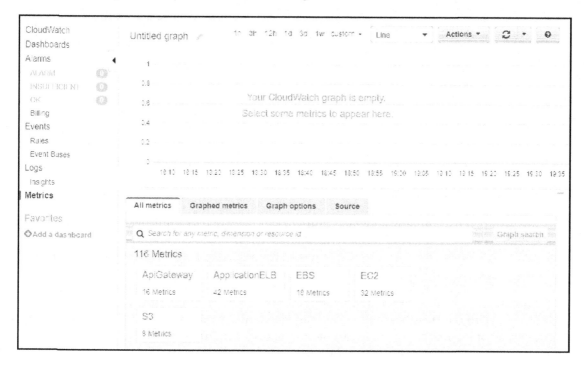

In the preceding screenshot, you can see that an overview of the metrics that are available in the region you selected. By clicking any of the metrics groups, you can drill down to the metric you would like to visualize. Simply select the metric, set the time range above the graph window, and the graph of your metrics will appear.

Logs

With CloudWatch, we can also collect logs from different sources, including services in AWS and external services, such as applications running on our **Elastic Compute Cloud (EC2)** instances or on-premise applications.

CloudWatch Logs have the ability to collect any types of logs from any type of service and display the logs in the management console, as demonstrated in the following screenshot:

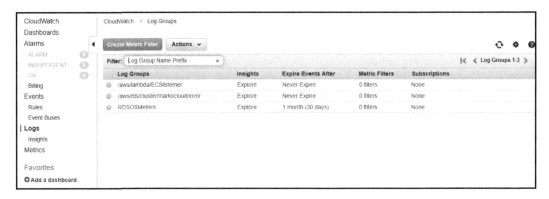

Logs are grouped by domains and each domain can have one or multiple streams in it. The logs service collects all logs indefinitely. Unlike metrics, there is no expiration of data in CloudWatch Logs and the service always has a cost associated with it. This implies that any unnecessary logs should be deleted once they are no longer needed.

Additionally, the CloudWatch management console allows us to perform a bit of analytics on our logs. With the **Insights** feature, we can also build expressions that will help us find an exact type of log matching the expression. The use of the **Insights** section is demonstrated in the following screenshot:

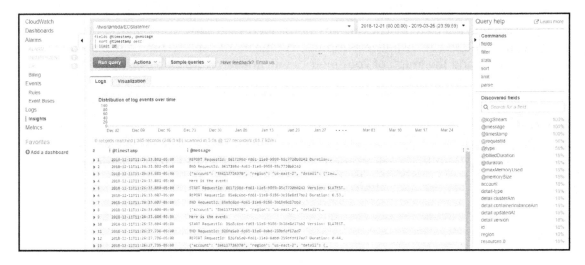

We can also use the same expression in an alarm to continuously monitor our logs and alert us when a certain log entry that matches the expression starts appearing in the log.

Alarms

CloudWatch also gives us the ability to perform actions based on any kind of pre-determined metric condition or threshold, or based on any kind of predefined log value or pattern. The metric threshold and log patterns can be configured in a CloudWatch alarm. Alarms will trigger an external function or action that can perform the following:

- **Notifications**: Integration with the **Simple Notification Service (SNS)** can help us notify response teams upon a certain metric or log.
- **Auto Scaling**: Integration with the AWS Auto Scaling service can help to auto scale EC2 instances and DynamoDB RCU/WCU configurations.
- **Auto Recovery**: Integration with the EC2 Auto Recovery service can help us recover instances where the health checks fail or instances that are affected by outages in EC2.
- **Event-based computing**: Integration with Lambda can help us push metrics and logs into Lambda functions that can perform custom actions based on these events.

CloudWatch alarms are designed to look for a condition for a certain amount of time or a certain amount of repetitions. For example, when Auto Scaling an EC2 instance group, we can use the CPU metric. An Auto Scaling policy will be configured with the percentage of the CPU that is determined as the threshold and for which the threshold must be breached before the alarm is triggered. This would commonly look like the following:

- When the CPU utilization is above 70%
- For 10 minutes
- Perform Auto Scaling by adding one more instance

The Auto Scaling mechanism uses a CloudWatch alarm to trigger the action. We can also use CloudWatch alarms by detecting patterns in a log file. A typical example would be a web application sending its connection logs to CloudWatch. The trigger for the alarm could be a 400 error in the log and the trigger threshold could be set to a certain number of occurrences in a specified amount of time:

- When 400 errors in the log appear
- With 10 or more occurrences
- Within the span of 10 minutes
- Send a notification to the response team via SNS

CloudWatch can be made to recover instances where the health check has failed. We can simply use the health check state metric of our instance, and, if the health of the instance changes, then the CloudWatch service can trigger an alarm that will, in turn, trigger a reboot of the instance where the health check has failed. This action will restart the instance on another hypervisor host and quickly enable the recovery of that instance in case of issues in the EC2 environment.

For event-based actions, alarms can feed metrics or logs to Lambda functions. The Lambda functions can perform the following actions based on the metrics and logs:

- Intelligent scaling actions on the metrics and logs, such as Auto Scaling EC2 with custom algorithms
- Predictive scaling or predictive failure analysis based on both metrics and logs
- The log format and data transformation
- The detection of threats in logs
- Forwarding the metric data to different targets such as DynamoDB, CloudSearch, or S3 for further analysis

The following screenshot demonstrates a billing alarm that is set up in this account:

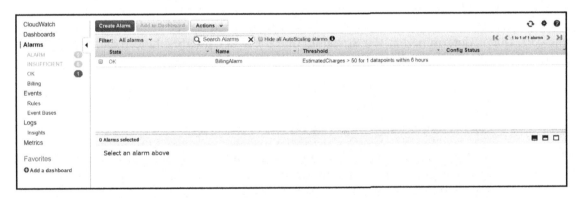

The billing alarm can be used to send a notification to a user or a group when a certain predefined threshold is exceeded. The threshold can be used to maintain control over your budget and catch any expenses that would otherwise cause the budget to be exceeded. For example, it would be wise to create several billing alarms that would alert a project manager once expenses have reached 50%, 80%, and 100% of the budget. By starting with 50%, the project manager can quickly determine whether the alert is coming in too soon in the month, and can take action accordingly as to not overspend the budget.

As you can see, the CloudWatch metrics and alarms can enhance the day-to-day operations of any application, help with scalability, produce cost savings by turning off the systems when not needed, and are a great benefit when troubleshooting and running system diagnostics.

Monitoring types – standard and detailed

Monitoring is only as effective as the interval the metrics are collected on. When our application experiences frequent changes in performance in very short intervals, it can be difficult to determine whether there is any kind of issue in our environment. For example, when our application experiences a spike in traffic for 2 minutes, our 5-minute metrics might not capture that spike. To allow for metrics that will suit every requirement of every application, CloudWatch allows for metrics collection in the following intervals:

- **Standard**: 5-minute metrics are output by all AWS services by default at no cost.
- **Detailed**: 1-minute metric collection on AWS services that can be enabled by the user and collected at an additional cost (10 detailed metrics are included in the free tier).
- **Custom**: Custom metrics are collected with an interval down to 1 second, at an additional cost.

With detailed metrics, we are able to detect any changes in our AWS services at a much shorter interval compared to standard metrics. We also have the ability to enable detailed metrics per service instance. For example, when we require detailed monitoring of a specific **Relational Database Service (RDS)** database, we can simply enable detailed metrics on just that database. Similarly, when a mission-critical application behind a load balancer requires us to act fast when the load balancer connection numbers spike, we can enable detailed metrics just on that load balancer. The cost of the detailed metric is then tied only to that instance of the service.

Additionally, when 1-minute metrics are not enough, we can supply custom metrics to CloudWatch with an interval down to 1 second. This can be very beneficial to containerized applications that can scale to requests in real time. For example, we previously scaled the EC2 instances and the scaling times were measured in minutes. That meant that we could collect 1-minute or 5-minute metrics and scale preemptively to a lower threshold. With 1 second metrics, we can scale containers at a moment's notice.

However, metrics of this detail are only available for custom metrics, so we need to output those metrics from our application and scale on the appropriate application-level metric. For example, we can scale on the number of connections per container. If your application can project the number of connections for each container, we can set a threshold that will take into account the average number of connections and scale the application within a second or two of the threshold being breached.

Creating a CloudWatch alarm

In this tutorial, we will be creating a new CloudWatch alarm. We need to log in to the management console and select **Alarms** from the menu:

1. The first step is to click the **Create Alarm** button to open the **Create new alarm** dialogue:

2. In the **Create new alarm** dialogue, select a **Metric** by clicking on the **Select metric** button:

3. The **Select metric** window will open and give us an option to select a metric. We can dig into the metrics and select the exact metric we would like to create an alarm for. For example, we can select **EC2** and then the **Per-Instance Metrics**. This gives us the ability to select a metric for exactly one instance. In the following example, we selected the **CPUUtilization** metric to use in our alarm. By using the pencil icon in the top-left corner, we can rename the metric if we would like to give it a more friendly name. When done, we simply click on the **Select metric** button:

4. This returns us to the **Create new alarm** dialogue, where we will scroll down to continue creating the alarm:

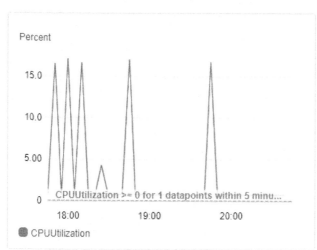

Create new alarm

Metric ✏ Edit

This alarm will trigger when the blue line goes up to or above the red line for 1 datapoints within 5 minutes

Namespace:	AWS/EC2
Metric Name:	CPUUtilization
InstanceId:	i-0412ecc8be43bbee5
InstanceName:	Markocloud-env
Period:	5 Minutes
Statistic:	Average

Percent

CPUUtilization >= 0 for 1 datapoints within 5 minu...

18:00   19:00   20:00

● CPUUtilization

5. In the **Alarm details** section, we need to name the alarm and can optionally give it a description. Here, we will also configure the threshold and duration of the threshold breach for the trigger. In this example, we selected the **CPUUtilization** above 80% for two data points (by default, these are 5 minutes apart). We also set the range of data points to be 5. This means that, in each 25-minute period, a breach of more than 10 minutes combined will trigger the alarm:

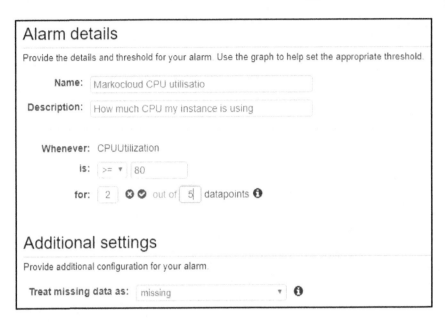

6. In **Actions**, we will select what kind of action is to be taken when the alarm is triggered. In our example, we simply set a notification to an SNS within our account. We can add multiple actions at this point; for example, to notify multiple topics or to add Auto Scaling, Auto Recovery, and other actions to this alarm:

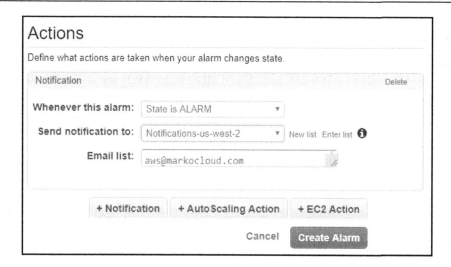

7. Once the alarm is created, it will be visible in the management console:

AWS CloudTrail

AWS CloudTrail is a fully-managed, serverless service that gives us the ability to collect an audit log of all API calls to AWS services. Since all calls to AWS are API calls, no matter what interface the client uses, the CloudTrail service gives us the ability to gain complete insight into **who** performed **what** action over **which** resource and **when**.

CloudTrail collects this information in the AWS API backend and can output the collected information to a collection bucket that we designate. All data collected by CloudTrail is automatically encrypted, and we can additionally protect all the logs in the bucket by enabling the CloudTrail log file integrity validation. The CloudTrail log file integrity validation enables you to determine whether the log file has changed or has been altered since the time it was collected and initially stored, whether any log file was deleted, and whether no logs have been delivered during a certain period of time.

This is a valuable forensic tool that can help identify any malicious activity by actors authorized to access the logs or due to the compromised credentials of those actors. When the log file integrity validation is enabled, a hash is created for every log that is delivered to the bucket. A separate hash inventory file is created to keep track of the files and their hashes. The file is created each hour and contains the listing of all the files delivered in the last hour. A separate hash is also created for the inventory file.

CloudTrail enables any account to use a free tier where all the API calls for the past 90 days are collected free of charge. In 2017, AWS also enabled the seamless integration of CloudTrail to all newly created accounts, which provides seamless collection of all the API calls for the past seven days within your account. This service is up and running and will not require you to make any configuration changes.

A combination of CloudWatch and CloudTrail gives us a complete picture of the environment and can be used when performing auditing, compliance, and validation of our environment and the historical usage of the account.

Working with VPC Flow Logs

To diagnose and troubleshoot the network connectivity at the **Virtual Private Cloud** (**VPC**) level, we can use VPC Flow Logs. The VPC Flow Logs feature provides us with the ability to capture information about the IP packets travelling through our VPC. When a VPC Flow Log is created, we are able to get an overview the logs created in the management console directly through the CLI, SDKs, or the API.

We can enable VPC Flow Logs on the level of a subnet, or we can log each and every network adapter in the subnet. This allows us to view the traffic and diagnose whether network packets are reaching the intended target and what the state of the packet flow during a certain collection period was. Flow logs can be used as a diagnostic tool when network traffic is not reaching a certain target; this can be a subnet, an EC2 or RDS instance, an **Elastic Container Service (ECS)** container with an **Elastic Network Interface (ENI)** attached, or another service that uses the ENI to connect to our VPC, such as a VPC interface endpoint. We can also use VPC Flow Logs as a security tool to monitor the state of the traffic reaching our instances.

When creating VPC Flow Logs, we will need to specify the target resource for the flow log. For an ENI, the service will create one log stream in CloudWatch, whereas, for a subnet, the service will create a log stream for every existing or future ENI in the subnet. When adding a new VPC flow log, it will take a few minutes before data starts to appear in the log stream. It is wise to remember that VPC Flow Logs do not record and display information in real time, but are rather historical records of network packet events.

VPC Flow Logs are stored to the CloudWatch Logs and are treated as any other CloudWatch Logs, meaning that we will incur CloudWatch Logs charges if we enable them on an object. This is why it is important to make sure that you disable any flow logs that are not required and delete any existing log streams so that you don't incur charges after the analysis is complete.

We have already discussed the structure of VPC Flow Logs in Chapter 3, *VPC Network Security*, so we will just do a quick overview of an example VPC Flow Log at this point:

Let's first look at the structure:

```
<version> <account-id> <interface-id> <srcaddr> <dstaddr> <srcport>
<dstport> <protocol> <packets> <bytes> <start> <end> <action> <log-status>
```

The entry is as follows:

```
2 888777666555 eni-abcd1234 10.0.0.121 10.0.0.147 22013 22 6 34 3366
1547812812 1547812888 ACCEPT OK
```

From the preceding example, we notice the following things:

- The flow log is telling us that the flow log version is 2.
- The account ID is 888777666555.
- The ID of the ENI is eni-abcd1234.
- The source address is 10.0.0.121.
- The destination address is 10.0.0.147.

- The source port is 222013.
- The destination port is 22.
- The protocol is 6 (TCP).
- The number of packets is 34.
- The combined size of the flow is 3366.
- The start timestamp is 1547812812.
- The end timestamp is 1547812888.
- The packet was accepted (ACCEPT).
- The status is OK.

Additionally, the packet could have been rejected with REJECT; there might have been no data collected (NODATA); or some records may have been skipped, due to the overwhelming load on the network, with SKIPDATA.

When flow logs are displaying REJECT as the action, then the packets are being rejected. If this a valid flow and the traffic should be passing to the target, it is due to a misconfiguration of a security group rule or a NACL. We have already covered security groups and NACLs in Chapter 3, *VPC Network Security*.

Flow logs recommendations and limitations

The flow logs service is fully integrated into the VPC core and can use the power of the custom **original design manufacturer** (ODM) hardware. However, due to the design limitations of the VPC backend, there are certain limitations with VPC Flow Logs that we have to be aware of when troubleshooting our environment. The following is a list of recommendations and limitations of VPC Flow Logs:

- **Recommendations**:
    - It is not recommended to run flow logs continuously on your production environment.
    - Flow logs do not perform packet inspection. When packet inspection is required, you can find a solution on the AWS Marketplace.
    - VPC Flow Logs are not intended for network performance collection. Use CloudWatch for performance metrics.

- **Limitations**:
  - When VPC Flow Logs are created, their configuration cannot be changed. You need to delete the flow log and create a new one if any configuration changes are required.
  - When a VPC is peered with a VPC from another account, VPC Flow Logs cannot be enabled.
  - VPC Flow Logs do not support tags.
  - VPC Flow Logs are not supported on EC2-Classic.
  - API permissions on VPC Flow Logs actions are not fine-grained. When permissions to VPC Flow Logs are required, the principal needs to be given the `ec2:*flowLogs` permission, meaning access to all flow logs.
  - When a network interface has multiple IP addresses and any secondary address is used, VPC Flow Logs will display only the primary IP address as the source or destination.

Additionally, VPC Flow Logs does not capture the following:

- Traffic to Amazon DNS servers
- Traffic to Amazon Windows License activation
- Traffic to the instance metadata and Amazon Time Sync Service
- Any **Dynamic Host Configuration Protocol** (**DHCP**) traffic
- Traffic to the VPC router
- Traffic between any VPC endpoint network (PrivateLink) interface and the **Network Load Balancer** (**NLB**)

Monitoring network components

To gain a deeper insight into the network flows and performance, you can use a combination of CloudWatch and VPC Flow Logs. While VPC Flow Logs give us a very fine-grained overview of a particular packet flow for a particular ENI, it would be difficult to get any kind of tangible information on the large-scale aspect of the state and performance of our network from VPC Flow Logs. For this purpose, we will be using the CloudWatch interface.

In the following example, we can use the CloudWatch environment to display network interface statistics for each EC2 instance in our environment. As you can see, we have two instances for which we are displaying network performance information.

In the CloudWatch interface shown in the following screenshot, we select only the network metrics and we are able to see the performance for each instance:

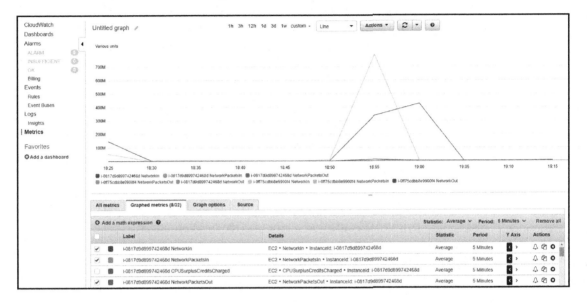

Sometimes, our network policy would mandate some additional network insight. For example, when deep packet inspection, traffic pattern analysis, and layer-7-based filtering are required, we can rely on a large offering of third-party networking tools from multiple vendors. Tools such as IPS/IDS systems, next-generation firewalls, and packet sniffers are available from the AWS Marketplace for deployment with just a few clicks.

Monitoring ELB

The CloudWatch management console gives us the ability to gain insight into the performance of ELB. Since the load balancer distributes the load across multiple instances, having the ability to view information on the load of our application at any given time is crucial.

One of the most important metrics when monitoring an ELB is latency of the response from our EC2 instances. The performance of our application is directly tied to the performance of the backend. The ability of the backend to respond as quickly as possible is going to increase customer satisfaction. Several studies have been done correlating the performance impacts of latency on user behavior. Amazon has conducted a latency study of how latency affects sales, available on their website. Every 10 milliseconds in latency, up to 100 milliseconds, was directly responsible for decreasing overall sales by 1%. Beyond 100 milliseconds, the sales dropped dramatically and user engagement beyond that point was not measured. Other studies described APIs with a 250 millisecond response time or longer to be completely unusable and will deter users from using them:

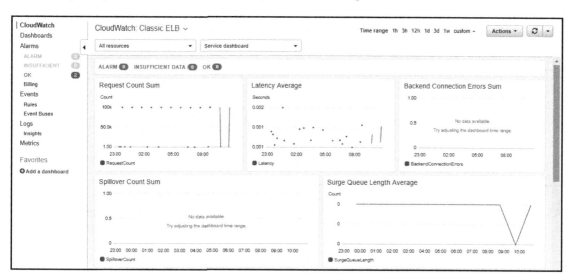

We should also be monitoring backend connection errors. On the right-hand side of the preceding screenshot we can see a combined sum of all backend errors, but we can also overview all the 400 and 500 error metrics separately. This can be done by going into the detailed metrics and selecting just the 400 or just the 500 errors. We will demonstrate detailed metrics in the next section when we discuss monitoring CloudFront, since the concepts for monitoring both services are the same.

Monitoring CloudFront

When monitoring CloudFront, the CloudWatch monitoring service allows us to get an idea of the performance of our CloudFront distribution and the consumption of our CloudFront resources by our distribution. The **CloudFront** dashboard also includes a nice feature that allows us to overview the error rates, as seen in the top-right corner of the following screenshot:

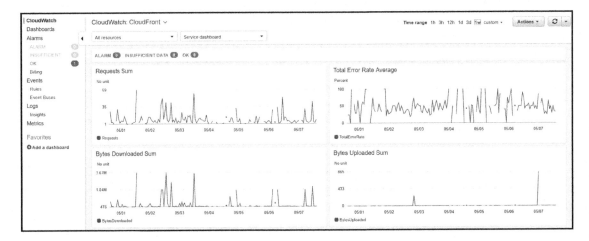

As this demo distribution seems to be error prone, we can drill down into the error metrics by clicking on the **Metrics** selection from the menu on the left and then view the detailed CloudFront metrics.

In this example, we have chosen just the requests and the 400 error rate to try and determine whether there is any correlation between the requests and the relatively high number of errors:

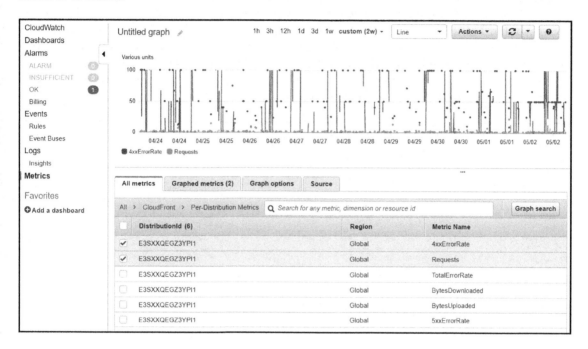

As you can see, CloudWatch can be a valuable tool for analyzing different types of metrics that are reported by AWS services and can be the first point of interest when performing an analysis or when troubleshooting an issue.

Monitoring the API gateway

Similarly to the ELB and CloudFront, we can monitor the performance of the API gateway by selecting the metrics related to each API. In this example, we have chosen to select all the metrics of the Test API. The API was tested externally during a 15-minute EST window and as we can see, traffic was recorded during that time. We have chosen to examine both 400 and 500 error codes, the latency of the API, and the integration latency, which measures the performance from the API gateway to the backend. We also have a count metric selected, but the counts are really small so they are not registering well on this chart:

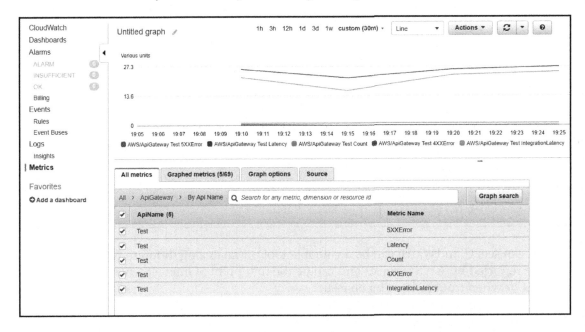

However, what we can see from this chart is a nice correlation between the integration latency and the overall latency of the API. This means that our API is performing well and the larger chunk of the latency is due to the backend responding slowly.

Monitoring Route 53

Route 53 is a bit different from other services, as we do not provision units of performance, thus we have no insight into the performance of the response times of our zones or the Route 53 service itself.

However, we can monitor the following specifics thorough CloudFront:

- **Domain registrations**: We can track the newly registered domains with this metric. For security reasons, we can create an alarm on this metric to notify our response teams of newly registered domains and verify that the registration was allowed and successful.
- **Route 53 resolver endpoints**: When using a Route 53 resolver to forward DNS requests to and from our networks, we can see the performance metrics, such as volume and latency, for each Route 53 resolver endpoint we create.
- **Route 53 health checks**: When our DNS records use advanced routing with health checks, we can view them in the CloudWatch console.

In the following screenshot, we can see two health checks configured for a Route 53 failover policy. In the current graph, two health checks are displayed – the top one has a status of **1** and the bottom one a status of **0**:

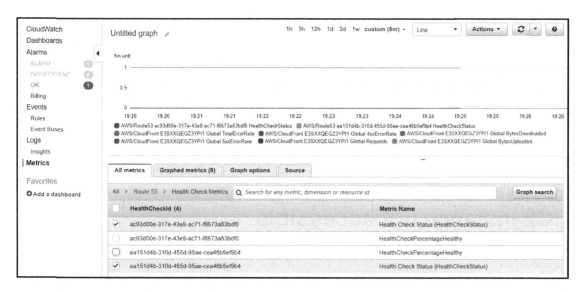

The status of **0** means the health check has failed. We can create an alarm to alert a response team of a health check failure. In the preceding example, the primary site stopped responding, and, due to a Route 53 failover policy, the traffic was seamlessly redirected to the secondary site.

Troubleshooting

Setting out to troubleshoot an issue can require us to look at the problem from different vectors of attack. As we have seen in this chapter, there are several tools that we can use to perform troubleshooting, including the following:

- **CloudWatch**: For collecting and analyzing metrics, application logs, and operating system logs
- **CloudTrail**: For collecting a log of all API calls and also for compliance and auditing
- **VPC Flow Logs**: To diagnose the connection and packet flow state

Each of those tools can help solve one piece of the puzzle when performing troubleshooting. In troubleshooting, the first step is to determine the problem, select the appropriate tool that will give us insight into the state of the unit experiencing the problem. and then decide on an approach to solve the problem.

Next, we are going to discuss some examples that will help you determine the right cause of action when troubleshooting connectivity, network, latency, and application error issues such as HTTP errors, which are as follows:

- EC2 instance not accessible
- ELB not responding or responding with 503
- CloudFront connectivity issues
- Route 53 issues

EC2 instance not accessible

When an instance is not accessible on the network, we need to troubleshoot from the outside. Since, in AWS EC2, we do not have any kind of access to the operating system other than the network, any cause of instances not responding on the network needs to be determined by checking the following:

- **Instance health check**: Is the instance running yet? Has it passed the health checks? You might be too eager to connect to a newly created instance, or an instance that has been running for some time is showing a degraded instance health. If the health check is indicating an issue, reboot the instance or redeploy it if it is stateless. For advanced instance health check troubleshooting, please refer to the *Further reading* section of this chapter.

- **Security groups and NACLs**: Are the security groups and NACLs set correctly? Remember, security groups are stateful and will allow any responses from the instance to pass, no matter what port the instance uses to return the response. NACLs are stateless, meaning that all return ports also need to be specified in a policy that will allow outgoing traffic.

ELB not responding or responding with 503

An ELB is just an extension of the instances on which the application is running. For any kind of ELB issues, you should always perform the following checks:

- **Target group instance health**: Are the instances in the target group responding? Are they marked as healthy in the ELB? When your instances are not responding, your ELB will respond with a 503 response.
- **Security groups**: Are the security groups selected in the load balancer configuration set correctly? The load balancer will not be available on the network if HTTP and HTTPS traffic are not permitted in the security groups.
- **Internal service error on ELB**: Check `https://status.aws.amazon.com` for the status of the service.

CloudFront connectivity issues

As CloudFront is just a caching engine, any issues will be coming from the backend that serves the application, unless the CloudFront service health is degraded. For any kind of ELB issues, you should always perform the following checks:

- **CloudFront responds with a HTTP error**: Check the backend of the distribution and ensure that it is performing correctly.
- **HTTPS certificate issues**: Check that the certificates attached to your distribution are configured correctly. Check whether you have all the certificates in the chain for our server and whether the chain is set up in an optimal manner.
- **Internal service error on CloudFront**: These are rare, but still check `https://status.aws.amazon.com` for the status of the service.

Route 53 issues

Route 53 is the only service that has an SLA defining 100% availability. Any issues in DNS resolution will be up to the content of the zone file and the configuration of the records. Here are some example issues and how to fix them:

- **The record is not resolving**: Check the entry in the zone file. Is the record correctly spelled? Is the record the correct type?
- **Routing issues – not failing over, weight of responses not correct**: Check that the backend to failover is healthy. Also check your weights are configured correctly.
- **TXT record has not changed since update**: Check the TTL. You can lower the TTLs down to 1 second if required.

In the rarest of cases, we can still check `https://status.aws.amazon.com/` for the status of the service.

Summary

We have taken a look at the motioning and troubleshooting aspects of AWS, as this pertains to network devices. At the end of this chapter, you should be familiar with CloudWatch and the capabilities it provides. We have taken a look at the metrics and alarms that we can use with CloudWatch. We have also looked at the services covered in this guide and how to perform monitoring and troubleshooting in CloudWatch.

In the next chapter, we will discuss network automation with CloudFront. We will see how we can automate every aspect of network service creation, management, and deployment, and how to unify the way we deploy networks in our environment.

Questions

1. Name the types of metrics that can be collected by CloudWatch and their collection intervals.
2. True or false: 1-minute metrics are discarded after 15 days.
3. When collecting logs with CloudWatch Logs, what is the default retention period?

4. Our application is going over budget frequently and the developers need a way to better predict the costs of AWS. How can this be achieved in a simple way?

5. When viewing metrics in CloudWatch, you need to combine multiple different instances in one graph. Is this supported by CloudWatch?

6. Your application is deployed in four regions: `us-east-1`, `us-west-2`, `ap-northeast-1`, and `eu-west-1`. You are trying to use CloudWatch to retrieve metrics from all ELBs in all the regions and graph them on one graph. How can this be done?

7. When troubleshooting network connectivity to your instances, you find a VPC Flow Log with the following entry: `2 888777666555 eni-abcd1234 10.0.0.121 10.0.0.147 22013 22 6 34 3366 1547812812 1547812888 REJECT OK`. What could be the root cause of your connectivity issues?

8. Your Windows EC2 instance in a VPC was started a minute ago and you have tried to ping it from a Linux instance in the same VPC but in a different subnet. There is no response. What would be the most likely cause of this instance not responding?

9. You have changed a Route 53 DNS record to a new version of your site, but your users are complaining that they are still seeing the old web content. What is the most likely cause of this behavior?

Further reading

Refer to the following references for further information:

- **CloudWatch documentation**: https://docs.aws.amazon.com/AmazonCloudWatch/latest/monitoring/WhatIsCloudWatch.html
- **CloudWatch regional endpoints**: https://docs.aws.amazon.com/general/latest/gr/rande.html#cw_region
- **Custom metrics**: https://docs.aws.amazon.com/AmazonCloudWatch/latest/monitoring/publishingMetrics.html
- **CloudWatch agent**: https://docs.aws.amazon.com/AmazonCloudWatch/latest/monitoring/install-CloudWatch-Agent-on-first-instance.html
- **CloudWatch enhanced monitoring scripts**: https://docs.aws.amazon.com/AWSEC2/latest/UserGuide/mon-scripts.html
- **CloudWatch alarms**: https://docs.aws.amazon.com/AmazonCloudWatch/latest/monitoring/AlarmThatSendsEmail.html

- **Troubleshooting EC2:** `https://docs.aws.amazon.com/AWSEC2/latest/UserGuide/TroubleshootingInstances.html`

- **Troubleshooting EC2 connectivity:** `https://docs.aws.amazon.com/AWSEC2/latest/UserGuide/TroubleshootingInstancesConnecting.html`

- **Troubleshooting ELB:** `https://aws.amazon.com/premiumsupport/knowledge-center/elb-connectivity-troubleshooting/`

- **Troubleshooting CloudFront:** `https://docs.aws.amazon.com/AmazonCloudFront/latest/DeveloperGuide/troubleshooting-distributions.html`

Section 5: Network automation in AWS

5

AWS CloudFormation is a service which helps you to describe and provision your AWS networks. A CloudFormation template provides a simpler and efficient way to manage your networks in the AWS cloud. This section provides an overview of the CloudFormation service as it relates to the network services.

We will cover the following chapter in this section:

- Chapter 10, *Network Automation with CloudFormation*

10
Network Automation with CloudFormation

Possibly the biggest advantage of the cloud is its ability to automate deployment from the infrastructure to the application to any tweaks and configuration changes in the application or the infrastructure over time. Complete and automated life cycle management of the whole environment is a key differentiation that allows us to deliver the application in a reliable, repeatable, and rapid manner. In regard to infrastructure automation, AWS provides us with the CloudFormation service, which allows us to deploy any component in AWS in a scripted and automated manner. In this chapter, we will take a look at the way in which we can use CloudFormation to automate and life cycle our network deployments.

The following topics will be covered in this chapter:

- Introduction to CloudFormation
- CloudFormation basic elements
- How CloudFormation works
- Creating network services with CloudFormation
- Best practices

Technical requirements

A basic understanding of orchestration and automation is required to follow along with this chapter. The ability to read and write **JavaScript Object Notation (JSON)** or **Yet Another Markup Language (YAML)** script, as well as experience of automating network deployments on-premise and in the cloud, is a benefit.

The CloudFormation template examples used in this chapter can be found at https:// github.com/PacktPublishing/AWS-Certified-Advanced-Networking-Specialty-Exam-Guide/tree/master/Chapter10.

Introduction to CloudFormation

CloudFormation is an **Infrastructure as Code (IaC)** service that gives us the ability to automate all aspects of infrastructure deployment in AWS. Infrastructure as code refers to the ability to create, manage, and delete resources in the same manner as our software code. Essentially, this means that we can do the following:

- Define the configuration of our infrastructure services in an IaC specification document
- Store the specification document in our version control system
- Deploy different versions of our IaC document to different, independent environments (such as `test`, `dev`, and `prod`)
- Verify the proper configuration and proper operation of the infrastructure in an IaC test environment
- Use the IaC in our code deployment process by allowing the deployment tools to both provision the infrastructure and then deploy the software on the newly provisioned infrastructure

IaC versus the traditional approach

To solidify the reason as to why we would use CloudFormation, let's compare a traditional approach to deploying infrastructure with the IaC approach. Traditionally, when designing new IT infrastructure, the following steps would need to take place:

1. We define a specification document. The specification document would encompass all the hardware, software, and network requirements of an application that we would be deploying.
2. The specification document is sent to the procurement team, and the procurement team would order the hardware.
3. After a few days, or possibly a couple of weeks of waiting, the hardware would be delivered.
4. The hardware would then be installed in the data center, connected to the power, the network, and possibly the **Storage Area Network (SAN)** by separate teams. Each team would perform a configuration on each of the physical boxes and then pass the task over to the next team.
5. Another day or two later, the hardware would be ready to install the operating system and underlying platform components, such as databases, DNS, and queues.

6. Platform verification starts. Depending on the level of complexity and automation, verification could take anything from minutes to hours.

7. Once verification is complete, software installation commences.

At this point, the teams would have spent hundreds of man hours, and the deployment of the software would have taken several days, perhaps several weeks. With infrastructure as code, the following steps would be taken:

1. We define a specification document. That document specifies the services to be deployed.

2. The specification document can be deployed to AWS within minutes.

3. Platform verification starts. Depending on the level of complexity, verification could take anything from minutes to hours.

4. Once verification is complete, software installation commences.

As you can see, we have sliced through the complete red tape and time of procurement, and we have eliminated all the steps that used to be required to install the hardware and verify it. IaC brings deployment times down from days and weeks in the case of traditional deployments to just hours or even minutes when the whole process is automated. We also have the ability to roll back any deployments in minutes and start again from scratch, whereas a traditional approach will have to resolve any issues that are encountered in the deployment process along the way, which could delay a traditional deployment process by days or weeks, or possibly even make the traditional deployment project fail.

Benefits of IaC

The IaC approach can be very beneficial to any environment that requires the infrastructure being deployed to be automated, reliable, verified, and deployed in a rapid manner. The CloudFormation service gives us the ability to completely automate deployments in the following scenarios:

- **Environments with rapid, agile development cycles**: We can use CloudFormation to define the way our infrastructure is deployed with each version of the application and how the infrastructure evolves over time with the evolution of the software.

- **Highly compliant environments**: CloudFormation gives us the ability to test the deployments and certify the infrastructure before pushing deployment to production.

- **Unify the environment across regions and applications**: With CloudFormation, we can create layers of specification documents that can conform to a certain standard and can be reused by different teams across accounts, regions, and applications.
- **Better utilization of our resources**: With CloudFormation, we have the ability to relieve our administrators of day-to-day repeatable tasks and utilize them to do tasks more suited to the human mind. Let the machines do the mundane, repeatable tasks that can be scripted, while our human brain thinks of new ideas, writes code, and gets creative!

On top of the main benefits mentioned here, you will find that there are many other benefits of using CloudFormation in your environment. It is one of those services that we start using, can see the benefits of, and then it just keeps making our job easier every day.

CloudFormation basic elements

Before diving deeper into how CloudFormation actually works, we need to familiarize ourselves with the components of CloudFormation and how they relate to each other. We will take a look at the following components of CloudFormation:

- Templates
- Stacks
- Change sets

Templates

A template is a specification document that describes the environment specifics that we would like to deploy in our AWS account. A template can be written either in JSON or in YAML. The template will precisely deploy those AWS services that we would like to deploy and which features of each service we would like to configure. We also specify relationships and can design the order in which we can deploy resources by specifying a DependsOn attribute in a condition.

Template sections

The CloudFormation template may contain one or more of the following sections:

- `AWSTemplateFormatVersion`: In this optional section, this specifies the CloudFormation template version that the template conforms to.
- `Description`: In this optional section, we can add any arbitrary string of text. This is designed to be the human-readable aspect of the template that will help us quickly understand what the template does.
- `Metadata`: In this optional section, we can specify any metadata that we would like to pass to the services and instances at the time of deployment.
- `Parameters`: In this optional section, we can specify any values that can be used in the `Resource` section at the time of deployment. We can specify parameters to create defaults, allowing users to select from several options that we permit.
- `Mappings`: In this optional section, we can specify mappings of parameters to the environment or region. For example, we can map a different image ID for `dev`, `test`, and `prod`, and this will determine the image to use depending on the deployment environment.
- `Conditions`: In this optional section, we can specify conditions that will determine which mapping to use or whether the resource will be created. The condition can define tags, IP address ranges, or time-based sequences, and can be used in combination with `DependsOn` to provide granular determination of when or how the resource will be deployed.
- `Transform`: In this optional section, we can specify any transformation, including additional templates and any type of specification from the AWS **Serverless Application Model (SAM)**.
- `Resources`: This is the only mandatory part of the template as it defines the actual resources that the CloudFormation service will be creating. Here, we specify all of our networks, routers, gateways, EC2 instances, databases, S3 buckets, and so on.
- `Outputs`: When required, we can use the `Outputs` section to return a certain piece of information at the point of deployment. For example, when creating a load balancer, we would like to know the address of the load balancer instead of having to look it up as a separate task. We can simply specify the URL of the load balancer to be output at the point of template creation.

Template policies

Additionally, there are several policies that we will learn about in the following subsections that will help us determine how the template is to be deployed, and how deployment or deletion impacts resources.

CreationPolicy

When certain resources have dependent subjects in the resource, we can use `CreationPolicy` to prevent resource completion from being displayed until the dependent subjects have also been created. For example, we will wait for a certain number of instances in an Auto Scaling group to be created before we return the signal for the successful creation of the Auto Scaling group. To perform this, we can add `WaitCondition` to `CreationPolicy`.

Here is an example of `WaitCondition` within `CreationPolicy`:

```
{
  "WaitCondition" : {
  "Type" : "AWS::CloudFormation::WaitCondition",
  "CreationPolicy" : {
  "ResourceSignal" : {
  "Timeout" : "PT30M",
  "Count" : "10"
  }
  }
  }
}
```

As you can see, `WaitCondition` can be used in any section of a CloudFormation template and defines a timeout and the number of resources to be created. In this example, the count is 10: `"Count" : "10"`, and the timeout is 30 minutes: `"Timeout" : "PT30M"`. This means that the CloudFormation template will wait for 10 successful deployments of dependent resources before it marks the tip level resource as completed, and if the count isn't reached in 30 minutes, it will time out.

DeletionPolicy

`DeletionPolicy` can be used to determine whether to retain a resource that was created within a CloudFormation deployment when the stack is terminated. `DeletionPolicy` will help us to retain any data that was created while the stack was operating.

There are three types of deletion policies:

- `Delete`: This deletes the resource.
- `Snapshot`: This creates a snapshot of supported resources, such as EBS volumes and RDS databases.
- `Retain`: This prevents the resource from being deleted when the stack is terminated.

Here is an example of a `DeletionPolicy` instance that will create a snapshot of the RDS database when the stack is deleted:

```
{
  "Resources" : {
  "myRDSdb" : {
  "Type" : "AWS::RDS::DBInstance",
  "DeletionPolicy" : "Snapshot"
  }
  }
  }
```

As you can see, the `DeletionPolicy` instance for the RDS database instance, `"Type"` : `"AWS::RDS::DBInstance"`, is set to snapshot the database volume before deletion with `"DeletionPolicy"` : `"Snapshot"`. This can be very helpful when you need to be able to retain the data generated in your stack, even after that application is decommissioned.

UpdatePolicy and UpdateReplacePolicy

In a similar manner to the `DeletionPolicy`, you can use the two update policies to determine what to do with the existing resources if a template update is set to overwrite them. You can use the snapshot and retain features found in the `DeletionPolicy`.

DependsOn

The `DependsOn` attribute allows us to control the order in which the resources will be deployed. By default, CloudFormation performs all resource deployments in parallel. We need to serialize deployment, for example, when a resource needs to be created before another resource can be deployed on top of it. Think of a VPC and its subnets. We cannot deploy those in parallel as we need to have the VPC created before we can create subnets.

Here is an example of a `DependsOn` attribute:

```
{
  "Resources" : {
  "myEC2" : {
  "Type" : "AWS::EC2::Instance",
  "Properties" : {
  "ImageId": "ami-1234wxyz",
  }
  },
  "DependsOn" : "myDB"
  }
  }
  }
```

Stacks

A stack is deployed from a template and represents a set of resources that are connected and belong to an application. A stack can also represent a part of an application if deployment is performed in layers. The ability to use CloudFormation to deploy our environment in separate stacks or in multiple stages can be very beneficial when we need a unified way of deploying resources for multiple applications, or when we need to deploy our application with the highest degree of agility.

For example, when you design your application, you can specify separate tiers of architecture and these tiers can be deployed with separate templates. This is good practice and can achieve most agility for your deployment. This approach is demonstrated in the following diagram:

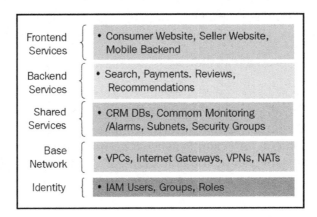

For each functional layer, we simply create a separate stack. To deploy an application from these stacks, we simply store the templates in a S3 bucket and use the `Transform` section to reference another stack that needs to be deployed, as demonstrated in the following code snippet:

```
{
 "Transform" : {
 "Name" : "AWS::Include",
 "Parameters" : {
 "Location" : "s3://cftemplatebucket/simple-network-stack.json"
 }
 }
 }
```

As you can see, the section simply specifies a location for a template named `simple-network-stack.json` that is located in a S3 bucket named `cftemplatebucket`.

Change sets

Once we have deployed our template and our stack has created successfully, we might have a need to introduce changes to the environment. There are several ways to approach upgrading an application, such as by performing an in-place upgrade or a blue-green deployment, and all of those depend on the level of disruption we can withstand during the updating of the application.

Within CloudFormation, we can use the change sets feature to perform updates on the infrastructure. With change sets, we have the ability to modify our running environment and view the modifications in the management console before we decide to deploy the changes to the running stack. Three possible levels of disruption a change set can cause once deployed to an active stack are as follows:

- **Non-disruptive updates**: Any operation with no impact on running objects; for example, changing CloudWatch alarms
- **Disruptive updates**: Any operation that will disrupt, but not delete or replace an object; for example, changing the instance type that requires a reboot will disrupt the instance
- **Replacement updates**: Any operation that deletes and replaces an object with a new ID; for example, changing an EC2 instance image from Linux to Windows

How CloudFormation works

The CloudFormation service reads all its input commands straight from the template. The template is stored in an AWS-managed S3 bucket, and a link to the template is provided to us when we deploy the stack. By default, the template is read in parallel, meaning that the service will try and create all the objects at once. It is very important to use the `DependsOn` attribute if any services need to be deployed in sequence. The following steps will be taken in CloudFormation when creating and managing an environment:

1. The user writes or visually designs a specification document called a template.
2. Using the management console, the CLI, the SDKs, or the CloudFormation API directly, the user sends the template to the CloudFormation engine.
3. The CloudFormation engine processes the template and verifies its syntax.
4. The CloudFormation engine deploys the resources specified in the template.
5. The user is able to see the resources that have been deployed in their account, as well as the template from which the resources have been created.
6. The user is able to create and view a change set that can then be applied to create changes in the resource configuration.
7. The user is able to decommission the deployed resources by deleting a CloudFormation environment.

Creating network services with CloudFormation

So, let's put all of this knowledge together. In this section, we will create a CloudFormation template that will create the following networking services:

- A VPC named `simpleVPC`
- Two public subnets with an internet gateway attached in two different availability zones
- Two private subnets with two different availability zones
- An NACL that will allow only MySQL traffic into and out of the private subnets

We will also create a key-value tag, `purpose : demo`, on all the resources so that we can easily identify them in the management console.

The VPC

To create the template, we will start with the `Description` and `Resources` sections, as shown in the following code block:

```
{
  "Description" : "Example Chapter 10: A Simple VPC template with two public
  and two private VPCs. A NACL permits only MySQL traffic in and out of the
  private networks",
  "Resources" : {
```

In the `Resources` section, we will be defining the resources. For the VPC, we will need to specify a name for the resource that we can use in the references and for the `DependsOn` attribute. We also need to define a CIDR block for the VPC. In our example, `10.0.0.0/22` will be the network CIDR for the VPC. As we stated previously, the `Tags` attribute adds the `purpose : demo` tag so that it is easily identifiable:

```
"simpleVPC" : {
  "Type" : "AWS::EC2::VPC",
  "Properties" : {
  "CidrBlock" : "10.0.0.0/22",
  "Tags" : [ {"Key" : "purpose", "Value" : "demo"} ]
  }
},
```

Always remember to close any bracket you opened with { at the end of your statement with } and add a comma , if there are more resources to specify.

Public subnets

Next, we need to create two public subnets. For each, we will specify their dependency on the VPC since they cannot be created before the VPC is created with `"DependsOn"  : "simpleVPC"`. We need to define which VP to create the subnet in, but since we don't have the VPC ID, we will need to pull this ID with the reference subroutine using the VPC resource name: `"VpcId" : { "Ref" : "simpleVPC" }`. We will also need to define two subnets, that is, `10.0.0.0/24` for the first subnet, and `10.0.1.0/24` for the second subnet, and, of course, tag the subnets appropriately.

For the first subnet, we will use the following script with a resource name of
`PublicSubnetOne`:

```
"PublicSubnetOne" : {
"Type" : "AWS::EC2::Subnet",
"DependsOn" : "simpleVPC",
"Properties" : {
"VpcId" : { "Ref" : "simpleVPC" },
"CidrBlock" : "10.0.0.0/24",
"AvailabilityZone" : "us-east-2a",
"Tags" : [ {"Key" : "purpose", "Value" : "demo"} ]
}
},
```

Similarly, for the second one, we need to simply change the resource name
to `PublicSubnetTwo`, and the CIDR accordingly:

```
"PublicSubnetTwo" : {
"Type" : "AWS::EC2::Subnet",
"DependsOn" : "simpleVPC",
"Properties" : {
"VpcId" : { "Ref" : "simpleVPC" },
"CidrBlock" : "10.0.1.0/24",
"AvailabilityZone" : "us-east-2b",
"Tags" : [ {"Key" : "purpose", "Value" : "demo"} ]
}
},
```

To make these subnets public, we need to create an internet gateway. We will do this with
the help of the following code with the resource name `simpleInternetGateway`:

```
"simpleInternetGateway" : {
"Type" : "AWS::EC2::InternetGateway",
"DependsOn" : "simpleVPC",
"Properties" : {
"Tags" : [ {"Key" : "purpose", "Value" : "demo"}]
}
},
```

Once created, the internet gateway needs to be attached to the VPC. This will be done with
the `AttachIGW` resource, which is simply specifying that our internet
gateway, `"InternetGatewayId" : { "Ref" : "simpleInternetGateway" }`, is
being attached to our VPC, `"VpcId" : { "Ref" : "simpleVPC" }`:

```
"AttachIGW" : {
"Type" : "AWS::EC2::VPCGatewayAttachment",
"DependsOn" : "simpleInternetGateway",
```

```
"Properties" : {
"VpcId" : { "Ref" : "simpleVPC" },
"InternetGatewayId" : { "Ref" : "simpleInternetGateway" }
}
},
```

Once the internet gateway is attached, we need to create a route table and establish a public route to the internet gateway we created. The `simpleRouteTable` resource creates the route table, and the `PublicRoute` resource creates the route to the internet, `"DestinationCidrBlock" : "0.0.0.0/0"`, through the `"GatewayId" : {` `"Ref" : "simpleInternetGateway" }` internet gateway in the `"RouteTableId" : {` `"Ref" : "simpleRouteTable" }` route that we created previously:

```
"simpleRouteTable" : {
"Type" : "AWS::EC2::RouteTable",
"DependsOn" : "simpleVPC",
"Properties" : {
"VpcId" : { "Ref" : "simpleVPC" },
"Tags" : [ {"Key" : "purpose", "Value" : "demo"} ]
}
},
"PublicRoute" : {
"Type" : "AWS::EC2::Route",
"DependsOn" : "AttachIGW",
"Properties" : {
"RouteTableId" : { "Ref" : "simpleRouteTable" },
"DestinationCidrBlock" : "0.0.0.0/0",
"GatewayId" : { "Ref" : "simpleInternetGateway" }
}
},
```

Note the different dependencies of the `"DependsOn" : "AttachIGW"` route and the `"DependsOn" : "simpleVPC"` route table – this is due to the fact that the route table can be created right after the VPC, while the route itself needs to wait for the internet gateway to be attached to the VPC.

Finally, we associate the routing tables with the public subnets with the `RouteTableAssociationOne` and `RouteTableAssociationTwo` resources:

```
"RouteTableAssociationOne" : {
"Type" : "AWS::EC2::SubnetRouteTableAssociation",
"DependsOn" : "simpleRouteTable",
"Properties" : {
"SubnetId" : { "Ref" : "PublicSubnetOne" },
"RouteTableId" : { "Ref" : "simpleRouteTable" }
}
```

```
},
"RouteTableAssociationTwo" : {
"Type" : "AWS::EC2::SubnetRouteTableAssociation",
"DependsOn" : "simpleRouteTable",
"Properties" : {
"SubnetId" : { "Ref" : "PublicSubnetTwo" },
"RouteTableId" : { "Ref" : "simpleRouteTable" }
}
},
```

Private subnets

Now, let's focus on the private subnets. The definition is the same as it is for the private subnets, except for their resource names, PrivateSubnetOne and PrivateSubnetTwo, and the CIDR IP ranges:

```
"PrivateSubnetOne" : {
"Type" : "AWS::EC2::Subnet",
"DependsOn" : "simpleVPC",
"Properties" : {
"VpcId" : { "Ref" : "simpleVPC" },
"CidrBlock" : "10.0.2.0/24",
"AvailabilityZone" : "us-east-2a",
"Tags" : [ {"Key" : "purpose", "Value" : "demo"} ]
}
},
"PrivateSubnetTwo" : {
"Type" : "AWS::EC2::Subnet",
"DependsOn" : "simpleVPC",
"Properties" : {
"VpcId" : { "Ref" : "simpleVPC" },
"CidrBlock" : "10.0.3.0/24",
"AvailabilityZone" : "us-east-2b",
"Tags" : [ {"Key" : "purpose", "Value" : "demo"} ]
}
},
```

Network access control lists

To automate **network access control list (NACL)** creation, we first need to create a NACL resource in the template. We will name it `PrivateSubnetACL` and attach it to `simpleVPC` with `"VpcId" : { "Ref" : "simpleVPC" }`. We are also adding the tags, as with all the other resources:

```
"PrivateSubnetACL" : {
 "Type" : "AWS::EC2::NetworkAcl",
 "DependsOn" : "simpleVPC",
 "Properties" : {
 "VpcId" : { "Ref" : "simpleVPC" },
 "Tags" : [ {"Key" : "purpose", "Value" : "demo"} ]
 }
 },
```

Next, we create the inbound `"Egress" : "false"` allow `"RuleAction" : "allow"` rule for the NACL. We will name it `PrivateSubnetACLIn`, make it dependent on the NACL we created before with `"DependsOn" : "PrivateSubnetACL"`, and allow protocol 6 (TCP) with `Protocol" : "6"` on port 3306 for MySQL with `"PortRange" : { "From" : "3306", "To" : "3306" }` from all the subnets in our VPC – `"CidrBlock" : "10.0.0.0/22"`:

```
"PrivateSubnetACLIn" : {
 "Type" : "AWS::EC2::NetworkAclEntry",
 "DependsOn" : "PrivateSubnetACL",
 "Properties" : {
 "NetworkAclId" : { "Ref" : "PrivateSubnetACL" },
 "RuleNumber" : "10",
 "Protocol" : "6",
 "RuleAction" : "allow",
 "Egress" : "false",
 "PortRange" : { "From" : "3306", "To" : "3306" },
 "CidrBlock" : "10.0.0.0/22"
 }
 },
```

Due to the fact that NACLs are stateless, we also need to create the outbound `"Egress"` : `"true"` allow `"RuleAction"` : `"allow"` rule for the NACL. We will name it `PrivateSubnetACLOut`, make it dependent on the NACL we created before with `"DependsOn"` : `"PrivateSubnetACL"`, and allow protocol 6 (TCP) with `"Protocol"` : `"6"` on all ephemeral ports that MySQL will return traffic on with `"PortRange"` : { `"From"` : `"1024"`, `"To"` : `"65535"` } from all the subnets in our VPC – `"CidrBlock"` : `"10.0.0.0/22"`:

```
"PrivateSubnetACLOut" : {
"Type" : "AWS::EC2::NetworkAclEntry",
"DependsOn" : "PrivateSubnetACL",
"Properties" : {
"NetworkAclId" : { "Ref" : "PrivateSubnetACL" },
"RuleNumber" : "10",
"Protocol" : "6",
"RuleAction" : "allow",
"Egress" : "true",
"PortRange" : { "From" : "1024", "To" : "65535" },
"CidrBlock" : "10.0.0.0/22"
}
},
```

Finally, we associate the NACL with each private subnet by creating the `PrivateSubnetOneACLAssociation` and `PrivateSubnetTwoACLAssociation` resources. Here, we will simply specify which subnet, `"SubnetId"` : { `"Ref"` : `"PrivateSubnetOne"` } or `"SubnetId"` : { `"Ref"` : `"PrivateSubnetTwo"` }, respectively, will be associated with the NACL – `"NetworkAclId"` : { `"Ref"` : `"PrivateSubnetACL"` }:

```
"PrivateSubnetOneACLAssociation" : {
"Type" : "AWS::EC2::SubnetNetworkAclAssociation",
"DependsOn" : "PrivateSubnetOne",
"Properties" : {
"SubnetId" : { "Ref" : "PrivateSubnetOne" },
"NetworkAclId" : { "Ref" : "PrivateSubnetACL" }
}
},
"PrivateSubnetTwoACLAssociation" : {
"Type" : "AWS::EC2::SubnetNetworkAclAssociation",
"DependsOn" : "PrivateSubnetTwo",
"Properties" : {
"SubnetId" : { "Ref" : "PrivateSubnetTwo" },
"NetworkAclId" : { "Ref" : "PrivateSubnetACL" }
}
}
```

Finally, we close off the JSON statements that we opened before the `Description` section, and after the `Resources` section:

```
    }
  }
```

The following diagram represents the final result of the CloudFormation template:

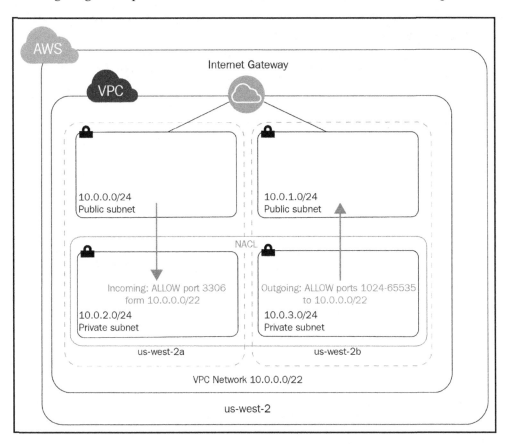

As you can see, we have a VPC created in **us-west-2** with two subnets (one public and one private in the **us-west-2a** and **us-west-2b** availability zones). The public subnets are attached to an internet gateway. A NACL protects the private subnets and only allows access to port `3306` from any subnet in the VPC and responses from the servers on all ephemeral ports to any subnet in the VPC.

Next, we will try and test this template in our AWS account.

Trying out the template

To test this functionality, you can download the template we discussed previously from the following link: `https://github.com/PacktPublishing/AWS-Certified-Advanced-Networking-Specialty-Exam-Guide/tree/master/Chapter10`. Follow these steps to get started:

1. Inspect the template and then log in to the management console. Open the **CloudFormation** console and click on **Create stack**. In the stack creation dialogue, select the stack from the file you downloaded from the preceding GitHub link with the **Choose file** button and then click **Next**:

2. Name the stack and click **Next**:

3. If you would like to add an additional key to the stack, you can do so in the next window. You can also simply leave this section blank as there is no need to add **Permissions**, **Rollback Triggers**, or any other options. Then, click **Next**:

4. In the **Overview** section, you will get the template URL where CloudFormation has stored your template. You can reuse this link if you choose to do so. Click **Create** to start the CloudFormation creation process:

5. Once the stack is created, the status will show as **CREATE_COMPLETE**. Please refresh the CloudFormation windows after several minutes if it is still showing **CREATE_IN_PROGRESS**:

6. Now, let's inspect the results. Navigate to **Your VPCs** and use a tag filter of `purpose : demo`—only the newly created VPC should be visible in the output:

7. Next, navigate to **Subnets** and use a tag filter of `purpose : demo`. This should show four subnets. If you select each subnet one by one and then click on the **Route Table** tab underneath, you should be able to see a route to `0.0.0.0/0` in the public subnets with CIDR `10.0.0.0/24` and `10.0.1.0/24`, but not in the private ones:

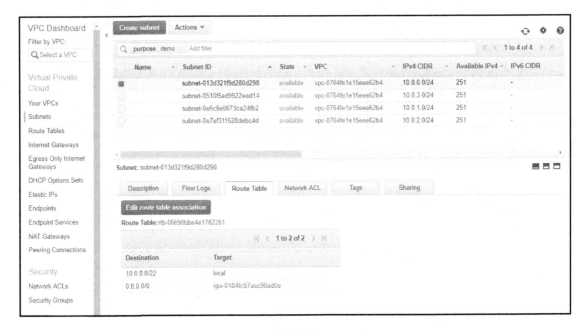

8. Next, navigate to **Route Tables** and use a tag filter of `purpose : demo`. This should show one newly created route table. If you select it and then click on the **Subnet Associations** tab underneath, you should see the two public subnets associated with the route table:

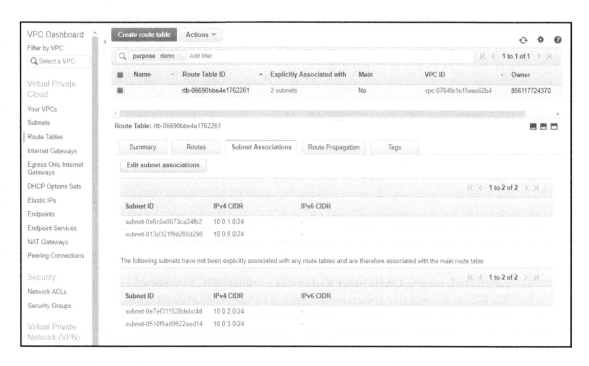

9. Next, navigate to **Internet Gateways** and use a tag filter of `purpose : demo`. This should show one newly created internet gateway:

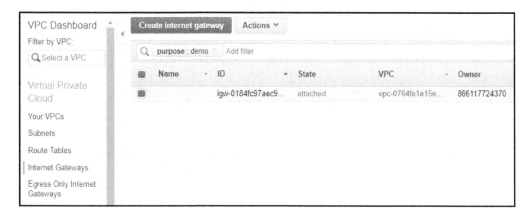

10. Next, navigate to **Network ACLs** and use a tag filter of `purpose : demo`. This should show one newly created NACL. If you select it and then click on the **Inbound Rules** tab underneath, you should see rule number **10**, which allows TCP port `3306`:

11. Next, click on the **Outbound Rules** tab underneath. You should see rule number **10**, which allows the ephemeral return TCP ports from `1024 - 65535`:

12. Next, click on **Subnet associations** to confirm that only the private subnets have been associated with the NACL:

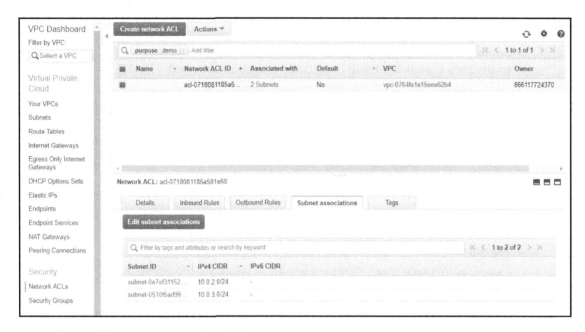

13. Once you are satisfied with the stack outcome, you can navigate to the **CloudFormation** management console and delete the stack. After the stack is deleted, verify that all the network objects it created have all been deleted:

As you can see, the CloudFormation service is an extremely powerful tool that can help us orchestrate and automate the creation, modification, and deletion of resources in AWS. For a network engineer, proficiency in JSON or YAML is becoming as popular as the leading switch and router command lines used to be.

Best practices

When working with CloudFormation, it is always good to remember the following best practices:

- Separate stacks into application tiers or by ownership so that a team that manages a certain unit will have complete control over it.
- Share stacks that create reusable resources, such as networks, security rules, and typologies. When using shared stacks, use the cross-stack references to reference IDs from other stacks.
- Always tightly control access to CloudFormation using IAM. CloudFormation is as powerful as all the other management tools, so make sure to only give permissions that the users require (least privilege).
- Do not embed any IDs unless you are explicitly referencing an existing resource.
- Use Mappings to map resources IDs to their regions.
- Do not embed any credentials in the template.
- Use the `Parameters` section to constrain users to certain object types; for example, instance types that they are allowed to use.
- Use stack policies for resources that must persist.
- When deleting stacks in a multi-layered application, look for any resources using the stacks resources because, if any dependencies exist, the deletion will fail. For example, an EC2 instance running in the VPC will not allow you to delete the VPC if the instance was not created with the same stack.
- Log all CloudFormation calls with CloudTrail.
- Always test your CloudFormation templates before using them in production. If available, use your CI/CD tool chain to test any changes that you make to your templates.

Summary

As you can see, using CloudFormation is relatively easy and allows you to perform any operation in AWS. CloudFormation is all about infrastructure as code and automation. We have taken a look at the structure of CloudFormation and looked into the details of a working example of a CloudFormation template. We have also looked at how to deploy that template and verify that the resources specified in the template were created correctly and connected to the correct entities.

With this chapter, we have now covered all the theoretical requirements laid out in the exam blueprint discussed in Chapter 1, *Overview of AWS Certified Advanced Networking – Specialty Certification*. In the next chapter, we will take a look at some exam tips and tricks that will help you prepare for the exam and pass it on your first try.

Questions

1. A CloudFormation deployment is called a ___.
2. Name the two scripting language formats supported by CloudFormation.
3. In CloudFormation, all resources are deployed in parallel. How can we serialize the template?
4. You have deployed a change set and are happy when viewing the changes. What needs to be done next to deploy the changes?
5. You have removed a subnet from your template and tried to deploy the changes to the running stack, but the change deployment failed. What could be the cause of this?
6. You are tasked with creating a network policy to deploy all VPCs with base subnets and security rules in the enterprise in the exact same fashion. What bad practice should you avoid when creating the template?
7. You are running an application that needs to be PCI compliant. How can CloudFormation be of benefit?

Further reading

Please refer to the following references for further information regarding what was covered in this chapter:

- **CloudFormation documentation**: https://docs.aws.amazon.com/cloudformation/index.html#lang/en_us
- **CloudFormation templates**: https://docs.aws.amazon.com/AWSCloudFormation/latest/UserGuide/template-guide.html
- **CloudFormation designer**: https://console.aws.amazon.com/cloudformation/designer

- **CloudFormation stacks**: https://docs.aws.amazon.com/AWSCloudFormation/latest/UserGuide/stacks.html
- **CloudFormation samples**: **https**://docs.aws.amazon.com/AWSCloudFormation/latest/UserGuide/sample-templates-services-us-west-2.html
- **CloudFormation resource attributes**: https://docs.aws.amazon.com/AWSCloudFormation/latest/UserGuide/aws-product-attribute-reference.html
- **CloudFormation custom resources**: https://docs.aws.amazon.com/AWSCloudFormation/latest/UserGuide/template-custom-resources.html
- **CloudFormation EC2 and network attributes**: https://docs.aws.amazon.com/AWSCloudFormation/latest/UserGuide/AWS_EC2.html

Section 6: The Exam

This section provides elaborated guidance on how you can prepare for the exam and provides tips and tricks on the topics covered in the book. This section also consists of two Mock Tests for readers to test their knowledge. It tries to cover all the topics from the scope of the exam and challenges the reader's understanding of the topics. Each Mock Test contains 60 questions. Readers should try to complete a Mock Test in 90 minutes of time.

We will cover the following chapters in this section:

- Chapter 11: *Exam Tips and Tricks*
- Chapter 12: *Mock Tests*

11
Exam Tips and Tricks

In this chapter, we will be looking at some general recommendations on what to do when taking the exam, and we will take a detailed overview of the requirements and each of the knowledge domains.

The following topics will be covered in this chapter:

- Introduction to the exam
- Domain 1: Design and implement hybrid IT network architectures at scale
- Domain 2: Design and implement AWS networks
- Domain 3: Automate AWS tasks
- Domain 4: Configure network integration with application services
- Domain 5: Design and implement for security and compliance
- Domain 6: Manage, optimize, and troubleshoot the network

Technical requirements

In this chapter, we will take a look at an overview of the technologies discussed in the previous chapters. By now, you should have familiarized yourself with all the aspects concerning networking in AWS.

Introduction to the exam

When looking at the requirements of this exam, you will quickly realize that the knowledge domains are not only geared toward the networking features of AWS, but represent a larger scope with management, automation, application services, and security composing a large section of the exam. For this reason, AWS recommends five years of experience with these technologies before attempting to take the exam. In five years, a typical network engineer will probably get hands-on experience with a broad range of technologies, or at least be highly proficient in most of them.

Due to the fact that your experience with AWS might not have covered each and every topic covered in the exam, you can use this book as a guide to discover the areas you need to do some work on and determine the knowledge confidence level of the areas that you are familiar with.

My recommendation to you is to approach passing the exam by identifying your strengths and weaknesses before attempting the exam and working on the weaknesses to build your knowledge to the correct confidence level. Building up your confidence level starts with reading this book, but, additionally, I would highly recommend that you start using the services mentioned in the book to get a real-world, hands-on grasp of the technologies, since being able to use the service or technology displays a much deeper level of knowledge than being able to describe it.

The AWS environment allows you to use the account with the free tier for the first 12 months, which means you can use most of these services at no cost and can easily experiment and try out the features described in this book. Additionally, I would suggest looking at the links provided in the *Further reading* section to get a more detailed overview of some subjects.

The AWS exam blueprint also recommends reading the whitepapers and the **frequently asked question (FAQ)** section of each service. The white papers can help you get a better idea of the case scenarios being presented in the exam. Additionally, AWS will use the FAQs to determine the level of knowledge required to pass the exam. So, one simple way to test your knowledge is to read the FAQs and try to answer them yourself. If you are able to answer correctly, then you are at the level of knowledge that AWS will require you to be at to pass the exam.

One additional resource is the practice questions. In this book, there will be two mock tests with 60 questions each that will simulate a real-world exam feel that can help you finalize the assessment of your preparedness for this exam. These questions are unique to this book, and the level of difficulty is designed to be at the level of the real-world exam. To determine whether you are ready to pass the exam, you should be able to answer more than 80% of the questions in each of the mock exams correctly. I like to call this the confidence level of knowledge for passing the exam, and when you are regularly reaching well over 80%, then you are ready to pass.

Good luck, keep calm, and make sure you answer as many questions as you can!

Domain 1 – Design and implement hybrid IT network architectures at scale

One of the biggest emphases of this exam is hybrid network implementation. You can expect about 14-15 questions that will test your ability to understand the connectivity options provided by AWS and their features. Namely, a large emphasis of this domain is on **Direct Connect (DX)**, the VGW, and BGP routing. You should familiarize yourself with the concepts of hybrid environments, how to make them highly available, and how to implement the BGP routing required to make those features work. When preparing for the exam, make sure you brush up on the following topics:

- Designing VPN connections with the VGW
- When to use the VGW and when to use a VPN instance
- The DX connectivity options including the network speeds
- The physical customer gateway features that need to be supported to connect to DX
- Making DX-connected environments highly available
- The automatic precedence of DX traffic over VGW regardless of BGP
- How to use ASN and specific route prioritization to send traffic through a desired link
- General BGP characteristics
- VPC peering and the characteristics/limitations of peering across regions

Domain 2 – Design and implement AWS networks

The other major part of this exam is testing your ability to design and implement networks in AWS. You can expect about 17-18 questions that will test your understanding of the way networking works in AWS, the design choices when implementing IPv4 vs IPv6, and the general knowledge of how to efficiently design the VPC, subnets, internet gateways, NAT instances, and VPC peering. Make a note of the following key points when preparing for the exam:

- Understanding the structure of the VPC networks and subnets
- IP address assignment with DHCP and the DHCP options sets
- The CIDR notation for IPv4 and IPv6 addresses
- How to perform DNS and name resolution from within the VPC, and how to use DHCP options sets to customize the way instances perform resolutions
- Using Route 53 to deliver DNS services to internal and external zones
- Using Route 53 to make cross-region applications highly available and to shape the traffic across multiple backends
- How security features tie into the VPC and how to use VPC flow logs to troubleshoot security
- Service ceilings for network components

Domain 3 – Automate AWS tasks

In the **automation** part of the exam, you can expect 5 or 6 questions on automation features that will test your ability to identify aspects of a deployment that could be automated, the understanding of the automation features in AWS, and the ability to read the automation template (either JSON or YAML). When preparing for the exam, make sure you brush up on the following topics:

- CloudFormation and its features
- Using CloudFormation to automate a network deployment
- Building reusable templates that can be referenced in future deployments in CloudFormation
- Implementing security throughout CloudFormation
- Understanding different deployment and automation options available in AWS

Domain 4 – Configure network integration with application services

Domain 4 covered a crucial part that any network engineer working in AWS will need to understand. This domain will test your skill with 9-10 questions on how to integrate an application running in a private VPC inside AWS or an application running in a hybrid environment to an AWS application service. The section covers features available in AWS and the ability to connect to those features in an efficient and cost-effective way. Look for questions about VPC endpoints, VPC peering, and connecting your on-premises application through a VPN or DX connection to an AWS service. Make sure you understand the following aspects of connecting your application to AWS application services:

- AWS services have public endpoints. Understand the flow of traffic to public endpoints when using VPNs and Direct Connect.
- The use of VPC endpoints and the availability of those endpoints to other sites such as peered VPCs and on-premises environments.
- Types and benefits of VPC endpoints.

Domain 5 – Design and implement for security and compliance

Security and compliance are a big part of networking in itself, since the network allows us to connect remotely to the service. This also implies that any attackers can connect to our application in the same manner. The domain will test your knowledge of implementing security and compliance within the AWS network and on top of the AWS network services. Expect 8-9 questions on security in the exam. Additionally, make a note of the following key points when preparing for the exam:

- Use the least privileged approach with permissions to resources that have resource-based policies.
- Ensure that each level of your application has the appropriate security controls in place.
- Create an onion approach to security—an onion has many layers, and the more you peel the layers the more it makes you cry. We want to put many layers of security in place and make the attacker cry enough to give up.

- Understand the use of the WAF, Shield, VPC Network ACLs, security groups, and the operating system firewall.
- Understand the use of API Gateway, CloudFront, ELB, and how they affect security.
- Minimize the attack surface by removing public access to services wherever possible.
- Use troubleshooting and monitoring tools, such as VPC flow logs, CloudWatch, and CloudTrail, to determine the security state of your environment.
- Understand encryption in transit and encryption at rest in AWS. Understand which service provides which type of encryption, and what protocol or encryption mechanism it uses.

Domain 6 – Manage, optimize, and troubleshoot the network

Lastly, managing, optimizing, and troubleshooting the network will look at your ability to measure the performance aspects of the network services you have deployed in AWS. The exam will lay out another 8-9 questions on this topic and will cover all aspects of testing your ability to use tools, such as CloudWatch and VPC flow logs, to determine the correct configuration, and identify inefficiencies in your architecture. Most of these questions will be looking to see you select the correct solution that will optimize the presented use case. When preparing for the exam, make sure you take a look at the following points:

- Using CloudWatch to monitor and determine the usage of resources
- Understand the billing aspects of the AWS services
- Identifying inefficiencies in your design as far as performance, billing, and security are concerned
- Identifying single points of failure in your design
- Using managed services to replace custom instances
- Using the troubleshooting features provided in AWS to determine the cause of a failure

Summary

As you can see, the way to prepare for the AWS Certified Advanced Networking - Specialty Exam is composed of the following:

- Determine the strengths and weaknesses of your knowledge on the domains covered by the exam—this book is designed to help you do exactly this.
- Get hands-on experience. Hands-on experience cannot be replaced by any book or training. As mentioned in this chapter, being able to use a service demonstrates more knowledge than being able to describe it.
- Focus on strengthening your knowledge through the use of the free tier in AWS and experimentation.
- Read the whitepapers and the FAQs to strengthen your familiarity of the background from which the exam questions will be formed.
- Determine your knowledge confidence levels by trying to answer the FAQs.
- Determine your exam preparedness with the mock exam by answering over 80% of the questions correctly.

The next chapter consists of two mock tests that you can attempt. Once you are confident that you can pass the real thing, make sure to keep calm, and take your time. Try to answer as many questions as you can, mark any questions that you are not sure of for review, and skip ahead to get a better overall coverage. Remember, you are not expected to pass with 100%, but you should be aiming to answer at least 80% of the questions correctly.

Finally, let me thank you again for choosing my book, and wish you good luck on your exam!

Further reading

- **The AWS Certified Advanced Networking - Specialty Exam Blueprint**: `https://aws.amazon.com/certification/certified-advanced-networking-specialty`
- **Exam Prep Guide**: `https://d1.awsstatic.com/training-and-certification/eligibilityupdates/AWS%20Certified%20Advanced%20Networking%20-%20Speciality_Exam_Guide_v1.2_FINAL.pdf`
- **Official Sample Questions**: `https://d1.awsstatic.com/training-and-certification/docs-advnetworking-spec/AWS_Certified_Advanced_Networking_Specialty_SampleExam.pdf`

12
Mock Tests

This chapter contains two mock tests that will simulate taking a real-world AWS Certified Advanced Networking - Specialty exam. The questions have been written to test the same domains in equal proportions as the real exam. The sample questions here are also designed to simulate the difficulty level of the real-world exam. You should be able to complete the exam within 90 minutes and achieve a score of 80% or above before attempting the real AWS Certified Advanced Networking - Specialty exam. Good luck!

Mock Test 1

1. You are connecting your on-premises environment to AWS. You need to connect to the `us-west-2` region where all your services are located. Your on-premise environment is located in New York on the East Coast. You are required to create a cost-effective solution that will be highly available. Which of the following options would satisfy those requirements?

>   A. Establish a Direct Connect link by using a provider that will connect your on-premises site with the us-west-2 region with a private link. The Direct Connect provider will ensure two connections are established, making the link highly available.

>   B. Establish a VPN between AWS and your on-premises site with the us-west-2 region using a VGW. The VGW will provide you with two tunnel endpoints, making the link highly available.

C. Establish two VPNs between AWS and your on-premises site with the us-west-2 region using two VGWs. The two VGWs will provide you with two tunnel endpoints, making the link highly available.

D. Establish a Direct Connect link by using a provider that will connect your on-premises site with the us-west-2 region with a private link. Establish a backup VPN between AWS and your on-premises site with the us-west-2 region using a VGW. Having both a Direct Connect and a VPN connection established will make the link highly available.

2. Your company has an existing environment with VPN connections across multiple sites. You are in charge of connecting an AWS VPC into the existing infrastructure. All the existing sites are using a GRE-based tunneled virtual overlay network that is terminated at the VPN gateway. What would be the most efficient way to integrate the VPC into the existing infrastructure?

A. Create a VGW with the GRE encapsulation option enabled to connect into the existing network using the GRE tunnel.

B. Redeploy the existing VPNs to IPSec. GRE is not supported on AWS.

C. Deploy a CloudHub VPN environment and connect all your on-premise sites to CloudHub VPN.

D. Create a custom EC2 instance or choose a solution from the marketplace.

3. When deploying a VPC, what part of the shared responsibility is AWS responsible for?

A. Making sure the VPC traffic is encrypted

B. Making sure the VPC security groups are correctly configured

C. Making sure the VPC internet gateway is highly available

D. Making sure the VPC networks do not overlap with other clients

4. Your SysOps team has deployed a Linux server to a VPC. They have configured a security rule and a network access control list to allow only incoming traffic to port 22. The SysOps team is unable to connect to the Linux server. They have tried redeploying the server to no avail. What is the most likely cause of the issue?

> A. The Linux server does not have the SSH service started.
>
> B. The network access control list policy for the outbound response is blocking the connection.
>
> C. The security group policy for the outbound response is blocking the connection.
>
> D. The Linux server firewall policy for the outbound response is blocking the connection.

5. You have been tasked with establishing a VPN connection for a Linux server in your on-premise environment that needs to use rsync to continuously mirror the contents of a volume to an identical Linux server running in AWS. You set up the VGW and configure two of your own customer gateways with the tunnel information provided by AWS. When looking at the state of the connection, you can see that the state of the connection to each of the customer gateways is down. What do you need to do to ensure the state tunnel changes to **UP**?

> A. Ping the AWS Linux host from the on-premise Linux host. This will bring the tunnel up.
>
> B. Remove one of the tunnel connections. Only one VGW tunnel can be up at once.
>
> C. Ping the on-premise Linux host from the AWS Linux host. This will bring the tunnel up.
>
> D. Set the state of the tunnel in the AWS management console to **UP**.

6. You have set up a direct connection to AWS from a partner collocation. Your data center is located in the same metro area and you would like to extend the private link from the collocation to your on-premise environment. One of the requirements of your compliance is that your data never traverses the internet. What is the correct way to approach this problem?

> A. Consult with the AWS partner and see whether they can help you establish an optical or MPLS link between the collocation and your on-premise environment.

> B. Use a VPN between your on-premise environment and your customer device in the collocation to establish a virtual private last mile link.

> C. Instead of locating your customer gateway in the collocation, move it to your on-premise environment and have the AWS partner terminate the Direct Connect connection directly in your on-premise data center.

> D. Consult with AWS Support and see whether they can help you establish an optical or MPLS link between the collocation and your on-premise environment.

7. Your VPC consists of both public and private subnets. The public subnets run the web frontend, and the private subnets run the backend and databases. To ensure greater security, a recommendation was given by the security team to remove the public subnets and put all the web frontends in the private networks behind load balancers. You deploy the public subnets and move the web servers to the private ones, but now you cannot reach the DynamoDB table that the web servers use to sync their sessions. What is the simplest way to allow the application to share cache information in DynamoDB?

> A. Set up a NAT gateway. The NAT gateway will route the traffic to the public endpoint for DynamoDB.

> B. Set up a VPC interface endpoint for DynamoDB. The interface endpoint will route the traffic to a private endpoint for DynamoDB.

> C. Set up a VPC gateway endpoint for DynamoDB. The gateway endpoint will route the traffic to a private endpoint for DynamoDB.

> D. Use ElastiCache instead of DynamoDB for session sharing.

8. You are designing a 10 GB Direct Connect link with a VPN backup over your 500 MB internet uplink to provide high availability for your hybrid deployment. How can you ensure that the traffic is always going to be sent via the Direct Connect link and utilize the performance and low latency of the Direct Connect link, while failing over smoothly to the VPN if the Direct Connect link goes down?

   A. In the Direct Connect console, and by making the VPN connection secondary.

   B. In the Direct Connect console, and by making the Direct Connect connection primary.

   C. In the Direct Connect console, and by enabling Bidirectional Forwarding Detection on the Direct Connect connection.

   D. In the Direct Connect console, and by enabling BGP as the routing protocol.

   E. All of the above.

9. Your company policy is to deploy each application into its own account in several different regions. Separate VPCs for development, testing, staging, and production are deployed in each account. A new global compliance requirement has been issued that will require the use of a centralized security VPC, which will contain services that need to be accessible from all VPCs, regardless of the account. VPC peering was recommended as the solution, and you are required to architect the design. What is the main concern when designing the solution?

   A. The VPCs are in separate accounts so this will not be possible. Use a VPN instead of VPC peering.

   B. The VPCs might have overlapping IP ranges.

   C. The applications deployed in the VPCs might not be compatible with VPC peering.

   D. The VPC peering connections only work within a region. Use a VPN instead of VPC peering.

10. You are troubleshooting a CloudFormation template that was designed by your DevOps team to deploy several VPCs for your test, your development, and production implementation. The VPC networks are as follows:
    - Development VPC: 10.0.0.0/24—Subnet 10.0.0.0/24
    - Test VPC: 10.0.0.0/23—Subnets 10.0.0.0/24 and 10.0.1.0/24
    - Production: 10.0.0.0/16—Subnets 10.0.0.0/16 and 10.0.1.0/16

    What is the reason for the CloudFormation deployment failing?

    A. The CloudFormation deployment is failing because the VPC ranges are overlapping. Change the development VPC to the 192.168.0.0/24 network and the Test to a 172.16.0.0/16 network so that the ranges do not overlap.

    B. The CloudFormation deployment is failing because you cannot deploy more than one VPC in one stack.

    C. The CloudFormation deployment is failing because the test VPC subnets should each have a suffix of /23.

    D. The CloudFormation deployment is failing because the production VPC subnets should each have a suffix of /24.

11. Your company has migrated the database server to a Multi-AZ RDS database that is deployed in your VPC private subnet. The database admin has changed the IP address from the custom instance to the primary RDS instance. While testing failover, the database admin has noticed that the requests are still being sent to the primary instance. How can this be fixed in the easiest possible way?

    A. Create a script that pings the primary instance, and if it is not responding, it should switch the IP in the application configuration to the secondary instance.

    B. Use the RDS DNS name instead of the IP.

    C. Enable the RDS autoswitch-IP option in the Multi-AZ configuration.

    D. Use an Elastic Network Interface on the primary RDS to quickly switch to the secondary if there is a failure.

12. You have been tasked with designing a solution that will isolate the management workload from the customer traffic in your VPC. What would be the best approach to achieve the desired functionality?

> A. Implement a marketplace solution that will allow virtual separation of networks within AWS.

> B. This is not possible due to the design of the VPC.

> C. Use an ENI on each of your instances to connect the second network subnet designated for management.

> D. Check the **Connect instances to management network** option in the VPC configuration. This feature allows you to connect your instances to the built-in VPC management network in AWS.

13. You are deploying a static website on an S3 bucket. You have decided to deploy it in the us-east-1 region. You test the performance of the website from different customer locations across the US and EU and find the performance is not adequate. What is the correct setup that will improve the performance of your application at the lowest possible cost?

> A. Mirror the S3 bucket to several US and EU regions so that the content is closer to your client locations.

> B. Enable a CloudFront distribution and point it to the bucket with the default price class (**All CloudFormation locations - best performance**) selected.

> C. Enable a CloudFront distribution and point it to the bucket with the price class 100 (**North America and Europe**) selected.

> D. Use an edge-optimized API Gateway to forward requests to the S3 bucket for the static content.

14. You have been tasked to manage version control in CloudFormation. The production stack has already been deployed in AWS. What is the least invasive way to implement version control at this point?

    A. Use CloudFormation change sets.

    B. Save your templates to a version control repository. Use a CI server to redeploy the production stack.

    C. Use OpsWorks instead of CloudFormation.

    D. Use Elastic Beanstalk instead of CloudFormation.

15. You are using an m5.2xlarge EC2 instance to ingest data from S3. The data is well distributed across tens of thousands of keys and reaches between 2 TB and 6 TB each day. You have deployed a VPC endpoint and ensured enhanced networking is enabled on the instance. Your developers are complaining that the data ingestion keeps failing to include data on days when the volume of data is higher than 4 TB. How could you ensure that the data is ingested in the most efficient manner possible?

    A. Use one m5.4xlarge instance to ingest the data.

    B. Use two m5.2xlarge instances to ingest the data.

    C. Use three m5.xlarge instances to ingest the data.

    D. Use four m5.large instances to ingest the data.

16. An application behind a load balancer is being deployed in your environment. Your manager is extremely wary about any DDoS attacks against your application. Your manager has asked you to recommend a solution to secure your application against DDoS attacks with the most comprehensive approach to DDoS mitigation. Which option would you recommend?

    A. Use the AWS WAF custom IP rules to implement DDoS mitigation.

    B. Use AWS Shield Advanced on your ELB to implement DDoS mitigation.

    C. Use NACL custom IP rules to implement DDoS mitigation.

    D. Use an AWS Marketplace solution to implement DDoS mitigation.

17. You are running an HPC workload on EC2 instances deployed in a cluster placement group. You have enabled enhanced networking and are looking to get the maximum performance out of the network. Which additional feature would enable you to get the most out of this setup?

> A. Open up your ACLs and security groups to **inbound:ALL** and **outgoing:ALL**. This will help speed up the traffic as no checks will be done on the packets.

> B. Set the VPC jumbo frame setting to **on startup**. Jumbo frames will add increased performance to your placement group.

> C. Deploy your instances in a spread placement group. This will spread the traffic over multiple network devices.

> D. Set a higher MTU in your operating system. Jumbo frames will add increased performance to your placement group.

18. You have a cluster of three EC2 instances with public IP addresses. The public IPs are mapped to a Route 53 DNS name for your application. Your application is slowing down and you need to increase the instance size to be able to accommodate the traffic increase. You power the instances off, change the size, and power them on. The instances pass the health checks and you can SSH into them but the application is still not available. What would be the reason?

> A. Redeploy the Route 53 public zone.

> B. Restart the instances; the services did not come up correctly.

> C. Restart the services in the instance to make sure they come up correctly.

> D. Public IPs have changed when the instances were shut down. Reconfigure the DNS name in Route 53.

19. When diagnosing a VPC Flow Log, you see the following entry:

```
2 123123456456 eni-12d8da8 10.0.0.121 10.0.1.121 3321 22 6 14 3218
1550695423 1550695483 REJECT OK
```

What does this VPC Flow Log mean?

    A. Instance `10.0.0.121` tried to SSH to instance `10.0.1.121` on port `22`, but the connection was not allowed.

    B. Instance `10.0.1.121` tried to SSH to instance `10.0.0.121` on port `22`, but the connection was not allowed.

    C. Instance `10.0.1.121` established an SSH connection to instance `10.0.0.121` on port `22`.

    D. Instance 10.0.0.121 established an SSH connection to instance `10.0.1.121` on port `22`.

20. You have peered VPC A with VPC B and VPC C with VPC A. Services in VPC B would require communication with VPC C. What options do you have to enable this? (Select all that apply.)

    A. Proxy the VPC B <-> VPC C traffic in VPC A.

    B. VPC A is a middle point where routing can be created to allow traffic to pass.

    C. Peer VPC B and VPC C.

    D. Use the CloudHub VPN to connect the VPCs.

    E. None of the above.

21. You have peered VPC A with VPC B. You try to ping the other side but there is no response. What could be the problem?

    A. You need to enable the ICMP protocol on the peering link.

    B. The routes for VPC A have not been created in VPC B and vica versa.

    C. You need to wait 15 minutes for the automatic route propagation from VPC A to propagate to VPC B and vica versa.

    D. The target on the other side is not available.

22. Company A is using a 10 GB Direct Connect link to store petabytes of data in S3 with a public VIF over HTTP. They have employed you to secure the data being transferred across the Direct Connect link with encryption. What would be the best option to encrypt all the data in transit immediately?

> A. Use HTTPS when connecting to S3. This will encrypt the data in transit.
>
> B. Deploy an IPSec VPN on the VIF. This will encrypt the data in transit.
>
> C. Use client-side encryption when uploading to S3. This will encrypt the data in transit.
>
> D. Nothing needs to be done. Data is encrypted automatically over Direct Connect.

23. Your company uses a gateway endpoint for all the private subnets to connect to the S3 service. The implementation consists of custom route tables for each subnet in the environment. Another network admin created the setup. There is a requirement for a new private subnet, and you are tasked to deploy it. Once deployed, the EC2 instances in the new subnet cannot access the S3 service. What is the solution?

> A. Create a new VPC gateway endpoint in that subnet.
>
> B. Create a new VPC interface endpoint in that subnet.
>
> C. Create a new security entry for the new subnet in the S3 gateway security policy.
>
> D. Create a new entry for the S3 gateway in the route table of the subnet.

24. You are deploying a VPN solution from the AWS marketplace on an EC2 instance. How can you ensure that the instance has optimal performance? (Select two.)

> A. Use IOPS-optimized EBS volumes.
>
> B. Use an instance type with lots of memory.
>
> C. Use an instance type with the appropriate amount of network throughput.
>
> D. Enable enhanced networking on the instance.

25. To ensure the highest network performance between two EC2 instances, which of the following would you select?

    A. Start the instances at the exact same time.

    B. Start the instances in a cluster placement group.

    C. Start the instances in a spread placement group.

    D. Start the instances in a network placement group.

26. You have set up two VPN connections with two VGWs to allow for aggregating the performance of multiple VPNs using BGP. You have created AS_PATHs of the same length for each VPN, but the traffic to your network seems to prefer one VPN over the other. What would make one VPN be preferred over another?

    A. The ASN of the preferred VPN is lower than the ASN of the second one.

    B. The MED property on the preferred VPN connection is higher than the second one.

    C. The second VPN is still configured as static.

    D. The prefix advertised on the preferred VPN is more specific than the second one.

27. While building a highly available application in AWS, a compliance requirement has been determined that requires end-to-end encryption to be implemented. Which solution would allow for implementing end-to-end encryption while remaining highly available?

    A. An ELB with SSL offloading serving an HTTPS endpoint. Highly available EC2 instances in an autoscaling group. An SSL-encrypted Multi-AZ RDS MySQL backend.

    B. Two ELBs with serving two HTTPS endpoints. Two EC2 instance autoscaling groups. An SSL Encrypted RDS MySQL backend.

C. An ELB with SSL offloading serving an HTTPS endpoint. Two EC2 instance autoscaling groups. An SSL Encrypted Multi-AZ RDS MySQL backend.

D. An ELB serving an HTTPS endpoint. Highly available EC2 instances in an autoscaling group. An SSL Encrypted Multi-AZ RDS MySQL backend.

28. A development team is planning on implementing blue-green deployment in their environment. Which service could you use to enable blue-green deployments?

 A. Use Route 53 with weighted routing.

 B. Use Route 53 with latency-based routing.

 C. Use the API Gateway with weighted routing.

 D. Use the ELB with latency-based routing.

29. Your team has written a CloudFormation template that deploys the VPC, the subnets, the IGW, and routing. The CloudFormation template syntax is correct and the template starts deploying. The template fails when creating the subnets. What could be the cause?

 A. The subnets are listed before the VPCs. Move the subnets down so they get created after the VPC.

 B. The resources are being created in parallel. Remove the **In-Parallel** tag on the subnets.

 C. The resources are being created in parallel. Add a **Depends-On** condition for the subnets.

 D. The resources are being created in parallel. Add a **Depends-On** condition for the VPC.

30. There is a Direct Connect connection set up with your on-premises environment. You are performing a high availability review that includes the connection. What recommendation would you give? (Choose all that apply.)

    A. No action is needed. The connection is highly available by default.

    B. Recommend setting up a backup VPN.

    C. Recommend setting up a backup Direct Connect link.

    D. Recommend setting up a backup connection via an ELB.

    E. Use an API Gateway.

31. Your company is deploying an authentication mechanism that will be used across all applications in AWS. The authentication application is hosted in a VPC with the IP address range 10.17.0.0/16. There are 11 other VPCs in your AWS account, and there are 3 more accounts with another 5, 8, and 12 VPCs each. You need to ensure a setup that will allow all the other VPCs to be able to use the authentication application. Considering that you are working across different accounts, which solution would you recommend?

    A. Use a marketplace solution to set up an overlay network across all your VPCs that will allow communication across all your VPCs.

    B. Use VPC peering and peer all the VPCs to each other.

    C. Use a marketplace solution to set up a VPN between your on-premise environment and all the VPCs. Route the traffic through your on-premise environment.

    D. Use VPC peering and peer all the VPCs to only the authentication VPC.

32. You have recently deployed an application to an EC2 cluster behind an ELB. You have an autoscaling group that scales between 8 and 48 instances. The application accepts HTTP connections, but due to a security review, you need to implement HTTPS on the internet portion of your application within the shortest time possible. Which solution would you recommend?

    A. Install an HTTPS certificate onto the instances and reconfigure the application to serve HTTPS.

    B. Use ACM to install a certificate on the ELB.

C. Move your application to S3 and serve the content directly from S3 via HTTPS.

D. Use CloudFront and terminate all the calls at CloudFront via HTTPS.

33. You have EC2 instances in four regions: us-west-2, us-east-1, eu-west-1, and ap-northeast-1. The instances download 1 TB of data daily from each input S3 bucket in their local region, and create a 100 Mb aggregate report to a new output S3 bucket within their region. You are connecting to the AWS via Direct Connect from your on-premise site to us-west-1, and you download the aggregate reports hourly from each region and upload the new 1 TB source for the jobs each day. During which part of the communication will you incur transfer charges?

    A. Downloading from S3 to the EC2 instances

    B. Uploading from the EC2 to the output S3 buckets

    C. Downloading from the output S3 buckets to your on-premise via Direct Connect

    D. Uploading to input buckets via Direct Connect

34. You are securing an application running in AWS. You need to identify the best practices for security for your application. (Select all that apply.)

    A. Reduce the attack surface of your application by removing any unnecessary entry points.

    B. Reduce the size of your application to the minimum number of instances.

    C. Implement security at all levels.

    D. Leverage AWS security features only.

    E. Implement detailed monitoring of your resources.

    F. Select the appropriate security controls for your application. Not all security features are applicable in all cases.

35. You are in charge of securing an application serving mobile clients behind an application load balancer. You are required to be able to control the traffic based on the IP address of the request and based on the expression used in the request. Which AWS solution could you implement to get the appropriate level of control?

   A. NACLs

   B. WAF

   C. Shield

   D. X-Ray

36. Your company has several accounts with consolidated billing. You are setting up an AWS Direct Connect connection with a Private VIF in one of the accounts. Where would the charges for any downloads across the Direct Connect be recorded?

   A. In the main AWS account that has the billing.

   B. In the account where the AWS Direct Connect was created.

   C. The are no download charges when using Direct Connect.

   D. The charges are split across the main AWs account and the subaccount, depending on the origin of the download request.

37. When planning to deploy a Direct Connect link, which features should your customer router support?

   A. Single Mode Fiber

   B. 802.1Q VLAN

   C. 802.11ac

   D. Multi Mode Fiber

   E. BGP with MD5 authentication

38. Your company has set up a Direct Connect connection that uses several different public and private VIFs to enable a connection with different services. A requirement for a new, L2-isolated and encrypted connection to a new VPC has been expressed by the PCI team, and you have been assigned to set this up. What would be the correct approach to do this?

    A. Deploy a new public VIF. Create a new VLAN to the new VIF. The connection will be encrypted with IPSec.

    B. Deploy a new private VIF. Create a new VLAN to the new VIF. The connection will be encrypted with IPSec.

    C. Deploy a new public VIF. Create a new VPN to the new VIF. The connection will be encrypted with IPSec.

    D. Deploy a new private VIF. Create a new VPN to the new VIF. The connection will be encrypted with IPSec.

39. You have been tasked with performing deep packet analysis on the VPC traffic. What would you use?

    A. VPC Flow Logs

    B. A third-party packet analyzer

    C. AWS WAF

    D. AWS CloudTrail

40. You have started up an instance in a private subnet in a VPC. You try and connect an elastic IP to the instance, but are unable to do so. Why?

    A. An IGW is not attached to the subnet.

    B. An ENI is not attached to the instance.

    C. A NAT gateway is not attached to the subnet.

    D. A Public IP is not attached to the instance.

41. You have deployed a VPC with an IPv6 network. Now, you need to remove the IPv4 network. What steps do you need to take?

> A. Take the VPC offline and remove the IPv4 range in the management console.
>
> B. Remove the IPv4 range in the management console.
>
> C. Remove the IPv4 range in the CLI.
>
> D. This cannot be done.

42. You are diagnosing the traffic flow from a VPC-enabled ECS container and need to understand which requests were accepted and rejected by this container. What can you do?

> A. Use VPC Flow Logs on the ENI of the container. Look for ACCEPT OK and REJECT OK entries in the log.
>
> B. Since ECS containers do not have ENIs, use VPC Flow Logs on the VPC network. Look for ACCEPT OK and REJECT OK entries in the log that point to the IP address of the container.
>
> C. Use VPC Flow Logs on the subnet. Look for ACCEPT OK and REJECT OK entries in the log.
>
> D. This cannot be done.

43. You are deploying an IPv6-only private subnet. To update the instances software, you are looking to deploy a NAT gateway for this subnet. Which option would you choose?

> A. Use the NAT gateway and select **Enable IPv6** on creation.
>
> B. Use an egress-only internet gateway instead.
>
> C. Use an internet gateway instead.
>
> D. Use a virtual private gateway instead.

44. You are creating a VPN from on-premise to AWs. Which firewall rules are required on the client side to connect a VPN? (Choose all that apply.)

    A. UDP port 50

    B. UDP port 500

    C. TCP port 50

    D. TCP port 500

    E. Protocol 50

    F. Protocol 500

45. A Lambda function needs to interact with an EC2 instance in a private subnet. Once the exchange of information is complete, the Lambda needs to store the data in a DynamoDB table. How can you enable this? (Select all that apply.)

    A. Deploy the lambda into the VPC. This will assign the lambda function a private IP to access the EC2 instance.

    B. The lambda will automatically have access to DynamoDB since Lambda has a public endpoint.

    C. Use a NAT gateway to allow access outside of the VPC.

    D. Use a DynamoDB VPC endpoint.

    E. Deploy a Route to the Lambda service in the private VPC.

46. How can you easily automate VPC peering in your AWS account for any newly created VPCs?

    A. Use an Elastic Beanstalk application with the **peer-VPCs** setting.

    B. Use a Lambda function to detect any newly created VPCs and peer them.

    C. Use a CloudFormation template and define peering in the template.

    D. This cannot be done.

47. Your EC2 instance is acting as an origin for a CloudFront distribution. You need to maintain end-to-end encryption of your traffic at all times. Which options can you configure on CloudFront to ensure end-to-end encryption?

> A. Set the viewer policy to redirect HTTP to HTTPS. Set the origin policy to match viewer.

> B. Set the viewer policy as HTTPS. Install an SSL certificate on the instance.

> C. Set the viewer policy as HTTP. Set the origin policy to match viewer.

> D. Set the viewer policy to redirect HTTP to HTTPS. Set the origin to HTTP.

48. To create a private VIF for a VPN on a Direct Connect connection, which of the following is required?

> A. The on-premise subnet ID

> B. The VLAN ID

> C. The VGW ID

> D. The IGW ID

49. In CloudFront, to optimize the performance of your application but still maintain PCI compatibility, which of the following can you use?

> A. End-to-end encryption with SSL

> B. Field-level encryption and SSL

> C. End-to-end encryption with SSL offloading

> D. Field-level encryption and SSL offloading

50. You have a CRM application running in your VPC. The setup has the following components:
>   - VPC with CIDR 10.0.0.0/16
>   - Subnets: A 10.0.0.0/24, B 10.0.1.0/24, C 10.0.2.0/24, D 10.0.3.0/24, E 10.0.4.0/24 and F 10.0.5.0/24—two in each AZ
>   - A VGW with the ID vgw-ad83aa7f

- A routing table with the following entries:
    - 10.0.0.0/16—local
    - 192.168.18.0/24—vgw-ad83aa7f
    - 192.168.19.0/24—vgw-ad83aa7f
- A default NACL that ALLOWS ALL traffic IN and OUT
- A default security group that ALLOWS ALL traffic OUT and DENIES ALL traffic IN
- A VPN security group that ALLOWS ALL HTTPS traffic IN from the 192.168.18.0/24 network
- The CRM instances are deployed in all subnets

Your CRM application requires access to S3. Which options would allow you to grant access to S3? (Select all that apply.)

A. Create a NAT instance in subnet A.

B. Attach a VPC endpoint to the VPC.

C. Attach an IGW to subnet A.

D. Create a NACL rule to allow access to S3 in the VPC.

E. Create a security group rule to allow access to S3 and attach it to the CRM instances.

F. Create a route in the default routing table to the VPC endpoint.

G. Create a route in a new routing table to the VPC endpoint and attach it to subnets B, D, and F.

51. You need to increase the performance of your application's read and write responses to the clients. Which service would you choose in your deployment to achieve that goal?

A. CloudFormation

B. CloudFront

C. API Gateway

D. S3

52. You have deployed your application behind a load balancer. You need to point your website, mywebsite.com, to the application using Route 53. How can you achieve this?

    A. Create an ALIAS record using the load balancer DNS.

    B. Create a CNAME record using the load balancer DNS.

    C. Create an A record using the load balancer IP.

    D. Create a PTR record using the load balancer IP.

53. You are establishing a Direct Connect link with AWS. Your customer gateway has been delivered and installed to the collocation and is ready for the cross-connect to be established. Who do you need to contact to get the cross-connect established?

    A. Contact AWS support.

    B. Contact the Direct Connect provider.

    C. Contact an AWS partner that can consult and help in this case.

    D. Raise a Direct Connect request in the management console.

54. You are connecting a Direct Connect to your on-premise site. The setup has over 300 /24 networks that need to be advertised across the Direct Connect link to the VPCs. What do you need to do to enable the connection across the Direct Connect link?

    A. Create public VIFs for each /24 network, and set up a separate VGW.

    B. Set up over 300 VLANs on the Direct Connect link.

    C. Create over 300 route entries in the BGP configuration.

    D. Summarize over 300 prefixes into less than 100 prefixes.

55. You are accessing the S3 bucket through a VPC endpoint. Your application keeps getting a 403 response from the bucket. You have checked the security groups, NACLs, and routes, and everything looks good. What is the solution to the problem?

    A. Enable enhanced networking on the EC2 instance.

    B. Ensure that the bucket name is resolving to the correct DNS name.

C. Ensure that the bucket policy allows access from the VPC.

D. Enable the S3 ACL propagation to the VPC.

56. You are deploying an application across regions. You need to be able to create the network configuration in a unified manner. Your company has chosen to build each part of the application with a separate CloudFormation template. What CloudFront feature would you use when deploying the stacks from these templates to correctly deploy to any region?

    A. When deploying the first stack, record the session ID. Use the session ID in the next stack.

    B. When deploying the first stack, record the outputs for use in the next stack.

    C. When deploying the first stack, export the outputs to the next stack.

    D. Use the AWS CLI to deploy; it will be simpler.

57. You are building a VPC that will host a highly available application. The application is required to have three nodes that determine the state of the application by comparing hashes across the network. When designing the infrastructure, which of the following assumptions are not true? (Select all that apply.)

    A. The application can be deployed into any region.

    B. The application requires three subnets in three availability zones to be created for high availability.

    C. The application cannot be deployed into any region.

    D. The application subnets should use the same routing table.

    E. The application requires two subnets in two availability zones to be created for high availability.

58. When connecting 20 branch offices that have 10 to 20 employees, what is the easiest solution to use?

> A. VPN CloudHub
>
> B: IPSec VPNs with VGW
>
> C. Direct Connect
>
> D. NACL

59. You have a requirement for highly available EC2 instances running in two VPCs to connect a mesh tunnel network with each other. The instances are deployed in VPC A with network 10.0.0.0/20 in us-west-1, and VPC B with network 10.0.0.0/16 in eu-west-1. You have decided on a marketplace instance that is capable of creating an overlay network for the mesh. What else should you consider when setting up this deployment?

> A. Peer the VPCs instead of using the marketplace solution, and mesh the instances directly through the peering connection.
>
> B. Use the VGW instead of using the marketplace solution, and mesh the instances directly through the VPN.
>
> C. Implement a second marketplace instance.
>
> D. Use DNS with public IPs on all instances for redundancy.

60. You are moving an application to AWS. The application requires sending broadcast packets to its peers to exchange the cluster state. When you deploy the cluster to the VPC, the cluster state on the instances is marked as unhealthy. Why could that be?

> A. The EC2 instances need to be deployed in a cluster placement group.
>
> B. The instances are in separate subnets, and broadcast packets are not being sent across the router.
>
> C. Broadcast is not allowed in the AWS VPC.
>
> D. The EC2 instances need enhanced networking to be enabled.

Mock Test 2

1. Your company has a requirement for a new Direct Connect link but the requirement is for a 100 Mb connection. Can this be achieved? (Select all that apply.)

   A. No. Direct Connect is only 1 GB or 10 GB.

   B. Yes. Use a Direct Connect Partner and ask for a 100 Mb hosted connection.

   C. Yes. In some cases, Direct Connect is available at 100 Mb.

   D. Yes. If you have a parent AWS account in the same company with an existing Direct Connect link, you can create a 100 Mb Hosted Virtual Interface for the subaccount.

2. The on-premises network of your company uses a next-generation firewall to perform traffic analyses and to determine the application from the pattern of packets on a switch port in promiscuous mode. You are designing the same architecture in AWS. You have found the vendor and the appliance on the AWS marketplace. How can you implement the next-generation appliance in AWS?

   A. Deploy the appliance in the same VPC as your application's VPC with promiscuous mode enabled on the primary network adapter of the appliance.

   B. Deploy the appliance in a separate security VPC. Enable promiscuous mode on a secondary ENI of the appliance.

   C. Deploy the appliance in the same VPC as your application's VPC. Route all the traffic from the application VPC to the appliance.

   D. Deploy the appliance in a separate security VPC. Route all the traffic from the application's VPC to the appliance.

3. You are deploying a third-party WAF in front of your application. To make the deployment highly available, which approach would you use?

    A. Use an autoscaling WAF group in the same subnet as the web frontend. Proxy the requests to the EC2 instance IPs.

    B. Use a WAF sandwich between two ELBs.

    C. Use a WAF layer cake between two ELBs.

    D. Deploy a standalone WAF instance in a separate VPC. Route the traffic from the separate VPC to the EC2 instances.

4. Your startup just got acquired by a multinational corporation. You are in charge of unifying the network infrastructure components. Both entities use multiple AWS accounts to deploy their application. The corporation that bought your startup is now enforcing the use of common authentication across all networks and applications. What would be the simplest way to enable your applications to authenticate to the corporate directory?

    A. Write an authentication broker running on two EC2 instances. Deploy one instance in the corporate directory VPC and one instance in your authentication VPC. Establish a secure way of exchanging credentials between the instances over the public IPs.

    B. Use VPC peering between your VPCs and the corporate authentication VPC.

    C. Establish a VPN between the accounts, as VPC peering is not supported across accounts.

    D. Move all your VPC resources into the corporate account.

5. You are deploying a custom NAT instance inside your VPC. What would you need to do to make sure the traffic passes correctly from the private network to the internet?

    A. Propagate the private subnet routes on the NAT instances.

    B. Enable source destination check on the NAT instance EC2 settings.

    C. Disable source destination check on the NAT instance EC2 settings.

    D. Enable enhanced networking on the NAT instance EC2 settings.

6. You are in charge of setting up a Direct Connect link from your on-premise to AWS. The core requirement is to have maximum fault tolerance and lowest latency for your connection. Which option satisfies those conditions?

A. One AWS Direct Connect link to one customer gateway, one virtual private gateway, and one backup VPN on a public VIF to a second customer gateway.

B. Two AWS Direct Connect link to two customer gateways and one virtual private gateway.

C. Two AWS Direct Connect links to two customer gateways and two virtual private gateways.

D. One AWS Direct Connect link to one customer gateway, two virtual private gateways, and one backup VPN on a public VIF to a second customer gateway.

7. A hybrid server environment is running between AWS and on-premises. For the on-premise servers to be able to simply resolve the DNS names of the EC2 instances, which service would you use?

A. A simple AD in your VPC.

B. A replica AD server of your on-premises AD in your VPC.

C. Route 53.

D. The on-premise DNS in your AD.

8. You have configured a health check on your Route 53 record for your Windows on-premise servers. The health check is reporting all those instances as unhealthy even though your application is working. What could be the cause?

A. On-premise servers are not supported for health checks in Route 53.

B. On-premise servers can be used, but only for the Linux operating system.

C. Check the on-premise firewalls and see whether the traffic from Route 53 is allowed.

D. Delete your Route 53 health checks and recreate them. Wait 15 minutes for the records to sync.

9. You are deploying an HPC application in the AWS cloud. You need the application to communicate with your on-premise site. The servers in your on-premise environment have 32 CPUs, 64 GB of RAM, and 500 GB of locally attached SSD for scratch space. Each server has two 10 GbE adapters with the MTU of 9,000. You are planning to set up a VPC with a cluster placement group of EC2 instances and connect the deployment via a VPN with your on-premises servers. In the current setup, are there any considerations that need to be addressed?

A. None, the setup will work fine.

B. There aren't any instances in AWS that will match your on-premise server configuration closely enough.

C. Using jumbo frames across VPN is not supported.

D. High availability of the environment is reduced when using a cluster placement group.

10. You are in charge of connecting your on-premise ETL environment to a data lake on S3. You need to download hundreds of terabytes of data from S3 in an efficient manner. What type of connection would you establish?

A. A VPN between AWS and your on-premises.

B. Connect directly to S3 over the internet.

C. A Direct Connect link with a public VIF.

D. A Direct Connect link with a private VIF.

11. You have an application that communicates via IPv6. You would like to migrate the application to AWS. In this case, are there any considerations that need to be addressed?

A. No, simply create a VPC with only an IPv6 address range.

B. No, simply create a VPC with a primary IPv4 and a secondary IPv6 address range.

C. Yes, IPv6 is not supported in the VPC.

D. Yes, IPv6 is only supported with enhanced networking instance types. Simply create a VPC with only an IPv6 address range and choose the correct instance type when deploying your application.

12. You are planning to deploy a Direct Connect connection with a VPN backup. To enable failover from Direct Connect to the VPN, what needs to be set up?

    A. Choose the correct AS_PATH prepending for both connections.

    B. Advertise a more specific prefix on the Direct Connect link.

    C. Advertise a more specific prefix on the VPN link.

    D. Advertise two identical prefixes on both links.

13. In a hybrid environment, how can you make sure your EC2 instances can resolve the on-premise hosts?

    A. Create a DNS-link on Route 53 with your on-premise servers. This way, Route 53 will advertise your on-premise network DNS.

    B. Create an instance that will forward your DNS queries to on-premise servers. Set up DHCP options for your VPC to point to this instance. This way, the instance can resolve your on-premise network DNS.

    C. Create a private zone in Route 53. This way, Route 53 will advertise your on-premise network DNS.

    D. Create an instance that will forward your DNS queries to on-premise servers. Set up DHCP options for your subnet to point to this instance. This way, the instance can resolve your on-premise network DNS.

14. When setting up an ELB, you are required to ensure that compliance procedures are followed. You decide to set up an **application load balancer** (**ALB**) that will automatically redirect HTTP to HTTPS. Your load balancer forwards all requests to your EC2 instances on port 443. What else could you do to increase the security of your application data in transit?

    A. The ALB cannot redirect your HTTP to HTTPS. You need to set up a redirect target group that will redirect any requests to HTTPS on the load balancer.

    B. The backend instances should be listening on the HTTPS port, not port 443.

    C. Block any HTTP requests on the ALB.

    D. Nothing. The setup is secure.

15. You have deployed CloudFront to cache public websites stored in an S3 bucket. You like the way this setup works, and you are looking to deliver some private content in the same way. What option would you choose to deliver a few specific private files from S3 via CloudFront?

> A. Use signed URLs.
>
> B. Use signed certificates.
>
> C. Use WebSocket connections.
>
> D. Use bucket policies.

16. An application is running in EC2. A new compliance policy has been introduced that will require stricter security in the VPC. An administrator eager for a promotion has quickly introduced a new security group and NACL policy that was not vetted by the security team. The application seems to be working, but your team lead has designated you with ensuring the packet flows are correct and the policies implemented are not going to break the application. What tools could you use to complete your task?

> A. Check the policies manually and then use the VPC Flow Logs to verify the packet flows.
>
> B. Use the policy simulator and then use the VPC Flow Logs to verify the packet flows.
>
> C. Check the policies manually and then use a third-party tool to sniff the packets and verify the packet flows.
>
> D. Use the policy simulator and then use a third-party tool to sniff the packets and verify the packet flows.

17. A new compliance policy has been introduced that will require you to set up an IDS/IPS system that can perform packet analysis in AWS. What tool would you recommend using to deliver this functionality?

> A. AWS WAF
>
> B. AWS IPS
>
> C. AWS Shield
>
> D. A third-party IDS/IPS product

18. There are several subnets in your VPC across several subnets. Your team is proposing using an EC2 instance that will be connected via an ENI to multiple subnets to perform compliance scanning in the local network. Are there any considerations with this setup?

     A. It will work, but make sure to choose an instance that allows for enough secondary ENIs to be attached.

     B. It will work, but only among subnets in the same availability zone.

     C. This will not work.

     D. It will work, but only among either private or public subnets.

19. Your company is running a single on-premise site that is connected to a VPC. Your company just got acquired by a larger company. They would like you to connect your environment to their security VPC, but the VPC IP address ranges overlap. What could you do to allow for connecting to both your VPC and the security VPC from your on-site deployment?

     A. Use BGP with a different AS_PATH for each VPC.

     B. Use a proxy instance in the security VPC that is out of the scope of your own VPC to pass traffic to the security tools.

     C. Redeploy your VPC to a new subnet.

     D. Use VPC peering between the VPCs.

     E. Use VRF on your on-premise router.

20. You have a VPC with a public and a private subnet. You deploy a NAT gateway and try to connect to the update services from the private instances. You are unable to connect to the update services. What could be the cause?

     A. The NAT gateway is still being created. It can take up to 30 minutes for the NAT gateway to become available.

     B. The NAT gateway has been created in the private subnet.

     C. The NAT gateway has been created in the public subnet.

     D. The NAT ENI is not connected to the private subnet.

21. You are looking at the ELB options. Your application requires extremely high performance at very high packet rates. Which would you choose?

    A. The ALB

    B. The Classic Load Balancer

    C. The NLB

    D. API Gateway

22. You would like to create a DNS service for a domain that you have registered with a third-party provider. Which option would you choose?

    A. Create a Route 53 private zone.

    B. Create a Route 53 public zone.

    C. Create a custom DNS server in EC2 and host your zone.

    D. Use the third-party DNS, since third-party domains are not supported on AWS.

23. When using a hosted virtual interface on a Direct Connect connection of another account, what does your account get charged for? (Choose all that apply.)

    A. Data transfer out of AWS

    B. Data transfer into AWS

    C. VIF uptime hours

    D. The Direct Connect link hours

    E. All of the above

24. Your company is using a NAT gateway in one of your public subnets to deliver updates and outgoing internet access to 10 private subnets. Recently, the updates have started failing. You discover that the NAT gateway is at capacity. Which option would enable you to mitigate this automatically?

    A. Replace the NAT gateway with a very large NAT instance.

    B. Add the NAT gateway to a NAT gateway autoscaling group and autoscale above the maximum of one NAT instance.

C. Write a CloudFormation script that will deploy an additional NAT instance in another public subnet. Create a CloudWatch trigger that will look at the aggregate performance of your NAT instance, and deploy another NAT gateway in case the existing NAT gateway is at maximum performance. Ensure that new routing tables are created by the CloudFormation script. Create a custom resource in the CloudFormation stack to trigger another lambda that will proportionally replace the routing tables in the private subnets.

D. There is no simple way to mitigate this automatically. A manual intervention will be required to scale a NAT instance.

25. You have two VPCs that you are trying to peer together. VPC A has a network of 10.0.10.0/24, and VPC B has a network of 10.0.20.0/24. You have created a peering connection with the ID pcx-f48a26. Which routes need to be created for the peering to be completed? (Select all that apply.)

   A. Add a route in VPC A for 10.0.10.0/24 on pcx-f48a26.

   B. Add a route in VPC B for 10.0.10.0/24 on pcx-f48a26.

   C. Add a route in VPC A for 10.0.20.0/24 on pcx-f48a26.

   D. Add a route in VPC B for 10.0.20.0/24 on pcx-f48a26.

   E. Add a route in VPC B for 10.0.10.0/24 on vgw-f48a26.

   F. Add a route in VPC A for 10.0.20.0/24 on vgw-f48a26.

26. To deploy an instance with up to 25 GBps network throughput, what would you need to do?

   A. Select an instance type that supports enhanced networking.

   B. Select an instance type with 10 GBps support and add a second ENI.

   C. Enable Enhanced networking in the instance.

   D. Use a cluster placement group to deploy the instance.

   E. Select an instance type with 10 GBps support and add two additional ENIs.

27. You have a VPC with an internet gateway with the ID igw-117aa5f attached, and two public subnets created. Your route table has the following entries:
    - 10.0.0.0/16 - local
    - 0.0.0.0/0 - igw-117aa5f

You have deployed an IPv6 network in the VPC and some instances with a dual stack. Since the IGW is attached to the VPC, you are expecting IPv6 unicast to kick in and make your instances available on the internet. However, the instances are not available on the internet. You try accessing them via IPv4, and they respond. What could be the problem?

   A. Dual stack is not supported in VPC.

   B. The IPv4 is always preferred. Remove the IPv4 addresses from the instances.

   C. You are missing the 0:0:0:0/0:0 entry in the route table.

   D. You are missing the ::/0 entry in the route table.

28. The following setup has been deployed by an ex-employee:
    - A virtual private gateway
    - A Direct Connect connection to your on-premise environment
    - A backup VPN between your on-premise site and AWS over the internet

The setup was designed to be highly available and the private resources are available to the on-premise users. However, AWS keeps sending you emails warning you that your VPN connection is not redundantly connected. What could be the cause of this?

   A. The Direct Connect connection does not offer a backup to the VPN link.

   B. The VPN connection gives you two tunnels to connect to for high availability. If only one tunnel is connected, AWS will periodically send out a notification that your VPN link is not redundant.

C. The Direct Connect connection gives you two tunnels to connect to for high availability. If only one tunnel is connected, AWS will periodically send out a notification that your Direct Connect link is not redundant.

D. The VPN connection does not offer a backup to the Direct Connect link.

29. When transferring S3 data across a VPN connection, what kind of transfer costs would be incurred?

    A. Increased VPN data transfer costs out of S3.

    B. Standard data transfer costs out of S3.

    C. Lower VPN data transfer costs out of S3.

    D. No transfer costs are incurred over a VPN.

30. When transferring S3 data across a Direct Connect connection, what kind of transfer costs would be incurred?

    A. Increased Direct Connect data transfer costs out of S3.

    B. Standard data transfer costs out of S3.

    C. Lower Direct Connect data transfer costs out of S3.

    D. No transfer costs are incurred over Direct Connect.

31. You are running an application behind an ALB. You have whitelisted the ALB IPs in your corporate firewall, but a few days later the users complain the application is not available anymore. You resolve the ALB DNS name, but see that the IPs have changed. Your firewall only supports whitelisting IPs, so how can you ensure your ALB will be available from your corporate network?

    A. Assign an Elastic IP to the ALB.

    B. Assign two Elastic IPs to the ALB. This is required for redundancy.

    C. Implement an NLB in front of the ALB.

    D. Implement two NLBs in front of the ALB.

32. There is a requirement to send all traffic in all your applications through a security VPC that will scan all the packets before letting them pass out of each VPC, on-premise site connected via Direct Connect, and branch office connected via VPN. What combination of services would you consider using to ensure this can be done properly?

   A. VPC Peering, WAF, ALB, and NLB

   B. VPC Peering, VPN, Direct Connect, and WAF

   C. VPC Peering, VPN, Direct Connect, a third-party packet scanner, and promiscuous mode

   D. VPC Peering, VPN, Direct Connect, a third-party packet scanner, and routing

33. There is a requirement for instances and services to programmatically exchange information on the network. Your applications use a mix and match of different technologies, and you would like to unify the way they communicate. What service would you choose to achieve this?

   A. The ELB

   B. The API Gateway

   C. The internet gateway

   D. The virtual private gateway

34. You are working for an ERP vendor. The company has just deployed their SaaS ERP solution and are looking for a way to integrate their system with other clients' networks in a secure and AWS-compatible manner. Which option would you evaluate as a possible solution?

   A. Implement VPNs with all the clients. Exchange the traffic across the VPN.

   B. Package the ERP into an AMI and let the clients deploy the AMI in their VPC.

   C. Peer the VPCs with your clients and exchange information over the peered connection.

   D. Use AWS PrivateLink to connect to the clients' VPCs.

35. You are connecting to services via a public VIF through a Direct Connect link. The security team looks at the deployment and has some concerns about using the public VIF. What could they be concerned about?

    A. There is nothing to be concerned about.

    B. Due to the way BGP works, all public IPs are advertised on the public network. When connecting over the public VIF, your private IP is also advertised and reachable by any instances with a public IP.

    C. Due to the way BGP works, all private IPs are advertised on the private network. When connecting over the public VIF, your private IP is also advertised and reachable by any instances with a private IP.

    D. Due to the way BGP works, all public IPs are advertised on the public network. When connecting over the public VIF, your public IP is also advertised and reachable by any instances with a public IP.

36. Your application is sitting in a pair of VPC private subnets. You use a NAT gateway to connect to the internet and transfer data mainly from S3 to the EC2 instances. You need to be mindful regarding the costs of your application. Which costs would you need to consider in this setup? (Select all that apply.)

    A. Cost of EC2

    B. Cost of NAT gateway hours

    C. Cost of S3 storage

    D. VPC hours

    E. S3 transfer-out costs

    F. NAT data processing costs

    G. IGW hours

37. You have deployed an application in a VPC with the 10.0.0.0/24 network and a 10.0.0.0/24 subnet. You seem to have made a mistake, and would like to increase the size of the VPC network to `10.0.0.0/20`. How can you do this?

> A. Stop all instances in the VPC. Put the VPC in maintenance and change the network CIDR.
>
> B. Terminate all instances in the VPC. Put the VPC in maintenance and change the network CIDR.
>
> C. Terminate all instances in the VPC. Remove the subnet and change the network CIDR.
>
> D. This is not possible. Create a new VPC and move the resources to the new VPC.

38. You are implementing a change in the management system that will track any changes to security groups and network access control lists in AWS. Which service would you be able to use to detect any of these changes?

> A. CloudWatch
>
> B. CloudTrail
>
> C. CloudFormation
>
> D. CloudFront

39. You are setting up an application in a VPC that will host a secure payment system. You have put security in place at all levels according to the requirements of the PIC DSS. You are worried about how to make sure that AWS is compliant with the PCI DSS standard before you roll out your application design. How could you get your hands on an AWS compliance report?

> A. Use AWS Artifact.
>
> B. Open a ticket on AWS support.
>
> C. Contact AWS by phone. Only phone support will be allowed to give you a compliance report.
>
> D. Compliance reports are internal and are not available to the public.

40. You are writing a CloudFormation template. You would like to use a third-party firewall appliance in your deployment. You have written a full stack for the VPC, subnets, and tested it. You find the solution on the marketplace and try to deploy it to EC2. Both of these work. How could you further automate the deployment?

>   A. Reference the third-party AMI in the template and deploy once the VPC and subnets are deployed.

>   B. You cannot use marketplace products in CloudFormation.

>   C. Reference the marketplace ID in the template and deploy once the VPC and subnets are deployed.

>   D. Use a custom resource that calls a Lambda function that deploys the solution from the marketplace.

41. The company you work for has a Direct Connect link to S3 through a public VIF. Some users in the company are trying to spin up instances in a private network and are trying to connect to them via their private IPs. They are getting a connection timed-out error. What would be the most likely cause?

>   A. The instance security group does not allow access to the instances.

>   B. The NACL does not allow access to the instances.

>   C. The public VIF does not allow access to the instances.

>   D. The instance operating system firewall does not allow access to the instances.

42. You need to implement a DevOps approach to deploying your networks. The core requirement is that you use an Infrastructure as Code approach. Which of the following services would you use to deploy the networks in a DevOps-compatible way? (Select all that apply.)

>   A. CodeDeploy

>   B. OpsWorks Stacks

>   C. AWS DevOps Stacks

>   D. CloudFormation

43. An EC2 instance cannot be pinged on the Elastic IP attached to it. You are able to log in but not ping. You attach the Elastic IP to another instance and you are able to ping it. What would be the most likely cause of this behavior?

   A. The second EC2 instance has enhanced networking enabled.

   B. The second EC2 instance has ICMP allowed in the security group.

   C. The first EC2 instance has ICMP denied in the NACL.

   D. The first EC2 instance has enhanced networking enabled.

44. When deploying a CloudFront distribution, you need to terminate both incoming and outgoing connections. Which option would you choose in the distribution settings to allow this?

   A. GET, HEAD, and option methods.

   B. GET, HEAD, OPTION, POST, PUT, UPDATE, and DELETE options.

   C. Read/write distribution.

   D. SSL offloading.

45. You are deploying a static website on S3. You are using AWS services to deliver the `mywebsite.com` domain. You want the site to be as secure and as fast as possible. What steps would you need to take to deploy the services? (Select all that apply.)

   A. Register the `mywebsite.com` domain in Route 53 and create a public zone.

   B. Create a public bucket policy.

   C. Create an origin access identity bucket policy.

   D. Deploy a CloudFront distribution with an origin access policy.

   E. Create a CNAME record for the distribution in Route 53.

   F. Create an ALIAS record for the distribution in Route 53.

   G. Create an ALIAS record for the S3 bucket in Route 53.

   H. Create a CNAME record for the S3 bucket in Route 53.

46. You have an OpenID central authentication VPC that is peered with your application VPC. You try and authenticate but get a **connection timed out** response from the OpenID resource. What would you need to do to fix this issue?

     A. Switch the VPC peering to a VPN.

     B. Deploy an ENI on the OpenID server in a public subnet of the central VPC.

     C. Configure the security group of the OpenID application with the IP ranges of your VPC subnets to allow access.

     D. Configure the security group of the OpenID application with the subnet IDs of your VPC subnets to allow access.

47. You have been called by your security response team because your EC2 application is under a DoS attack. What can you do to quickly block the IP addresses that are sending the DoS traffic?

     A. Use VPC Flow Logs to discover the offending IPs and deploy a WAF to implement the IP-based rules.

     B. Use VPC Flow Logs to discover the offending IPs and deploy NACL-based blocking rules.

     C. Use VPC Flow Logs to discover the offending IPs and deploy Shield Advanced to implement the IP-based rules.

     D. Use VPC Flow Logs to discover the offending IPs and deploy a third-party marketplace solution to implement the IP-based rules.

48. You are deploying a cluster of instances behind an ELB that uses a custom UDP-based communication. Which option would be appropriate for this deployment?

     A. The ALB

     B. Classic Load Balancer

     C. Network Load Balancer

     D. None of the above

49. You are deploying a VPC with the 10.0.0.0/28 CIDR. How many subnets can you deploy into this VPC?

    A. 1

    B. 0

    C. 2

    D. 28

50. What is the most important consideration when connecting VPCs via VPC peering?

    A. The account that the VPCs belong to

    B. The IP address ranges

    C. The regions that the VPCs are in

    D. The ASN of the VPC peer

51. When creating a VPC, which of the following is NOT true? (Select all that apply.)

    A. You can create a primary IPv4 network address range to a VPC.

    B. You can create a primary IPv6 network address range to a VPC.

    C. By default, you can create four additional IPv4 network address ranges to a VPC.

    D. You can create one secondary IPv6 network address range to a VPC.

    E. By default, you can create four additional IPv6 network address ranges to a VPC.

    F. By default, you can create as many subnets as a CIDR notation will allow in a VPC network.

52. You are creating a network CloudFormation template. Which CloudFormation type would you use to assign an IPv6 address to?

        A. AWS::EC2::NetworkInterface

        B. AWS::EC2::IPv6Address

        C. AWS::VPC::ENI

        D. AWS::VPC::IPv6Address

53. In CloudFormation, what does the following snippet of code do?

```
"MyRule" : {
 "Type" : "AWS::EC2::NetworkAcl",
 "Properties" : {
 "VpcId" : { "Ref" : "MyVPC" },
 }
 },
```

        A. The snippet attaches a security group rule to a VPC.

        B. The snippet attaches a NACL rule to a VPC.

        C. The snippet creates a NACL within a VPC.

        D. The snippet creates a security group in a VPC.

54. You are creating a subnet in a VPC. To make the subnet highly available, which of the following would you need to do?

        A. Spread the subnet across at least two availability zones.

        B. A subnet cannot be highly available.

        C. Spread the VPC across at least two availability zones.

        D. Create a secondary subnet IP range that can exist in another availability zone and attach it to the subnet.

55. When deploying a VPN service in AWS, you need to consider all levels of high availability of your application. One of the factors proposed by your routing team is to make sure you have two VPN devices on two distinct ASN backends. You decide this is doable in AWS and start building the solution. Which option would help you achieve this?

> A. Deploy two AWS VPNs via a VGW. The ASN is assigned randomly so you will likely get two different ASNs assigned.

> B. Deploy two custom VPN devices on EC2. Choose two Elastic IPs that map to two different ASNs.

> C. Deploy two AWS VPNs via a VGW. Select a different ASN for each VGW.

> D. Deploy two custom VPN devices on EC2. Select a different ASN for each instance public IP.

56. You need to ensure encryption in transit is configured correctly on your AWS deployments. You only use managed services to connect to AWS. Which encryption technology is available across all services for data in transit protection on AWS?

> A. ESP

> B. GRE

> C. TLS

> D. DH

57. When deploying a Direct Connect link, your company has found that some of the devices in the on-premise location are not compatible with the BGP routing protocol. What is the alternative approach when using Direct Connect to using BGP? (Select all that apply)

> A. Static routing

> B. BGP with encapsulated static routing

> C. RIPv2

> D. BGP with encapsulated RIPv2

> E. None of the above

58. You have created a highly available, public/private VPC with the VPC wizard. Which of the following objects will NOT get created?

    A. Two public subnets in two availability zones

    B. Two private subnets in two availability zones

    C. Two internet gateways

    D. A NAT instance with an Elastic IP

    E. Two routing tables

59. Which on-site connection type would you recommend to a bioengineering startup that would like to get the following:
    - 1 GBps throughput
    - Reliable link
    - Use of BGP

    A. Direct Connect

    B. AWS VPN with VGW

    C. A custom third-party VPN

    D. VPC peering

60. Your company has a legacy corporate website on EC2 instances. The website has had some issues in the past, and the users visiting the site have seen some 503 error responses on the browser. The business has decided to invest in a redesign that will take three months. In the meantime, they would like you to improve the experience of the users visiting the site. As a network engineer, what simple and cheap workaround could you recommend?

    A. Put the EC2 servers behind a load balancer.

    B. Deploy a static copy of the site to S3 and use Route 53 health checks to fail over to S3 in case the site is down.

    C. Clone the EC2 instances into another deployment, and use Route 53 health checks to fail over to S3 in case the site is down.

    D. Use autoscaling to increase the performance of the EC2 instances.

Assessments

Chapter 2 – Networking with the Virtual Private Cloud

1. Choose from the following: the network, subnets, routes, internet gateway, NAT gateway, egress only gateway, ENI, VPC Endpoint, VPC Peering connection, NACLs, and security groups.
2. Routing is performed via the NAT gateway or an instance in IPv4, whereas an egress-only gateway is used in IPv6.
3. A VPC cider cannot be changed once created. CIDR sizes should accommodate current and future application needs.
4. IPv4 uses 1:1 NAT between Public or Elastic IPs and the subnet IPs, whereas IPv6 addresses are reachable directly.
5. A gateway uses routing to route traffic to a private network from the AWS service, while the interface endpoint connects directly into the VPC with a VPC private IP attached to it.
6. Implement a proxy in VPC B to pass traffic from A to C.
7. Create a VPC. Create 8 subnets – three pairs of private subnets in different AZs for each private application tier and one pair of public subnets for the web application. Subnets will only communicate on Layer 3. Create a VPC endpoint for the SQS service so that the private subnets can communicate with the SQS.

Chapter 3 – VPC Network Security

1. Security groups.
2. Your NACL only allows incoming traffic. You need to open all the required ports for the outgoing traffic in the NACL.
3. `ufw disable` disables the firewall service. This is not recommended. Consult with your Linux administrator so that they can provide you with a command that will open the required ports instead of disabling the firewall.
4. The NACL or security groups are blocking the traffic, as can be seen by the `REJECT` action in the output.

5. The WAF Sandwich architecture approach.
6. Add a load balancer and put your EC2 instances in an autoscaling group. This will make sure that the instances can scale to handle the traffic when the spike occurs. Although you know the IP range, blocking the IP range would be wrong as you have not identified whether the traffic is legitimate or not.
7. Implement a CloudFront Distribution for the website and protect it with AWS Shield – Standard.

Chapter 4 – Connecting On-Premises and AWS

1. IPv4 private networks are defined as private by default. IPv6 uses unicast addressing, which is essentially public by default.
2. Lower cost.
3. Autonomous system.
4. IPSec.
5. 1.25 Gbps.
6. BGP, MD5 BGP authentication, 1000BASE-LX or 10GBASE-LR fibre connector, 802.1Q VLAN encapsulation.
7. 1Gbps DirectConnect for low latency with an IPSec VPN on top for encryption.
8. Use a VPN – it has two tunnels and is inherently highly available. No requirements for bandwidth, latency, and so on have been specified, so VPN should do the trick!

Chapter 5 – Managing and Securing Servers with ELB

1. Distribution of traffic across multiple instances.
2. Application Load Balancer and Network Load Balancer.
3. The Network Load Balancer.
4. The Application Load Balancer.
5. No, the NLB cannot pass traffic across a peered VPC connection.
6. The AWS Certificate Manager.
7. AWS Shield.

Chapter 6 – Managing and Securing Content Distribution with CloudFront

1. All HTTP method types can be configured and read, write, update, and delete HTTP operations are supported.
2. It can increase the TTL for applications that define the default TTL for the caching behavior.
3. An origin.
4. AWS Shield Advanced with WAF rules.
5. Signed URLs.
6. The AWS Certificate Manager.
7. `Lambda@Edge`.

Chapter 7 – Managing and Securing the Route 53 Domain Name System

1. The management entry point is an API that stores the DNS information on an extremely fast database layer. The SLA is 100% and it supports routing and health checks.
2. Use geolocation routing.
3. Build a S3 static copy of your site. Use Route 53 failover routing to failover to the S3 bucket in the case of major outages.
4. Create a DNS record with all the node IPs and a health check based on TCP port 443. If the port is unreachable, then the Route 53 service will remove the node from the response. Direct the provider so that they connect to the DNS name.
5. Transfer the domain to Route 53 and enable domain transfer locking.
6. Use a route 53 multi-value record for the cluster. Use the cluster DNS name in the lookup of peer nodes. Use a health check on the record to only determine healthy nodes. Route 53 will always return up to 8 hosts in the lookup response.
7. You need to provide the NS names to your registrar so that they can switch DNS over to Route 53.

Chapter 8 – Managing and Securing API Gateways

1. REST and WebSocket.
2. Any application running in AWS or outside AWS, any AWS HTTP addressable service like S3, DynamoDB, and so on.
3. Create a resource policy and allow only traffic from any development IP or endpoint.
4. Use federation with IAM or Cognito if it's supported by a third party. If federation is not supported by the third party, you can also implement a Lambda authorizer that can check the authentication data in the API request.
5. Use ACM for API Gateway and ELB and use a self-signed certificate, a private CA, or a public CA for the EC2 instances.
6. Yes, this kind of behavior is supported by WebSocket.
7. Connect the clients to the API Gateway. Use API keys for requests from the mobile clients and then send the backend request directly to DynamoDB. To prevent over-use of DynamoDB, you can implement a usage plan that will throttle the request from each user.

Chapter 9 – Monitoring and Troubleshooting Networks in AWS

1. Standard, detailed, and custom.
2. True.
3. The logs are kept indefinitely.
4. Use billing alarms and create alerts when the budget has exceeded 50%, 80%, and 100%. Make sure that the alert notifies the developers through an SNS subscription.
5. Yes, this is supported.
6. Not with CloudWatch, you need to use a third-party tool as CloudWatch is regionally bound.

7. A security group or NACL is denying traffic to the instance.
8. You are not waiting for the operating system to start. Wait five minutes and then try again. If there is no response, then check the security group and NACL.
9. The TTL on the record is set too high and you need to lower it. The clients also need to flush their resolver cache.

Chapter 10 – Network Automation with CloudFormation

1. Stack.
2. JSON and YAML.
3. With the DependsOn attribute.
4. Just execute the changeset on the existing stack. This will deploy the changes.
5. Look for any EC2 instances or other services using the subnet. Until the subnet is empty, you will not be able to delete it.
6. Hard code any defined values. Always use references and map any specific resources to regions with mappings.
7. CloudFormation can help you test and ensure that your configuration is PCI compliant before deploying to production.

Mock test 1

Question	Answer	Explanation
1	B	The VGW provides you with two tunnel endpoints for high availability. No need for a secondary link.
2	D	You will need a custom solution to connect to a GRE tunneled VPN network as GRE is not supported in AWS. You could redeploy everything to IPSec or the CloudHub VPN, but it could be very complicated. We are looking for the simplest way of doing this.
3	C	AWS is responsible for making the internet gateway highly available.
4	B	The NACLs are stateless. For every inbound rule, an outbound rule needs to be created to allow access.
5	A	To establish an initial VPN connection, simply initiate traffic from the on-premise site.
6	A	AWS direct connect partners can help you establish private optical or MPLS links from the collocation to your on-premise environment.

7	C	DynamoDB supports a gateway VPC endpoint. A will not work as you have removed the public subnet. D could work, but it would require a redesign of the application, and the question is asking for the simplest way.
8	C	DirectConnect always takes priority over a backup VPN, so nothing needs to be done to make it the preferred link. Bi-directional Forwarding Detection on the Direct Connect connection will help detect a failure and smoothly fail over traffic to a backup Direct Connect or VPN link. Direct Connect always uses BGP as the routing protocol.
9	B	VPC peering requires the VPCs to have unique IP ranges, and any overlapping will prevent you from establishing a peering connection. VPC peering is available across regions and across accounts, and using VPN would not make a difference if IPs are overlapping. There is no application support required to peer VPCs.
10	D	From the ranges of the production subnets, the addresses should have a/24 suffix – 10.0.0.0/24 and 10.0.1.0/24.
11	B	Using the RDS DNS will allow for the automatic failover of traffic in case of the primary instance failure. A would work but it is cumbersome; the C option doesn't exist and you can't use an ENI with a RDS instance.
12	C	You can use an ENI to connect to a secondary network in a VPC. Although a solution described in answer A could exist. it would use the same mechanism. B is incorrect while D does not exist.
13	C	The cheapest option to accelerate your website will be a CloudFront distribution. You can select price class 100 (North America and EU), which will help you save a bit on request pricing.
14	A	You can use change sets to manage the versions of a deployed stack from within CF.
15	C	A 2xlarge instance has up to 10 Gbit/s. This instance cannot ingest more than 4 TB of data per day, so the bottleneck is the compute power. Two instances would work, and so would an instance double the size, but to be more efficient, we could reduce the instance size by half and use three xlarge instances. Four large instances would simply mean that we have the same compute power as a 2xlarge and would not be able to ingest more than 4 TB of data.
16	B	AWS Shield Advanced is an advanced DDoS mechanism that can be deployed to protect Amazon EC2, Elastic Load Balancing (ELB), Amazon CloudFront, AWS Global Accelerator, or Amazon Route 53 services, and includes a host of features to protect your infrastructure. Although other services can be used to protect from DDoS Shield Advanced, this is most comprehensive way.
17	D	Set the MTU to 9000. Instances that are collocated inside a cluster placement group, such as jumbo frames, help to achieve the maximum network throughput possible. No need to enable this on your VPC.
18	D	The public IPs always change when the instances are shut down. Using elastic IPs might be a better idea in this case.
19	A	The 10.0.0.121 instance tried to SSH to instance 10.0.1.121 on port 22, but the connection was not allowed.

20	A, C	You can either proxy traffic from B to C in A, or you can peer B and C together. Other options are not viable since transient routing in VPC peering is not supported and CloudHub wouldn't be useful for this.
21	B	After you create a VPC peering link, you need to create routes in both VPCs for the other VPC.
22	A	Data is not encrypted across Direct Connect. Using HTTPS when accessing S3 encrypts the data in transit. IPSec VPN is an option, but will decrease the bandwidth of the Direct Connect link. The client is transferring PB of data, so performance is key. Client encryption would work, but only for newly uploaded data.
23	D	Each private subnet needs an entry to the S3 gateway endpoint if it is using a different routing table.
24	C, D	Make sure that you understand the EC2 network's performance and ensure that enhanced networking is enabled.
25	B	Cluster placement groups ensure the best network performance between EC2 instances.
26	D	The most specific entry in your route table will determine which route will be used.
27	D	ELB is highly available and should not offload SSL due to end-to-end encryption requirement. One autoscaling group should be highly available. One RDS Multi-AZ deployment provides high availability. SSL encryption to MySQL enables end-to-end encryption.
28	A	Route 53 with latency-based routing allows us to deploy and application according to the blue-green model. We can increase the weight of the green deployment while decreasing the weight of the blue one, thus moving traffic from blue to green.
29	C	All the resources in a CloudFormation stack are built in parallel. Use Depends-On conditions to provide the ordering of dependent resources, like subnets, which depend on the existence of the VPC.
30	B, C	A backup VPN or Direct Connect connection is required to make the primary Direct Connect connection highly available.
31	D	VPC peering with just the authentication VPC will work across accounts and regions. While other solutions might work, they might allow direct access to all VPCs, which is not required.
32	B	Adding a certificate to the ELB via ACM would be the least effort and cheapest solution. Additionally, it has the advantage of the ELB offloading traffic, and no reconfiguration is needed on the EC2 side.
33	C	Transfers out of AWS will incur charges, even if they're running over Direct Connect.
34	A, C, F	Make sure that you choose the appropriate security tools at each level. Leverage both AWS and other tools, like the operating system firewall and other vendor products. Minimize the attack surface by reducing the number of entry points to your application.

35	B	The Web Application Firewall (WAF) can help you maintain security at the level of the requester IP range and by implementing regular expressions that are allowed in your application to protect from injection attacks.
36	A	When consolidated billing is created, all the charges are aggregated in the main billing account.
37	A, B, E	You customer router needs to support a single mode fiber connection via the use of VLANs and BGP.
38	C	Use a VPN to encrypt the connection on the Direct Connect link. Use a private VIF to connect to a VPC.
39	B	A third party packet analyzer is required to perform deep packet inspection.
40	A	Private subnets do not have IGWs attached and thus do not support Elastic IPs.
41	D	You cannot remove the default IPv4 range of your VPC.
42	A	If an ECS container is VPC enabled, it has its own ENI. You can use VPC flow logs on the ENI to diagnose the traffic.
43	B	An egress only internet gateway can perform the same function in IPv6 as a NAT gateway does in IPv4 for private networks to allow outbound traffic to the internet.
44	A, E	For an IPSec VPN, you will need to open UDP port 500 and allow protocol 50 (ESP).
45	A, C, D	The lambda can be deployed in the VPC to access private resources. Once the lambda is private, we will need to use a DynamoDB VPC endpoint or a NAT gateway to enable access to DynamoDB from the private VPC subnet.
46	C	You can use peering defaults to peer any newly created VPCs to your existing VPCs.
47	A	Always redirect traffic from HTTP to HTTPS with a viewer policy, which means that all requests to CloudFront will be redirected to HTTPS. On top of that, setting the origin policy to match the viewer will also guarantee that only HTTPS is used in the communication since the viewer is always redirected to HTTPS.
48	B, C	To create a private VIF, the VLAN ID of the Direct Connect link and the virtual private gateway ID of the VGW are required. The IGW is not part of Direct Connect. An on-premise subnet ID does not exist.
49	D	You can use field-level encryption with SSL offloading to increase the performance of your application but still maintain the encryption of sensitive data in the encrypted fields.
50	B, F	You need to maintain the instance subnets private, so the only option is a VPC endpoint. You also need to create a route to the VPC endpoint in the default VPC routing table to grant access to S3. All the security groups and NACLs allow outbound access, so no security configuration is required.
51	B	CloudFront can accelerate the performance of your application by caching and terminating the incoming connections at the edge.
52	A	An ALIAS record can help you direct traffic from a domain apex record (no prefix to domain.com) to an AWS resource. It works similarly to CNAME, but allows the use of the apex entry. You cannot use a CNAME record when using an apex in route 53.

53	B	The Direct Connect Partner will be the one establishing the cross-link once the device is in the collocation rack.
54	D	When using Direct Connect, the prefixes need to be summarized below 100 for the connection to work.
55	C	403 means that you have reached the bucket but don't have permission to access it.
56	C	You can export stack output values to the next stack when a complex infrastructure is deployed.
57	A, E	You will need to ensure that the application is deployed in three AZs. If the application is deployed in less than three AZs, then the state of the application might not be determined correctly (for example, two nodes in one AZ go down). Not all regions support 3 AZs.
58	A	VPN CloudHub can help you easily connect multiple sites with VPNs in the easiest manner.
59	C	The marketplace solution will not be highly available if they're running on one instance. Make sure to deploy another instance to make it highly available.
60	C	Broadcast and multicast are not allowed in the AWS VPC.

Mock test 2

The VPN connection gives you two tunnels to connect to for high availability. If only one tunnel is connected, AWS will periodically send out a notification stating that your VPN link is not redundant.

Question	Answer	Explanation
1	A, D	A hosted connection can be provided by a partner, as well as a hosted virtual interface, if your organization already has another Direct Connect link.
2	D	Promiscuous mode is not allowed in AWS. If you are scanning traffic, you will need to route all the traffic from the VPC to a separate VPC where the appliance will intercept and monitor your traffic.
3	B	To make a WAF deployment highly available, you can use the WAF sandwich approach.
4	B	VPC peering will allow you to communicate with the other account and authenticate.
5	C	Each EC2 instance performs source/destination checks by default. This means that the instance must be the source or destination of any traffic it sends or receives. However, a NAT instance must be able to send and receive traffic when the source or destination is not itself. Therefore, you must disable source/destination checks on the NAT instance.
6	B	You need to set up one virtual private gateway in AWS to provide the endpoint connection for your Direct Connect links. You can then attach two Direct Connect links from two customer gateways to achieve high availability.
7	A	A simple AD can forward requests for Amazon DNS servers from your VPC.
8	C	Make sure that you are allowing the health check traffic from route 53 to your instances.
9	C	While jumbo frames up to 9,000 are supported in the VPC, VPNs support a MTU of 1500. Although answer D points out a fact, no requirements for high availability have been outlined in the question.
10	C	Using Direct Connect with a public VIF will be the most efficient way of delivering S3 data to the data center as the transfer costs are reduced over Direct Connect.
11	B	You can add an additional IPv6 address range to a VPC. However, you cannot disassociate the primary IPv4 block from the VPC.
12	D	AWS will always prefer Direct Connect when the same prefix is advertised on a VPN link. This can help failover to the VPN link when the Direct Connect link is down.
13	B	An EC2 instance can be added to the VPC DHCP options set to override the AWS DNS servers. You will need to create a forwarder that will forward requests to the on-premise servers.

14	D	Nothing needs to be done; this setup is secure.
15	A	You can use signed URLs to deliver private content from otherwise public resources. This would be the easiest way to provide access to those specific files.
16	A	To verify the policies, look at what they do. Verify that the policies are configured correctly by enabling VPC flow logs and checking the packet flows. Look for ACCEPT OK and REJECT OK in the flows to determine which packets are being allowed and denied.
17	D	To perform packet analysis, a third party tool needs to be used in AWS.
18	B	An ENI can be used to connect to multiple subnets, but only within one availability zone.
19	E	Virtual Routing and Forwarding VRFs can help your router maintain two overlapping routing tables to connect to two distinct VPCs over VPN. VRF is recommended when a supported router is used to connect to multiple VPCs with overlapping IPs.
20	D	If a NAT gateway is created in a private network, it will not have an access to the internet. Always make sure that you create the NAT gateway in a public subnet with an Elastic IP.
21	C	NLB allows maximum network performance and can handle tens of millions of requests per second.
22	B	To host a domain registered at a third party, use a public hosted zone. You can also transfer the registration to AWS if you so desire.
23	A	On a hosted VIF, your account only gets charged with the transfer out costs. The main account pays for the Direct Connect link hours.
24	C	A CloudFormation script can be used in this way to add resources. Since existing resources cannot be modified by CloudFormation, the CloudFormation script can issue a request to a Lambda Function through a custom resource request that will update the existing subnet routing configuration.
25	B, C	VPC A needs a route to the VPC B network and vice versa.
26	A, C	Select an instance that supports enhanced networking and turn it on to get 25 GBits/s and more.
27	D	The ::/0 default route is required for IPv6 instances to be able to communicate with the internet.
28	B	The VPN connection gives you two tunnels to connect to for high availability. If only one tunnel is connected, AWS will periodically send out a notification that your VPN link is not redundant.

29	B	Standard data transfer costs out of S3 over a VPN.
30	C	Lower data transfer costs out of S3 over a Direct Connect link.
31	C	A network load balancer can be implemented with an elastic IP in front of the ALB so that the elastic IP of the NLB can be used in the white list.
32	D	To connect VPCs together use VPC peering, peer all VPCs into the central VPC, and route all the traffic from the peered VPCs and the VPNs and Direct Connect connections to the third-party device in the central VPC to perform packet scanning.
33	B	API Gateway provides a unified API interface for applications to exchange information
34	D	PrivateLink offers vendors the ability to connect to their client's VPC using an ENI. PrivateLink also stands behind interface VPC endpoints.
35	D	When connecting over the public VIF, your public IP is advertised via BGP and is reachable by any instances with a public IP.
36	A, B, C, F	We need to be mindful of the EC2 instance and S3 storage, as well as NAT instance operating hours and the GB of data that's processed by the NAT instance.
37	D	Once created, a network VPC cannot be altered.
38	B	CloudTrail can log all API calls against AWS and capture any changes that are made to security groups and NACLs.
39	A	Access to all AWS compliance reports is available on AWS Artifact through a self-service portal.
40	A	Since the deployment is to EC2, the marketplace solution will have an AMI. You can specify the AMI ID in your CloudFormation template.
41	C	You need a private VIF to connect to a VPC.
42	D	Use CloudFormation to deliver an Infrastructure as Code approach to deploy your networks.
43	B	The most likely cause is that the second instance allows ICMP while the first doesn't.
44	B	To use CloudFront to terminate both incoming and outgoing connections, use the GET, HEAD, OPTION, POST, PUT, UPDATE, and DELETE options when creating the distribution. This will allow CloudFront to terminate all the methods of the HTTP calls.
45	A, C, D, F	To make the site as secure and as fast as possible, always deploy it behind a CloudFront distribution. B and G would be needed if CloudFront wasn't used, while E and H are not possible.
46	C	Only IP ranges of your VPC subnets can be used in security groups of other VPCs that are peered.
47	B	Although all but Shield can help, the simplest solution is to implement IP blocking NACL rules.
48	D	UDP is not supported on any of the ELBs.

49	A	10.0.0.0/28 is the smallest CIDR. Only one 10.0.0.0/28 subnet can be deployed in this setup.
50	B	IP address ranges in VPC peering should not overlap.
51	B, E, F	You can create only one secondary IPv6 range within a VPC. You can create up to 200 subnets in a VPC by default. CIDR notation will allow for many more.
52	A	You can use a AWS::EC2::NetworkInterface property to assign an IP address.
53	C	The snippet creates a NACL within a VPC.
54	B	A subnet is always tied to exactly one availability zone.
55	C	You can choose to select a two different ASNs when creating a VGW.
56	C	TLS can be used to encrypt any data in transit to all services in AWS.
57	E	BGP is a prerequisite to using Direct Connect. Encapsulated protocols in BGP do not exist.
58	C	Only one internet gateway is created, since an IGW is highly available.
59	B	AWS VPN over VGW would satisfy all these requirements.
60	B	Deploying a static S3 site copy would be the most cost-efficient and simple workaround. Since you don't know if it is a performance issue or if the site is already load balanced, putting the site behind a load balancer or in an autoscaling group might not help. Cloning the site might help, but could be expensive.

Other Books You May Enjoy

If you enjoyed this book, you may be interested in these other books by Packt:

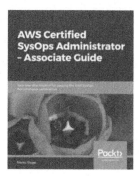

AWS Certified SysOps Administrator - Associate Guide
Marko Sluga

ISBN: 978-1-78899-077-6

- Create and manage users, groups, and permissions using AWS IAM services
- Create a secure VPC with public and private subnets, Network Access Control, and security groups
- Get started with launching your first EC2 instance, and working with it
- Handle application traffic with ELB and monitor AWS resources with CloudWatch
- Work with S3, Glacier, and CloudFront
- Work across distributed application components using SWF
- Understand event-based processing with Lambda and messaging SQS and SNS in AWS
- Get familiar with AWS deployment concepts and tools including Elastic Beanstalk, CloudFormation and AWS OpsWorks

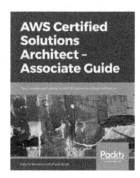

AWS Certified Solutions Architect - Associate Guide
Stuart Scott, Gabriel Ramirez

ISBN: 978-1-78913-066-9

- Explore AWS terminology and identity and access management
- Acquaint yourself with important cloud services and features in categories such as compute, network, storage, and databases
- Define access control to secure AWS resources and set up efficient monitoring
- Back up your database and ensure high availability by understanding all of the database-related services in the AWS Cloud
- Integrate AWS with your applications to meet and exceed non-functional requirements
- Build and deploy cost-effective and highly available applications

Leave a review - let other readers know what you think

Please share your thoughts on this book with others by leaving a review on the site that you bought it from. If you purchased the book from Amazon, please leave us an honest review on this book's Amazon page. This is vital so that other potential readers can see and use your unbiased opinion to make purchasing decisions, we can understand what our customers think about our products, and our authors can see your feedback on the title that they have worked with Packt to create. It will only take a few minutes of your time, but is valuable to other potential customers, our authors, and Packt. Thank you!

Index

Made in the USA
Middletown, DE
28 October 2020